D1614643

1100 MARK I 1962–67 AUTOBOOK

Workshop Manual for
Austin 1100 Mk I 1963–67
Austin 1100 Countryman Mk I 1966–67
Morris 1100 Mk I 1962–67
Morris 1100 Traveller Mk I 1966–67
MG 1100 Mk I 1962–67
Riley Kestrel 1100 Mk I 1965–67
Vanden Plas Princess 1100 Mk I 1963–67
Wolseley 1100 Mk I 1965–67

by

Kenneth Ball G I Mech E
and the
Autopress team of Technical Writers

AUTOPRESS LTD   GOLDEN LANE   BRIGHTON   BN1 2QJ   ENGLAND

The AUTOBOOK series of Workshop Manuals
covers the majority of British and Continental
motor cars.

For a full list see the back of this manual.

CONTENTS

ISBN 0 85147 211 7

First Edition   1968
Second Edition, fully revised 1968
Third Edition, fully revised 1969
Fourth Edition, fully revised 1969
Fifth Edition, fully revised 1970
Sixth Edition, fully revised 1971
Reprinted   1972

© Autopress Ltd 1972

Printed in Brighton England for Autopress Ltd by G. Beard & Son Ltd

ACKNOWLEDGEMENT

My thanks are due to The British Motor Corporation Ltd for their unstinted co-operation and also for supplying data and illustrations.

I am also grateful to a considerable number of owners who have discussed their cars at length and many of whose suggestions have been included in this manual.

Kenneth Ball G I Mech E
Associate Member Guild of Motoring Writers

Ditchling Sussex England.

INTRODUCTION

This do-it-yourself Workshop Manual has been specially written for the owner who wishes to maintain his car in first class condition and to carry out his own servicing and repairs. Considerable savings on garage charges can be made, and one can drive in safety and confidence knowing the work has been done properly.

Comprehensive step-by-step instructions and illustrations are given on all dismantling, overhauling and assembling operations. Certain assemblies require the use of expensive special tools, the purchase of which would be unjustified. In these cases information is included but the reader is recommended to hand the unit to the agent for attention.

Throughout the Manual hints and tips are included which will be found invaluable, and there is an easy to follow fault diagnosis at the end of each chapter.

Whilst every care has been taken to ensure correctness of information it is obviously not possible to guarantee complete freedom from errors or to accept liability arising from such errors or omissions.

Instructions may refer to the righthand or lefthand sides of the vehicle or the components. These are the same as the righthand or lefthand of an observer standing behind the car and looking forward.

CHAPTER 1

THE ENGINE

1 : 1 Description

Although the engine is combined with the transmission system, this chapter will deal with those operations which, apart from the removal of the complete unit from the car, concern the engine alone.

The usual BMC features of engine design are again quite distinctive in all models covered by this manual, and the following description will apply to any one of the cars, whether it is fitted with one or two carburetters according to the power output required. There is, however, one feature which will affect the removal and dismantling procedure and that is the type of transmission which is fitted. The differences between normal and automatic transmission operations will be fully covered under separate headings.

The splendid cutaway drawing in **FIG 1 : 1** shows the engine and transmission unit in the twin carburetter version. From this it can be seen that the engine is in unit construction with a fourspeed gearbox, the transmission casing also forming the sump. The engine capacity of the 1100 Mk I is 1098 cc. Details of bore and stroke and compression ratios are given in Technical Data at the end of this manual together with an extensive coverage of further technical information.

Vertical pushrod-operated valves are set in line along the cylinder head, the valve stems being fitted with oil seals. The camshaft runs in three plain whitemetal bearings and is driven by chain from the crankshaft. Synthetic rubber rings on the camshaft chainwheel act as chain silencers and tensioners. The oil pump is driven from the other end of the camshaft and a transverse shaft driven by camshaft gearing turns the distributor.

Gudgeon pins are fully floating in the 1098 cc engine. The pistons have three compression rings and one slotted oil control ring. The connecting rods are fitted with renewable steel-backed bearing shells lined with special alloy. The crankshaft runs in similar bearings but end thrust is taken by washers on either side of the centre bearing.

The oil pump draws oil from the base of the transmission casing and delivers it to an external fullflow filter. By drilled passages the oil then passes to the main, big-end and camshaft bearings. From the front camshaft bearing oil is fed to the overhead rocker gear, returning to the sump down the pushrod holes to lubricate the tappets. A relief valve in the circuit restricts oil pressure to a safe maximum when the oil is cold and thick, returning the surplus back to the sump.

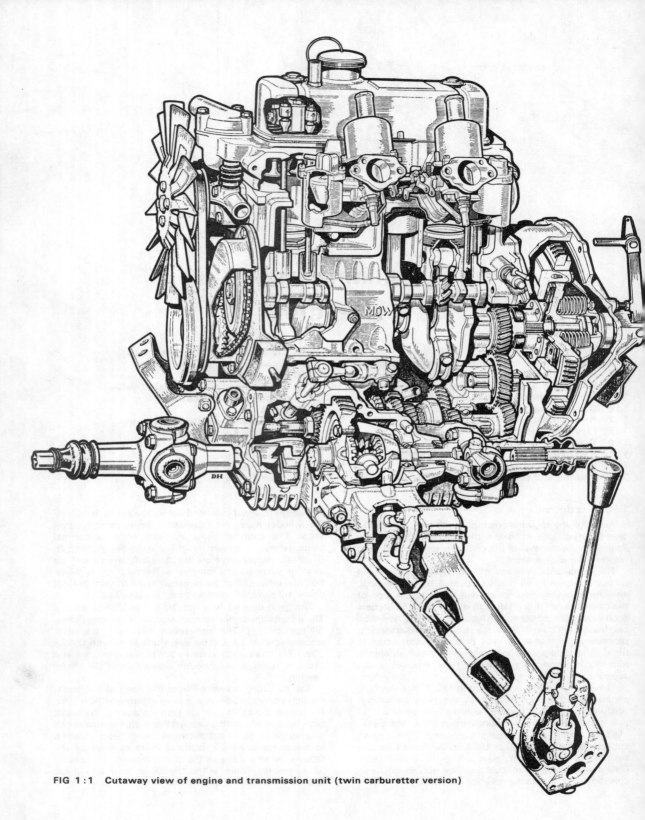

FIG 1:1   Cutaway view of engine and transmission unit (twin carburetter version)

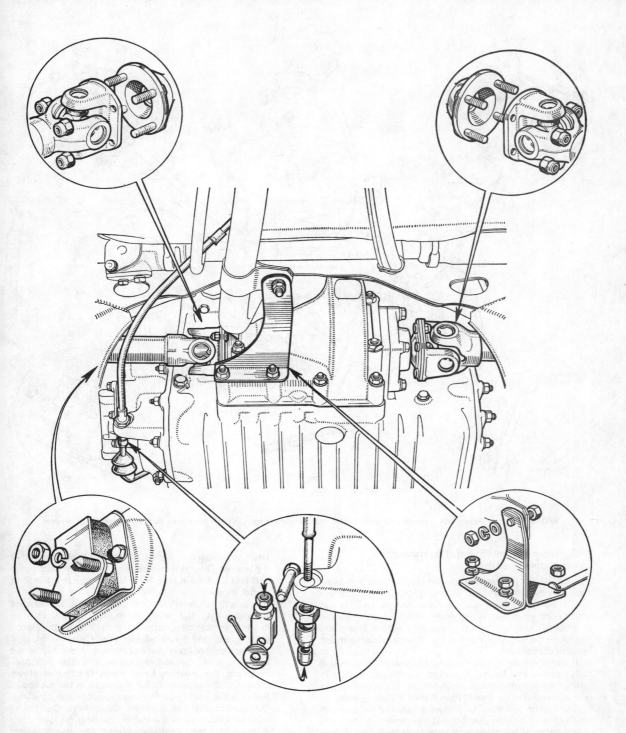

FIG 1 : 2   Removing the engine and automatic transmission unit. Work on these components from below

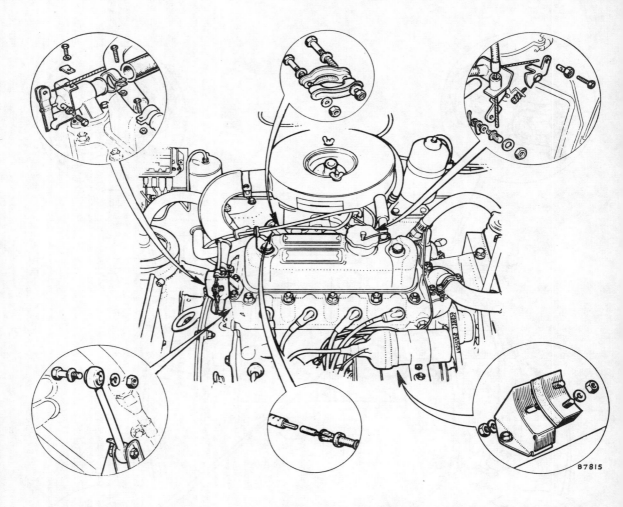

FIG 1 : 3 Removing the engine and automatic transmission unit. Work on these components from above

1 : 2 Removing engine and transmission, synchromesh gearbox

The usual operations of decarbonizing and top over-haul can be done without removing the power unit, but unlike normal engine and gearbox assemblies it is not possible to work on the big-ends unless the transmission is dropped out of the way, and this entails lifting the complete assembly out of the car. **The subframe must not be disturbed.**

If the operator is not a skilled automobile engineer it is suggested that he will find much useful information in 'Hints on Maintenance and Overhaul' at the end of this manual, and that he should read it before starting work.

The engine and transmission assembly can be removed and refitted through the bonnet aperture but the front subframe must be raised high enough for working under-neath. **It must be stressed that any supports must be firmly based and not likely to collapse during the operation or serious injury could result.** Then proceed as follows:

1 Drain the cooling system if a heater is fitted and remove the bonnet. Disconnect leads from generator, distributor and coil, and earth lead from clutch housing. Remove starter motor.

2 Remove the carburetters (see **Chapter 2**). Disconnect the cable from the heater valve on the head and the hoses from the valve and return pipe. Release the clutch lever spring and slave cylinder (see **Chapter 5**), pull the slave cylinder pushrod out and wire the cylinder out of the way on the suspension system. **Do not disconnect the clutch fluid hose from the slave cylinder.** Release the exhaust pipe from the manifold.

3 Release the spill hose from the radiator and cowling. Disconnect the speedometer cable from the trans-mission casing or at the cable coupling on later cars. Remove the dust excluder, extract the two retaining plate screws and withdraw the gearlever. Release the changespeed extension from the floor tunnel (two screws). Place sturdy supports under the frame sidemembers.

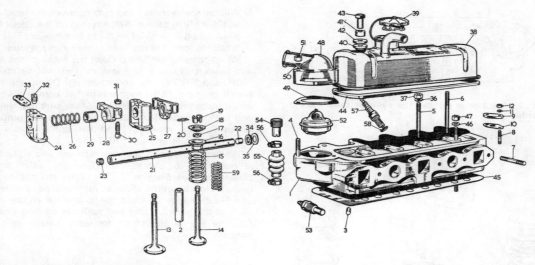

FIG 1 : 4   Components of the cylinder head

Key to Fig 1 : 4   1 Cylinder head   2 Valve guide   3 Plug   4 Water outlet elbow stud
5 Rocker bracket stud (short)   6 Rocker bracket stud (long)   7 Manifold stud   8 Stud   9 Cover plate
10 Cover joint   11 Washer   12 Nut   13 Inlet valve   14 Exhaust valve   15 Outer spring
16 Guide shroud   17 Packing ring   18 Spring cup   19 Valve cotter   20 Circlip   21 Rocker shaft
22 Rocker shaft plug   23 Rocker shaft plug (screwed)   24 Rocker bracket (tapped)   25 Rocker bracket
26 Spacing spring   27 Valve rocker (pressed type)   28 Valve rocker (forged type)   29 Rocker bush (for forged type)
30 Tappet adjusting screw   31 Locknut   32 Locating screw   33 Bracket plate   34 Double-coil washer
35 Washer   36 Washer   37 Nut   38 Valve rocker cover   39 Oil filler cap   40 Rubber bush
41 Distance piece   42 Cup washer   43 Nut   44 Cover joint   45 Cylinder head joint   46 Washer
47 Nut   48 Water outlet elbow   49 Elbow joint   50 Washer   51 Nut   52 Thermostat
53 Thermal transmitter   54 Bypass adaptor   55 Rubber connection   56 Clip   57 Sparking plug
58 Gasket   59 Inner spring (twin carburetter application)

4 Release the exhaust pipe from the transmission casing. Separate the extension from the differential casing (two shouldered setscrews low down on each side).

5 Remove the U-bolts to disconnect both drive shaft couplings. Push the sliding joints onto the shafts to separate the couplings. Release the lefthand engine mounting from the bearer plate (two nuts). Fit two lifting eyes to the cylinder head in place of two right-hand side nuts. Take the weight of the engine and remove the righthand engine mounting bracket and the screws securing the rear bracket to the subframe. Check that all cables and pipes connecting the unit to the car frame have been detached and then lift the unit from the car.

Refitting is the reverse of the removal procedure. Upon completion fill the cooling system.

1 : 3 Removing engine and automatic transmission

1 Remove the battery and tray. Drain the cooling system.

2 Study **FIG 1 : 2** and remove or disconnect the components shown. Before parting the drive shaft flanges indicated by the top insets, raise the car until the front wheels are clear of the ground. Lastly remove the engine rear mounting nuts, bottom right.

3 **FIG 1 : 3** shows the main components to remove or disconnect from above. First disconnect the stay and tie back the bonnet. Disconnect all electrical cables and the earth lead where they join the starter, generator, coil and car body and remove the distributor cap.

4 Remove the air cleaner, disconnect the controls top right, and the fuel pipe. Do operations top left and bottom left, then top and bottom centre. Release the cooling system spill hose from the radiator cowling.

5 Fit a lifting attachment to the cylinder head nuts and lift the engine vertically, just enough to release the drive shafts from the driving flanges and then remove the complete unit from the car.

When refitting, reverse the removal operations but note the following:

Lower the unit until the drive shafts can engage the driving flange studs and screw on the nuts about four threads, then lower the unit completely. Adjust the gearchange cable and selector rod by referring to **Chapter 6a**.

1 : 4 Removing and replacing the cylinder head

This can be done with the engine either in or out of the car.

1 Drain the cooling system (see **Chapter 4**). Disconnect the negative battery cable. Refer to **FIG 1 : 4** and pull the top hose off outlet elbow 48. Remove the upper support plate for the radiator.

2 Remove the carburetter(s) as instructed in **Chapter 2**. Remove the rocker cover 38 (two nuts 43). Remove the sparking plugs and release the distributor suction pipe clip from the water control valve housing. If a heater is fitted, remove the hose and cable from the valve at the rear righthand top of the head. Slacken top clip 56 on the rubber bypass connection.

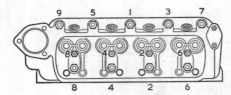

FIG 1 : 5 Slacken or tighten the cylinder head nuts in this order

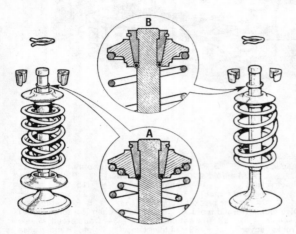

FIG 1 : 6 The valve assembly. 'A' shows double valve springs, and 'B' a single spring. Inset shows seal location at bottom of cotter groove

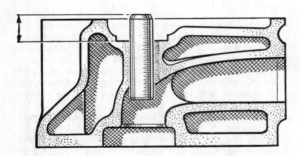

FIG 1 : 7 Drive in valve guides until $\frac{1}{32}$ inch projects above the valve spring seat as indicated

3 Release the exhaust pipe to manifold clamp. When fitted, remove the closed-circuit breather control valve by slackening the adaptor hose clip and removing the support bracket. Remove the nuts and washers securing the manifold(s) to the head and withdraw the manifold(s).

4 Remove the rocker assembly. **It is most important to slacken the external cylinder head nuts at the same time as the rocker bracket nuts or the head may be distorted and water subsequently find its way down the bores. The correct order is given in FIG 1 : 5.** Having lifted off the rocker assembly complete with brackets, lift out the pushrods and store them in the correct order for replacement.

5 With all the cylinder head nuts removed the head may be lifted off. In case of difficulty, tap on the sides of the head, using a block of wood to hammer on. This will break the joint. Lift the head squarely up the studs.

When refitting the head, clean the faces of the head and block and use a new gasket. This will be marked 'TOP' and 'FRONT' for correct fitting. Do up the head nuts finger tight, fit the pushrods in their correct positions and replace the rocker assembly. Make sure that the top and bottom ends of the pushrods are located properly. Do up all nuts finger tight and then tighten a turn at a time in the order given in FIG 1 : 5.

Whenever the head has been removed and replaced it is necessary to check and adjust the valve rocker clearances (see **Section 1 : 20**). After the engine has been run for some time, the head nuts must be retightened and the clearance checked again. Replace all the other parts in the reverse order and refill the cooling system. Run the engine and check for leaks. Finally, refit the bonnet.

1 : 5 Servicing the head and valve gear

1 Remove the head as in the preceding section. If decarbonizing is intended, plug all the waterways in the top face of the cylinder block with pieces of rag. Scrape the carbon from the combustion spaces in the head before removing the valves to avoid damage to the seats.

2 **FIG 1 : 6** shows the valve assembly on the 1098 cc engine. Use a spring compressor after removing the cotter clip at the top. With the spring(s) compressed, remove the split taper collets, release the compressor and lift off the cap, spring(s) and rubber sealing ring. Note in **FIG 1 : 4** that shroud 16 is no longer fitted. Remove the valve after marking it to ensure correct reassembly. Clean the ports free from carbon and examine the valve seats and stems.

3 Valve stems must show no signs of 'picking up' or wear, neither should they be bent. If satisfactory, but the valve seats show pitting too deep for removal by grinding paste, have the seats reground at a garage. If the seat is too far gone or has been burnt, fit new valves. Head seatings may also be badly worn or pitted and these may be recut after the glass-hard glaze has been removed. If the seats are then too wide they can be reduced by a facing cutter. Seatings which are beyond recutting can be restored by having inserts fitted.

4 To grind-in valves put a light spring under the head and use medium-grade carborundum paste unless the seats are in very good condition, when fine-grade paste may be used at once. Use a suction-cup tool and grind with a semi-rotary movement, letting the valve rise off the seat occasionally by pressure of the spring under the head. Use paste sparingly. When both seats have a smooth grey matt finish clean away every trace of the grinding paste from both port and valve.

5 If, on inspection, the valve guides are found to be worn they may be renewed. Use a drift $\frac{7}{16}$ inch in dia. to drive the old guide downwards into the head combustion space. The drift must have a spigot $\frac{9}{32}$ inch in dia. by 1 inch in length to locate in the guide bore. Drive new guides in from the top, inlet guides

being inserted with the largest chamfer uppermost. Exhaust guides should have their counterbored ends at the bottom. When fitted, the guides should project $\frac{19}{32}$ inch above the machined valve spring seating in the head as shown in **FIG 1 : 7**. When new guides are fitted the seatings must be recut to ensure concentricity.

6 To strip the rocker gear refer to **FIG 1 : 4** and remove locating screw 32 from the front rocker bracket 24. Mark the rockers and brackets for correct replacement, remove the splitpin and washers from the end of the shaft and slide off all the parts. To clean the oilway in the shaft remove plug 23.

7 Worn rocker bushes may be renewed on forged rockers only. The pressed type of rocker, which has an inserted tip for contact with the valve stem, must be renewed as an assembly. To fit a new bush to a forged rocker it must be drilled and aligned very carefully so that the hole will finish **up** coincident with the oil hole leading to the adjuster end of the rocker. The oil hole in the rocker boss must be continued by drilling through the bush with a No. 47 drill. Finally, burnish-ream the bore of the bush to .5630/.5635 inch.

8 To reassemble the rocker gear, secure the front bracket in place with the locating screw. Then reassemble the parts in the correct order, using lubricant. The screwed plug in the shaft must be at the front.

9 Finish decarbonizing by cleaning carbon from the piston crowns. Spring an old piston ring into the bore on top of the piston and scrape with a blunt tool so that a ring of carbon is left round the periphery to prevent excessive oil consumption. Clean off thoroughly and make sure that the faces of the head and the block are free from particles.

When reassembling the valves, fit new springs if the old ones are found to be shorter than the sizes specified in Technical Data. Also renew the rubber sealing rings, pressing them over the stem until they reach the bottom of the cotter recess as shown in **FIG 1 : 6**. Lubricate the valve stems before insertion. Refit the head as in **Section 1 : 4**.

1 : 6 Overhauling the valve timing gear

Refer to **FIG 1 : 8** for details of the timing gear and camshaft. To remove the timing gear proceed as follows:

1 Remove the radiator as described in **Chapter 4**. Slacken the generator mounting bolts, press the generator towards the block and remove the belt. Unlock and remove the crankshaft pulley securing screw. Carefully lever off the damper and pulley assembly. Remove screws 29 and 32 and pull off the cover 27. Note the seal in the cover.

2 Remove oil thrower 15. Unlock and remove camshaft nut 25. Using short levers, ease both chainwheels

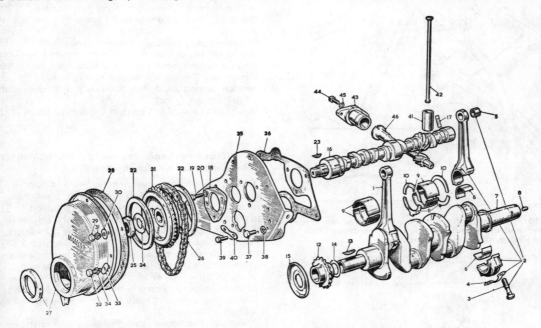

FIG 1 : 8 Timing gear and engine internal parts

Key to Fig 1 : 8 1 Connecting rod (Nos. 1 and 3) 2 Connecting rod (Nos. 2 and 4) 3 Screw 4 Washer 5 Small-end bush 6 Big-end bearing 7 Crankshaft 8 Plug 9 Crankshaft main bearing 10 Main bearing thrust washer (upper) 11 Main bearing thrust washer (lower) 12 Crankshaft gear 13 Key 14 Washer 15 Oil thrower 16 Camshaft 17 Pump driving pin 18 Camshaft locating plate 19 Screw 20 Washer 21 Camshaft gear 22 Tensioner ring 23 Gear key 24 Lockwasher 25 Nut 26 Timing chain 27 Timing chain cover 28 Cover joint 29 Cover screw 30 Washer 31 Washer 32 Screw 33 Washer 34 Washer 35 Mounting plate 36 Plate joint 37 Screw 38 Washer 39 Screw 40 Lockwasher 41 Tappet 42 Pushrod 43 Distributor housing 44 Screw 45 Washer 46 Drive spindle

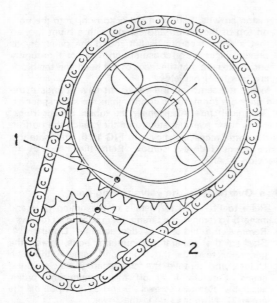

FIG 1:9 Replace timing gears with marks 1 and 2 opposite each other

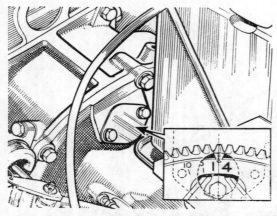

FIG 1:10 To see the flywheel timing marks, remove the cover and use a mirror. Mark 1/4 indicates TDC. 5, 10 and 15 deg. marks are also provided

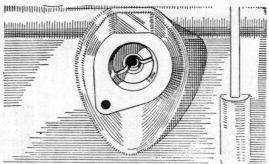

FIG 1:11 Distributor driving spindle correctly located, with large offset uppermost

forward complete with chain. Note the packing washers 14 behind crankshaft wheel 12.

3 When replacing the components in the reverse order be careful to fit the packing washers. If either of the chainwheels is renewed, check for thickness of packing by placing a straightedge across the sides of the camshaft wheel teeth. Measure the gap between the straightedge and the sides of the crankshaft wheel teeth with feeler gauges. This measurement is the thickness of the packing required behind the crankshaft wheel.

4 If the timing chain is noisy but not worn, fit new tensioner rings 22. Do not renew a chain alone but always the set of two wheels and a chain. To replace the parts set the crankshaft with its keyway at TDC and the camshaft keyway at one o'clock as shown in **FIG 1:9**. Assemble the wheels and chain with the timing dimples 1 and 2 opposite each other and fit the crankshaft wheel to the crankshaft key. Turn the camshaft to align the key and camshaft wheel keyway and press both wheels home. Fit lockwasher 24 and tighten the camshaft nut, locking it by turning up a tab.

5 Later oil thrower 15 is marked 'F' for front. Early unmarked throwers must be fitted with the concave side facing forward. **The early-type timing cover and oil thrower must be used together.** The next step must be taken with care. Fill the lips of the oil seal with grease and insert the pulley hub squarely. Turn the pulley as it enters to avoid damaging the lips of the seal.

6 Offer the pulley and timing cover to the crankshaft and line up the key and keyway. Push the pulley home and turn the cover carefully until the securing screw holes are aligned. Tighten the screws evenly, using a torque wrench setting of 6 lb ft for the $\frac{1}{4}$ inch ones and 14 lb ft for the $\frac{5}{16}$ inch.

7 Replace the rest of the parts in the reverse order.

1:7 Removing and replacing the camshaft, meshing distributor driving spindle

FIG 1:8 shows the components. See **Section 1:21** for procedure on cars with automatic transmission.

Start by removing the rocker assembly (**Section 1:5**), and then remove the manifolds. Remove the side covers and lift out tappets 41, storing them in the correct order for replacement. Remove the timing gear (**Section 1:6**). Do the following on models with a synchromesh gearbox:

1 Disconnect the high-tension leads from the coil and plugs and the thinner low-tension wire from the side of the distributor. Remove the distributor but do not slacken the clamping plate bolt or the timing will be lost (see **Chapter 3**).

2 Take out the screw and withdraw the distributor housing 43 from the block. Screw a $\frac{5}{16}$ inch UNF bolt $3\frac{1}{2}$ inches long into the tapped end of the distributor drive spindle 46 and withdraw it.

3 Remove camshaft locating plate 18 and withdraw the camshaft. Check the condition of the journals, the cams and the gear. Replacing bearing liners in the block is a skilled job which entails line-reaming with special equipment and the removal of the flywheel and transmission case.

4 Check the end float of the camshaft by reassembling the locating plate and chainwheel on the camshaft. Use feeler gauges to measure the clearance between the locating plate and the front face of the front camshaft journal. Excessive end float calls for renewal of the locating plate.

5 Lubricate the journals before replacing the camshaft and check that the rear end driving pin 17 will engage the oil pump spindle slot.

When the camshaft is in place it will be necessary to mesh the distributor driving spindle correctly.

6 Set No. 1 piston at TDC on the compression stroke. No. 4 inlet valve will then be just opening. Set the 1/4 mark on the flywheel in line with the pointer on the clutch cover as shown in **FIG 1 : 10**. Alternatively set the camshaft wheel dimples in line as in **FIG 1 : 9**. Screw the long $\frac{5}{16}$ inch bolt into the end of the distributor drive shaft and hold the shaft with the slot just below the horizontal with the large offset uppermost. Enter the gear. It will rotate as it engages with the camshaft gear until it is in approximately the two o'clock position as shown in **FIG 1 : 11**. Remove the long bolt, insert the distributor housing and secure it with the special bolt and washer. The head of the bolt must not protrude above the face of the housing. Refit the distributor. If the clamp bolt has been slackened and the timing lost, refer to **Chapter 3**.

7 Replace the remaining parts in the reverse order to that adopted when dismantling. If the tappets are found to be worn, fit new ones by selection. A tappet should just fall slowly into its guide when lubricated. Do not use too much force when tightening the side-cover bolts. Early shallow covers are easily distorted and a torque of 2 lb ft is enough. Later deep-pressed covers will stand a bolt torque of 5 lb ft.

1 : 8 Removing and replacing flywheel and clutch, synchromesh gearbox

Coil spring clutch:

1 Remove the battery and carrier. Remove the starter (see **Chapter 11**).

2 Release the clutch operating lever from the clutch cover, pulling the pushrod out of the slave cylinder. Refer to **Chapter 5** if necessary. Remove the slave cylinder and tie it to the engine bulkhead without disconnecting the flexible hose.

3 Remove the exhaust pipe clamp and the radiator cowling steady bracket. Release the rear engine mounting from the subframe sidemember. Extract the bolts securing the clutch cover to the flywheel housing.

4 Raise the engine enough to enable the cover to be removed, **but make sure that the fan blades cannot damage the radiator core.** Remove the clutch thrust plate from the pressure spring housing (three nuts).

5 **Do not remove the flywheel until Nos. 1 and 4 pistons are at TDC.** In this position the C-washer locating the primary gear is fitted with the bridge linking the two flats above the crankshaft and it cannot drop. Otherwise the washer can fall and wedge behind the flywheel oil seal with the probability of serious damage to the seal. Knock up the locking washer and slacken the flywheel retaining screw three or four

threads. Use Service Tool 18G.304 with adaptor set 18G.304M to free the flywheel from its taper.

As the flywheel is removed, oil may spill from the annulus at the back of the flywheel oil seal and run down the face of the flywheel onto the clutch driven plate. Watch for this to avoid assuming that the oil has passed the seal while in service. Keep the flywheel vertical to prevent the oil from contaminating the clutch facings.

6 Screw the three adaptor studs into the flywheel through the recessed holes in the clutch spring housing. Fit the plate of Tool No. 18G.304 over the studs, fit the nuts and screw them down evenly to keep the plate parallel with the flywheel. Insert the centre screw and withdraw the flywheel. Remove the extractor immediately the taper is broken.

7 Remove the flywheel retaining screw and the keyed driving washer. Withdraw the flywheel and clutch assembly. Refer to **Chapter 5** for clutch dismantling procedures.

8 The crankshaft primary gear cannot be removed without the flywheel housing being removed. This operation is covered in **Section 1 : 9**.

9 Refitting is a reversal of the preceding instructions. The oil seal must be lubricated before assembly to prevent burning before normal lubrication reaches the point.

Wipe all traces of oil from the crankshaft and flywheel tapers and ensure that the primary gear C-washer is positioned correctly in its groove. The best plan is to degrease the tapers so that they are perfectly dry before assembly. Turn the crankshaft so that the circlip is at the top of the shaft so that it cannot fall out, or it may prevent the flywheel from being pushed home. Tighten the flywheel retaining screw to a torque of 110 to 115 lb ft.

Diaphragm spring clutch:

Follow the preceding instructions but note that the clutch thrust plate is retained by a spring ring. Remove the flywheel and clutch assembly with Tools 18G.304 and 18G.304N. Refitting is a reversal of the removal instructions.

1 : 9 Removing flywheel housing

Remove the engine as in **Section 1 : 2** and the flywheel and clutch assembly as in **Section 1 : 8**. Then do the following:

1 Remove the setscrews and nuts holding the housing to the block and transmission case. Note the position of the fixings for correct replacement.

2 To avoid damaging the housing oil seal as it is withdrawn over the primary gear splines, use Service Tool 18G.570, which is fitted over the splines as shown in **FIG 1 : 12**.

3 When refitting in the reverse order make certain that the thrust washer behind the primary gear has its chamfered bore against the crankshaft flange as shown. Check end float of the primary gear according to the instructions in **Section 1 : 11**. Clean off all old jointing from mating faces and fit a new BMC gasket. This is important. Examine the sealing lips of the oil seals and renew any seals which are faulty or have been leaking.

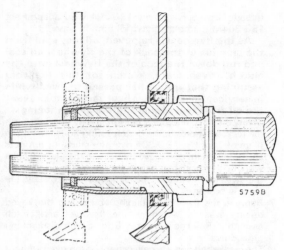

FIG 1:12 Removing and refitting the flywheel housing. Use Service Tool 18G.570 over the splines on the crankshaft primary gear to protect the oil seal

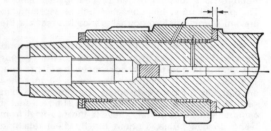

FIG 1:13 First type of crankshaft primary gear. Adjust end float with suitable thrust washer, indicated by arrows

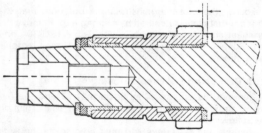

FIG 1:14 Later type of crankshaft primary gear. Adjust end float with suitable thrust washer, indicated by arrows

4 Continue reassembly by packing the first motion shaft rollers with high-melting-point grease to stop them tilting when the housing is being refitted. Use Tool 18G.570 over the primary gear splines as in dismantling and screw the two pilot bars which are part of the set into the two bottom tapped holes in the crankcase. These will pilot the housing into position and take the weight off the seal. If, during dismantling, it is found necessary to renew the gear train, the transmission casing must be removed as in the next Section. This will enable the idler gear end float to be determined.

5 Make quite sure that the correct short setscrew is fitted in the top righthand position in the housing as a long screw might damage the oil gallery in the block. Tighten the fixings to a torque of 18 lb ft. which will give the required compression of the gasket to a thickness of .030 inch. A small cutaway in the gasket enables a feeler gauge to be inserted between the machined faces to check this figure.

1:10 Removing the transmission, synchromesh gearbox

Remove the engine as in **Section 1:2** and the flywheel and clutch as in **Section 1:8**. Remove the starter motor, and the flywheel housing as in **Section 1:9**. Remove the setscrews from the flange of the transmission case, lift the engine and separate the two. Dismantling of the transmission is covered in **Chapter 6**. Refit as follows:

1 Remove all traces of old jointing materials. Check the end float of a new idler gear, if one is fitted, before the transmission case is put back (see **Chapter 6**).

2 Tighten all fixings finger tight at first, and then a turn at a time to ensure even pressure all round. This will make an oiltight joint and keep the gears in correct relationship.

3 Make sure that the front bearing cork oil seal remains correctly positioned as the crankcase and transmission case are brought together.

1:11 Servicing the crankshaft primary gear, synchromesh gearbox

This is an operation which follows on from removal of the flywheel housing in **Section 1:9**. There are two types of gear, the early one with lubricated bushes and a later type with non-lubricated bushes to obviate oil leakage into the clutch. These are shown in **FIGS 1:13** and **1:14** respectively. Remove the gear as follows:

First type with lubricated bushes

1 Extract the retaining C-washer and backing washer and withdraw the gear together with the thrust washers. If the bushes are worn, new ones can be fitted and burnish-reamed in line to a bore of 1.5015 to 1.5020 inch, as shown in **FIG 1:15**.

2 When refitting the gear check the end float between the inner thrust washer and the gear. Thrust washers are available in various thicknesses to obtain the correct clearance of .0035 to .0065 inch. The washer is indicated by arrows in **FIG 1:13**. When the gap is .1295 to .1315 inch, use a washer .125 to .127 inch thick. When the gap is .1315 to .1335 inch, use a washer .127 to .129 in thick. When the gap is .1335 to .1345 inch, use a washer .129 to .131 inch thick. The rear thrust washer must be fitted with its treated face against the thrust face of the backing washer.

Note that this type of gear is pressure-lubricated through drillings in the crankshaft.

Second type with non-lubricated bushes

With this type there is no oil feed from the crankshaft and no oil seal in the flywheel. Remove the gear by removing the flywheel housing as in **Section 1:9** and following the preceding instructions. The end float must be the same as given for the early type with lubricated bushes but the thrust washer selection is as follows:

When the gap is .1175 to .119 inch, use a washer .112 to .114 inch thick. When the gap is .119 to .121 inch, use a washer .114 to .116 inch thick. When the gap is .121 to .123 inch, use a washer .116 to .118 inch thick. When the gap is .123 to .125 inch, use a washer .118 to .120 inch thick.

1 : 12 Pistons and connecting rods, 1098 cc engine

It is important to remember that the piston with gudgeon pin and connecting rod with small-end bush can only be obtained as assemblies. The small-end bush and the gudgeon pin must not be renewed separately.

Removing (synchromesh gearbox):

See **Section 1 : 21** for changes when automatic transmission is fitted.

The cooling system, the transmission case and the external oil filter must be drained and then the engine removed from the frame as in **Section 1 : 2**. Remove the flywheel and clutch as in **Section 1 : 8**, the flywheel housing as in **Section 1 : 9**, the transmission as in **Section 1 : 10**, and the cylinder head as in **Section 1 : 4**. Then proceed as follows, referring to **FIG 1 : 8**:

1 Unlock and remove the big-end bolts 3 and remove the caps, after marking both cap and rod for bore and position. Remove any carbon ring from the top of the cylinder and push the rod and piston up and out. Refit the cap.
2 The gudgeon pins are fully floating. Remove the two circlips and press out the pins, but first mark the pistons so that they will be reassembled in their correct bores and the right way round.

Piston rings:

To remove the rings slide a piece of thin steel like a disused .020 inch feeler gauge under one end and pass it round under the ring, at the same time gently pressing the raised part onto the piston land above. Always remove and refit rings over the top of the piston. Clean carbon deposit from the rings grooves with a piece of broken ring but do not remove metal or oil consumption will increase.

Before fitting new rings remove the cylinder bore glaze with garage equipment and check the ring gap in the bore. Place a piston about 1 inch down the bore and press the new ring down onto it. Measure the gap between the ring ends with a feeler gauge and file the ends if necessary until the gap is .006 to .011 inch. The second and third rings are tapered and must be fitted with the narrow taper upwards. The narrow face is stamped with a 'T' for identification.

Piston sizes:

During production the pistons are fitted by selective assembly as shown by markings on the crown (see **FIG 1 : 16**). A piston stamped with a figure 2 in the diamond is for a bore with the same stamp.

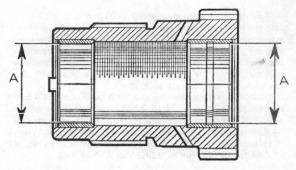

FIG 1 : 15 Crankshaft primary gear bushes. Line-ream to 1.5015 to 1.5020 inch

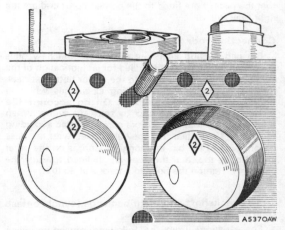

FIG 1 : 16 Piston graded sizes are stamped in a diamond. Piston and bore marks must coincide. Oversize dimensions are stamped in an ellipse

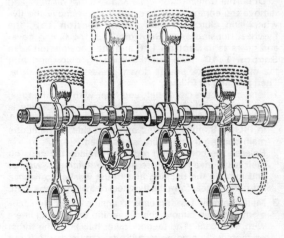

FIG 1 : 17 The offset connecting rods correctly assembled. Longer boss faces away from adjacent main bearing

Two oversizes are available, +.010 and +.020 inch and the piston crowns are stamped with the actual oversize dimensions in an ellipse. This dimension is the bore size for a piston so marked and the running clearance is allowed for in the piston machining. When fitting oversize pistons, stamp the block adjacent to the bore with the oversize. Piston sizes are as follows:

Standard pistons are suitable for a bore size of 64.576 to 64.635 mm or 2.5424 to 2.5447 inch. Pistons which are +.010 inch oversize are suitable for a bore size of 64.830 to 64.889 mm or 2.5524 to 2.5547 inch. When the pistons are +.020 inch oversize, a suitable bore size is 65.084 to 65.143 mm or 2.5624 to 2.5647 inch

Refitting pistons:

Lubricate all parts and set the rings with their gaps at 90 deg. to each other. Check all markings to ensure that the pistons are fitted to the correct bores and are the right way round.

Connecting rods:

Big-end bearing liners are renewable and new ones are interchangeable, being drilled for jet lubrication of the cylinder walls whether fitted to the top or bottom. Check for bearing material and running clearances with the figures given in Technical Data. **On no account file either the rod or the cap to take up wear.** When refitting, check that the rods are correctly fitted according to **FIG 1 : 17**. Notice that they are offset, with the boss on one side of the big-end longer than it is on the other side. Notice too, that the caps are inclined towards the camshaft. Tighten the bolts to a torque of 35 lb ft.

1 : 13 Crankshaft and main bearings (synchromesh gearbox)

For variations from the following procedure when automatic transmission is fitted, refer to **Section 1 : 21.**

Removing:

Drain the transmission case and external oil filter and remove the engine as in **Section 1 : 2.** Remove the flywheel and clutch assembly as in **Section 1 : 8,** the flywheel housing as in **Section 1 : 9,** the timing cover and gears as in **Section 1 : 6** and the transmission as in **Section 1 : 10.** Take out the sparking plugs and turn the cylinder block upside down, preferably in a fixture. Then proceed as follows:

1 First check the crankshaft end float with a dial gauge, levering the shaft endwise. The correct clearance is .002 to .003 inch and new thrust washers 10 and 11 in **FIG 1 : 8** must be fitted on either side of the centre main bearing if this figure is exceeded.

2 Release the connecting rods and replace the caps on their respective rods. Prise out the retaining C-washer and remove the backing and thrust washer to release the primary gear from the flywheel end of the crankshaft.

3 Mark the main bearing caps to ensure correct replacement and then remove them, keeping the bearing liners with their caps. The tagged lower halves of the thrust washers will come away with the centre cap. Lift out the crankshaft, the top halves of the thrust washers and the top half-bearing liners from the block.

Check the crankpins and main bearing journals for wear, scoring and ovality. The shaft may be reground to undersizes of −.010, −.020, −.030 and −.040 inch and suitable bearing liners are available for those sizes. **Never file the bearing caps in an attempt to take up wear.**

Force paraffin through the oilways in the shaft, followed by clean thin engine oil. This is particularly important if a bearing has 'run' as every trace of bearing metal must be removed from the lubricating system. Renew the bearing liners if they are scored, pitted or breaking up.

Refitting:

Replace the thrust washers with the oil grooves facing outwards and the tagged halves in the centre cap. The bearing liners are notched to fit in recesses in the top housing and the cap. Lubricate all running surfaces liberally with engine oil during reassembly. Tighten the bolts to a torque of 60 lb ft.

1 : 14 Flywheel starter ring (synchromesh gearbox)

Remove a worn starter ring gear from the flywheel by splitting it with a cold chisel, taking care not to damage the flywheel. Check that the mating surfaces of gear and flywheel are clean and free from burrs.

Heat the new ring evenly to a light blue colour, which is equivalent to a temperature of 300°C to 400°C or 572°F to 752°F. Do not exceed this temperature or the gear teeth will be softened. Drop the ring over the flywheel register with the lead on the teeth towards the register. Tap lightly into place and allow to cool naturally. The shrink fit so obtained will make the ring immovable.

1 : 15 The oil pump (synchromesh gearbox)

For details of the oil pump when automatic transmission is fitted, refer to **Section 1 : 21.**

To remove the oil pump, remove the engine as in **Section 1 : 2,** the flywheel and clutch assembly as in **Section 1 : 8** and the flywheel housing as in **Section 1 : 9.** Bend back the locking washers and remove the bolts securing the pump to the crankcase. Note the position of the driving slot in the shaft to facilitate replacement.

Two types of pump are fitted, as shown in **FIG 1 : 18** and only the top one, which is the Hobourn-Eaton, is capable of being dismantled. The other must be renewed as an assembly.

Servicing the Hobourn-Eaton pump:

Remove setscrew 4 and lift off cover 3, noting the locating dowels. With the rotors in place, check the end float by placing a straightedge across the face of the pump and using feelers to measure the clearance between the top face of the rotors and the underside of the straightedge. This clearance must not exceed .005 inch and excessive clearance can be reduced by removing the dowels and lapping the face of the pump body, keeping it square and flat.

With the rotors installed, measure the clearance of the rotor lobes in the positions shown in the illustration at **A.** Renew the rotors if the clearance exceeds .006 inch.

Reassemble in the reverse order and check the pump for freedom of action. Refit to the block by aligning the drive slot with the pin in the end of the camshaft. Use a new gasket and make sure it does not obscure the intake and delivery ports. Use new tab locking washer(s).

1 : 16 Lubrication, oil filter and relief valve

Drain oil from the engine and transmission by removing the magnetic plug on the righthand rear side of the transmission casing. Do this when the oil is hot as it flows more freely. Renew the plug washer on alternate oil changes.

Oil pressure warning light on early Morris and MG models:

With the ignition switched on the warning light should glow and go out when the engine is running. If it does not, the cause may be lack of oil, low oil pressure, need for an oil change or a clogged filter. Locate the trouble as follows:

1 Check the oil level.
2 Disconnect the lead from the filter head. If the light then goes out fit a new filter element and change the oil. **If the light still glows with the lead disconnected and the engine running, stop the engine at once.** Then check that the oil strainer in the sump is not choked with sludge. Check that the pressure-fed bearings have the correct working clearances as excessive play will allow oil to escape more readily. Check that there is no air leak at the pump pickup union on the suction side of the pump and that the pump is in good condition.

Oil pressure warning lights on all models except early Morris and MG:

If the oil filter warning light continues to glow when the engine is running at or above a fast-idle, fit a new element and change the oil before another 300 miles have been run. If the oil pressure warning light glows when the engine is running check preceding Operation 1 and also Operation 2, starting with the oil strainer.

Changing filter element:

Disconnect the battery before starting work on the filter. Refer to **FIG 1 : 19** and unscrew the centre bolt which is arrowed. Hold the bowl upright as it will be full of oil. Remove the element and internal parts and clean the inside of the bowl in fuel. **Do not attempt to clean the element as nothing useful can be done with it.**

Refit parts 1 to 5 in the order shown, making sure that the new element is the correct replacement, and that seating washer 3 is a good fit on the bolt. Check the sealing washers in the head and on the bolt and renew them if necessary. Use a torque of 10 to 15 lb ft on the centre bolt. It is essential that there is no leakage from the filter as this could lead to complete failure of the engine lubricating system. Fit the assembled bowl after filling it with clean engine oil, run the engine and check for leaks at once.

On the '1100' with automatic transmission it will be necessary to slacken the ignition coil mounting bracket clamp to remove the filter bowl.

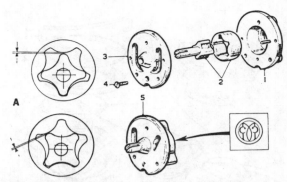

FIG 1 : 18 The two types of oil pump which may be fitted. Pump 5, made by Concentric (Engineering) Ltd, is serviced as an assembly only. 'A' indicates lobe positions for checking clearance on Hobourn-Eaton pump

Key to Fig 1 : 18 (Hobourn-Eaton)
1 Body 2 Shaft and rotor 3 Cover 4 Screw, cover to body

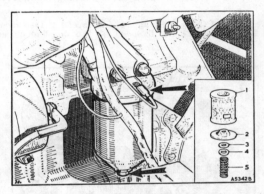

FIG 1 : 19 Oil filter on engines without automatic transmission

Key to Fig 1 : 19   1 Filter element   2 Seating plate
3 Seating washer   4 Steel washer   5 Spring

Lubrication:

Note that on cars fitted with automatic transmission the method of checking the oil level is to run the engine for one or two minutes. Then switch off and wait a minute before using the dipstick.

Oil pressure relief valve

This valve deals with excessive pressure when the oil is cold and thick. It is to be found on the rear righthand side of the cylinder block under a domed nut. This nut may have one copper washer or two fibre washers and the correct type must be fitted to give the required lifting pressure. Take out the spring and valve cup and check the spring against the figures given in Technical Data. Fit a new cup if the seating is worn.

1 : 17 Closed circuit breathing

When fitted, this device will appear as in **FIG 1 : 20**. To dismantle, remove clip 1. Clean all metal parts in fuel. Difficult deposits can be removed by first boiling the parts before cleaning with fuel. Do not use abrasives.

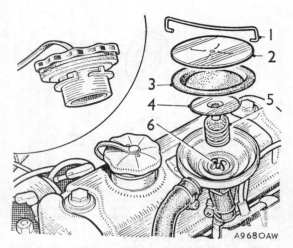

FIG 1 : 20 Closed circuit breathing arrangement, later type

Key to Fig 1 : 20   1 Spring clip   2 Cover   3 Diaphragm
4 Metering needle   5 Spring   6 Cruciform guides

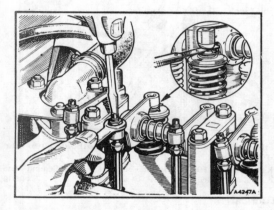

FIG 1 : 21 Adjusting the valve rocker clearance, with inset showing the feeler gauge in use

Clean the diaphragm with detergent or methylated spirits. Renew parts which are worn or damaged, but note that the early type of valve assembly without the cruciform guides 6 can only be serviced as an assembly.

When reassembly the later type, make sure the metering needle is in the cruciform guides and that the diaphragm is seated correctly.

1 : 18 Valve timing

Set No. 1 cylinder inlet valve to .029 inch clearance with the engine cold and turn the crankshaft until the valve is about to open. The 1/4 TDC mark on the flywheel should then be opposite the pointer in the clutch cover inspection aperture as shown in **FIG 1 : 10**. The inlet valve should be about to open and No. 4 piston should be at TDC on its compression stroke.

Having completed the check, do not forget to restore the inlet valve clearance to the normal running figure. It is not possible to check the valve timing accurately when the clearance is normal, and it is increased to .029 inch so that the valve starts to open at TDC. With automatic transmission the timing marks are on the converter.

1 : 19 Reassembling a stripped engine

All dismantling and reassembling operations have been given in detail in the various Sections, so that it is simply a matter of tackling the tasks in the correct sequence. Always fit new gaskets, which are available in complete sets. Lubricate all running surfaces with clean engine oil.

Start by fitting the crankshaft, followed by the pistons and connecting rods. Fit the oil pump and camshaft, then the timing gear and cover, not forgetting the distributor driving spindle. With the engine the right way up, fit the tappets and pushrods, followed by the assembled head and then the rocker gear. Replace the sidecovers but first check that all the pushrods are correctly located at both ends. Fit the crankshaft primary gear, the transmission, the flywheel housing and the flywheel and clutch assembly. If the engine is out of the frame, replace it by following the instructions in **Section 1 : 2** or **1 : 3** in reverse order. Torque wrench figures for all important fixings are given in Technical Data.

When all refitting operations are completed it is time to adjust the valve rockers as follows. Finally, refill the systems with oil and water.

1 : 20 Valve rocker adjustment

The method of adjusting the clearance is shown in **FIG 1 : 21**. The correct clearance for both inlet and exhaust valves is .012 inch with the engine cold and no departure from this figure is permissible. Press down on the adjusting screw when checking in order to disperse any oil film inside the pushrod cup, and hold it with a screwdriver while tightening the locknut. Check after tightening in case the screw has shifted. Note that accurate setting is impossible if the valve stem end of the rocker arm is pitted with wear, as the feeler gauge will simply be bridging the depression.

The clearance of each valve must be set with its tappet on the back of the cam, opposite to the cam peak. This is readily done by working to the following sequence:

Adjust No. 1 rocker with No. 8 valve fully open.
Adjust No. 3 rocker with No. 6 valve fully open.
Adjust No. 5 rocker with No. 4 valve fully open.
Adjust No. 2 rocker with No. 7 valve fully open.
Adjust No. 8 rocker with No. 1 valve fully open.
Adjust No. 6 rocker with No. 3 valve fully open.
Adjust No. 4 rocker with No. 5 valve fully open.
Adjust No. 7 rocker with No. 2 valve fully open.

Notice that the numbers in each line add up to nine. Remembering this, it is easy to go on checking without constant reference to the table.

If the head has been off and a new gasket fitted, run the engine for about 100 miles and then tighten the head nuts and check the rocker clearance again. Every time extra tightening is carried out on cylinder head nuts it will affect the clearance, so always check it.

1 : 21 Operations affected by automatic transmission

The removal of an engine fitted with automatic transmission has been covered in **Section 1 : 3.** The following operations detail all the procedures to be used when servicing the engine, where they differ from similar operations carried out on an engine with synchromesh gearbox.

Working on the cylinder head :

This is fully covered in **Sections 1 : 4** and **1 : 5** and rocker clearance adjustment is to be found in **Section 1 : 20.**

Overhauling the valve timing gear :

Refer to **Section 1 : 6.** Note when checking the valve timing as in **Section 1 : 18** that turning the crankshaft is done by inserting a screwdriver through the hole in the converter housing shown in **FIG 3 : 6** in the Ignition Chapter. The screwdriver is used to lever against the starter ring gear teeth. With the 1/4 mark on the converter in line with the pointer on the cover, the piston will be at TDC.

Removing and replacing the camshaft :

Follow the instructions given in **Section 1 : 7,** but remove the engine and transmission as instructed in **Section 1 : 3.**

Be extremely careful when removing the camshaft. The oil pump drive coupling may stick by oil adhesion to the camshaft and possibly fall into the transmission unit. Ensure therefore, when refitting the camshaft, that this coupling is correctly located on the oil pump spindle splines. Renewal of the camshaft bearings entails the removal of the converter, converter housing and transmission unit.

When removing and refitting the distributor driving spindle, turn the engine over by the method just given under 'Overhauling the valve timing gear'.

Removing and replacing the transmission unit :

This is necessary in order to work on the oil pump, the pistons and connecting rods and the crankshaft, operations which will be covered after the following instructions are completed.

Removing the transmission unit :

1 Remove the engine and transmission as in **Section 1 : 3.**
Remove the radiator mounting bracket, the starter motor and the converter cover. Drain the transmission. Unlock the converter centre bolt, stop the converter from turning with a screwdriver inserted through the hole in the housing and remove the centre bolt. Unlock and remove three equally spaced setscrews from the converter centre and set the crankshaft slot horizontal.
2 Remove the converter with Special Tool 18G.1086 as shown in **FIG 1 : 22** and also the low pressure valve indicated by the bottom arrow. Fit Tool 18G.1088 on the converter output gear and remove the self-locking nut from the input gear. **FIG 1 : 23** will help when identifying parts.

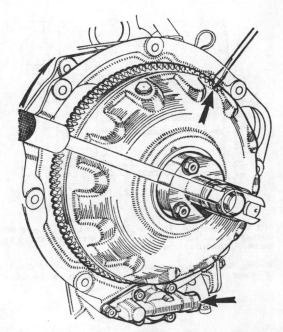

FIG 1 : 22 Removing the converter with Service Tool 18G.1086. Top arrow shows screwdriver preventing converter from turning. Lower arrow points to the low pressure valve. Automatic transmission

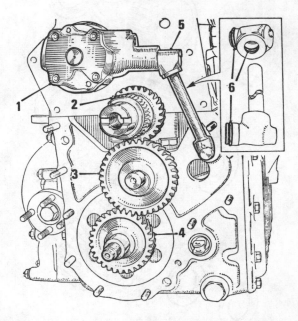

FIG 1 : 23 The converter housing removed. Automatic transmission

Key to Fig 1 : 23 1 Main oil pump 2 Converter output gear 3 Idler gear 4 Input gear 5 Oil feed pipe 6 Sealing rings

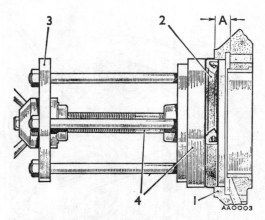

FIG 1 : 24 Service Tool in use to fit the converter output gear oil seal. 'A' is the depth measurement to be taken. Automatic transmission

Key to Fig 1 : 24   1 Converter housing   2 Oil seal
3 Service tool 18G.1068   4 Service tool adaptor set 18G.1068.A

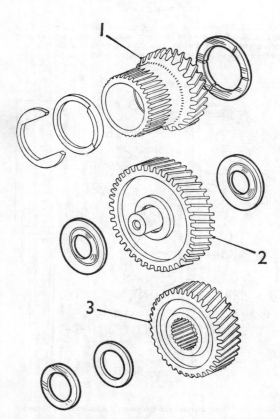

FIG 1 : 25 Converter output gear 1, idler gear 2, and input gear 3, showing their respective thrust washers. Automatic transmission

3 Remove the gearchange bellcrank lever and the lever pivot. Fit protector sleeve 18G.1098 over the output gear and remove the converter housing. Lever the main oil feed pipe from transmission and oil pump. Remove idler gear, thrust washers and output gear. Disconnect governor control rod at carburetter.

4 Remove oil filter and engine oil feed pipe with rubber seal and spring washer. Remove nuts and setscrews and lift engine away from transmission. Inspect all seals and bearings and renew if necessary. Replacing the converter output gear oil seal needs special care as it is possible for it to blank off the oil drain hole behind. Mark the housing bore anywhere on the periphery and take all measurements from that point. Take measurement A in FIG 1 : 24. If it is $\frac{3}{8}$ inch press the new seal in flush with the housing face. If it is less, fit the seal proud of the housing face by the difference between the two measurements and vice-versa if A is more than $\frac{3}{8}$ inch. The reason for taking all measurements from a single point is that the converter housing face is not machined. Fit the seal, using the Special Tools named in the illustration, after lubricating it well.

Refitting the transmission unit:

1 Immerse the front main bearing cap rubber seal in oil and fit with the lip facing the rear of the engine. Fit the rubber sealing ring to the main oil strainer pipe and fit new gaskets to the transmission case (see FIG 1 : 23). Locate the moulded rubber seal correctly and fit the engine to the transmission. Tighten the setscrews and nuts as lowering takes place.

2 Refit the main oil feed pipe with the spring washer beneath the rubber seal. Refit the oil filter, with its two rubber sealing rings and gaskets. Refit the main oil pump to transmission oil pipe.

3 Trim off excess transmission jointing from the rear of the unit, clean the surfaces and fit a new converter housing gasket. Refit the converter output gear. Apart from small differences in design, it is possible to use FIG 1 : 14 for reference and the 'Second type' operation in Section 1 : 11 when making certain that the correct running clearance of .0035 to .0065 inch is maintained. Fit the chamfered inner edge of the thrust washer facing the crankshaft. (See also FIG 1 : 25).

4 Referring to the same illustration, assemble idler gear 2 to the transmission with any nominal washer from the range of washers available fitted on the transmission side of the gear. Refer to FIG 1 : 26 and assemble Service Tool 18G.1089 with a dental wax washer interposed onto the converter housing side of the gear. Fit the Service Tool to input gear 3 with a dental wax washer interposed. If the input gear will not fully mesh with the idler gear it indicates that the third speed reaction gear thrust washer has become displaced. This must be remedied by removing, dismantling and reassembling the gear train; an operation which must be entrusted to a Service Station equipped to do such work.

5 Fit protector sleeve 18G.1098 over output gear 1 and refit the housing, tightening the bolts to 18 lb ft. Do not fit the input shaft nut. Then remove the housing.

6 Measure the thickness of the idler gear thrust washer plus the thickness of the Service Tool and its dental wax washer. Subtract .004 to .007 inch to give the total thickness of thrust washers required for the correct end float. Washers are available in thicknesses of .132 to .133 inch, .134 to .135 inch, .136 to .137 inch and .138 to .139 inch.

7 Measure the thickness of the input gear Service Tool and its dental wax washer. Add .001 to .003 inch to give the total thickness of thrust washers required to give the correct 'nip' on the input bearing. Input gear thrust washers are available in thicknesses of .128 to .130 inch, .132 to .134 inch, .140 to .142 inch, .148 to .150 inch and .152 to .154 inch.

8 Divide the total thickness by 2 to find the thickness of each washer fitted on either side of the **idler gear.** Fit two washers to make up the calculated thickness onto the **input gear shaft,** fitting them on the outside of the gear with the chamfered inner edge of one washer towards the gear.

9 Refit the converter outlet pipe, checking that it is square with the casing. Refit the housing, tightening the fixings to a torque of 18 lb ft. Tighten the input gear nut to a torque of 70 lb ft. Service Tool 18G.1088 will hold the converter output gear while Tool 18G.592 tightens the nut. Fit new locking plates to each pair of converter bolts in turn, tightening the bolts to 22 to 24 lb ft. Lock with the tabs. Lubricate the oil seal and fit the converter. Refit the washer (offset pegs), centre bolt and lockwasher. Tighten to 110 to 115 lb ft. and lock. Refit the low pressure valve and gasket. Refit the gear selector bellcrank lever, clevis pin and rubber boot. Refit the converter cover, starter motor and rear engine mounting.

Removing the oil pump:

1 Remove the engine and transmission. Follow the preceding instructions under 'Removing the transmission unit' as far as levering off the main oil feed pipe in Operation 3. Remove the pump securing screws and withdraw the pump.

2 Service the pump as in **Section 1 : 15** but refer to **FIG 1 : 27** which shows the later type of Hobourn-Eaton pump.

Pistons and connecting rods:

1 Follow **Section 1 : 12** but note that it is necessary to remove the engine and transmission according to **Section 1 : 3.**

2 Remove the converter, converter housing and transmission unit from the engine as in the preceding instructions on 'Removing the transmission unit'. Refit in the reverse order.

Crankshaft and main bearings:

1 Follow **Section 1 : 13** but remove the engine and transmission unit as in **Section 1 : 3.**

2 Remove the converter, converter housing and transmission unit from the engine as in the preceding instructions on 'Removing the transmission unit'.

3 Inspect and refit the crankshaft and bearings according to **Section 1 : 13.** Inspect and refit the transmission unit according to the preceding instructions.

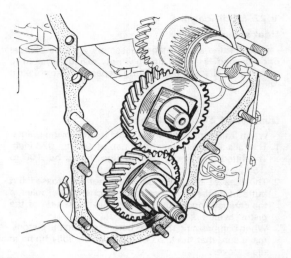

FIG 1 : 26   Input and idler gears fitted with Service Tool 18G.1089. Tool is two sets of washers with a wax washer between each pair. Automatic transmission

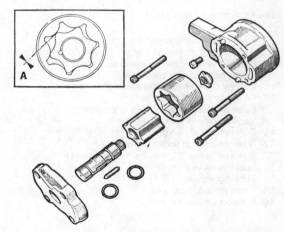

FIG 1 : 27   Main oil pump for engine with automatic transmission. 'A' shows lobe position for checking clearance

Converter output gear:

Remove the engine and transmission (see **Section 1 : 3**). In Operation 1 of 'Removing the transmission unit' in the instructions just given, begin with the removal of the starter motor and carry on to the point in Operation 3 where the converter housing has been removed. Then remove the idler gear, thrust washers and the converter output gear assembly (see **FIG 1 : 25**). Adjust by starting at 'Refit the converter output gear' in Operation 3 of the preceding instructions on 'Refitting the transmission unit', and complete that Operation. Refit by completing Operation 9.

1:22 Modifications

Heat shield:

This is fitted as an integral assembly with the silencer on later models. When fitting a new exhaust system to earlier cars, discard the existing separate heat shield if one is fitted.

Dualflex 61 oil control rings:

When fitting this type of ring note the following points:
1 The rails should have a fitted gap of .012 to .028 inch. The fitted gap of the side springs should be .100 to .150 inch.
2 The lugs of the expander must not be crossed but butted together and inserted into one of the holes in the scraper ring groove on the non-thrust side of the piston, which is the camshaft side.
3 When compressing the rings before refitting the pistons, make sure that the ends of the rings are fully home in the grooves.
4 Remove any glaze from the bore.

1:23 Fault diagnosis

(a) Engine will not start

1 Defective coil
2 Faulty distributor capacitor (condenser)
3 Dirty, pitted or incorrectly set contact breaker points
4 Ignition wires loose or insulation faulty
5 Water on sparking plug leads
6 Battery discharged, corrosion of terminals
7 Faulty or jammed starter
8 Sparking plug leads wrongly connected
9 Vapour lock in fuel pipes
10 Defective fuel pump
11 Overchoking or underchoking
12 Blocked petrol filter or carburetter jet(s)
13 Leaking valves
14 Sticking valves
15 Valve timing incorrect
16 Ignition timing incorrect

(b) Engine stalls

1 Check 1, 2, 3, 4, 5, 10, 11, 12, 13 and 14 in (a)
2 Sparking plugs defective or gaps incorrect
3 Retarded ignition
4 Mixture too weak
5 Water in fuel system
6 Petrol tank vent blocked
7 Incorrect valve clearances

(c) Engine idles badly

1 Check 2 and 7 in (b)
2 Air leak at manifold joints
3 Carburetter jet setting wrong
4 Air leak in carburetter
5 Over-rich mixture
6 Worn piston rings

7 Worn valve stems or guides
8 Weak exhaust valve springs

(d) Engine misfires

1 Check 1, 2, 3, 4, 5, 8, 10, 12, 13, 14, 15 and 16 in (a) 2, 3, 4 and 7 in (b)
2 Weak or broken valve springs

(e) Engine overheats, see Chapter 4

(f) Compression low

1 Check 13 and 14 in (a), 6 and 7 in (c) and 2 in (d)
2 Worn piston ring grooves
3 Scored or worn cylinder bores

(g) Engine lacks power

1 Check 3, 10, 11, 12, 13, 14, 15 and 16 in (a); 2, 3, 4 and 7 in (b); 6 and 7 in (c); and 2 in (d). Also check (e) and (f)
2 Leaking joint washers
3 Fouled sparking plugs
4 Automatic advance not operating

(h) Burnt valves or seats

1 Check 13 and 14 in (a), 7 in (b) and 2 in (d). Also check (e)
2 Excessive carbon around valve seats and head

(j) Sticking valves

1 Check 2 in (d)
2 Bent valve stem
3 Scored valve stem or guide
4 Incorrect valve clearance

(k) Excessive cylinder wear

1 Check 11 in (a) and see Chapter 4
2 Lack of oil
3 Dirty oil
4 Piston rings gummed up or broken
5 Badly fitting piston rings
6 Connecting rod bent

(l) Excessive oil consumption

1 Check 6 and 7 in (c) and check (k)
2 Ring gaps too wide
3 Oil return holes in piston choked with carbon
4 Scored cylinders
5 Oil level too high
6 External oil leaks
7 Ineffective valve stem oil seals

(m) Crankshaft and connecting rod bearing failure

1 Check 2 in (k)
2 Restricted oilways
3 Worn journals or crankpins

4 Loose bearing caps
5 Extremely low oil pressure
6 Bent connecting rod

(n) Internal water leakage, see Chapter 4

(o) Poor water circulation, see Chapter 4

(p) Corrosion, see Chapter 4

(q) High fuel consumption, see Chapter 2

(r) Engine vibration

1 Loose generator bolts
2 Mounting rubbers loose or ineffective
3 Exhaust pipe mountings too tight
4 Fan blades out of balance
5 Misfiring due to mixture, ignition or mechanical faults

CHAPTER 2

THE FUEL SYSTEM

2 : 1 Description

All the models use SU electric fuel pumps and SU carburetters. There are two types of fuel pump to be covered, one is designated SP and the other AUF.200. Basically they are identical in operation, but there is some difference in the design of the inlet and outlet valves, as can be seen in **FIG 2 : 1**.

On 1098 cc synchromesh transmission engines the carburetter(s) may be a single or twin HS2 type, according to the car. On all automatic transmission engines the carburetter is a single HS4.

2 : 2 Routine maintenance

Every 3000 miles, unscrew the damper unit from the top of the carburetter and pour thin 20W engine oil into the hollow piston rod until the level is $\frac{1}{2}$ inch above the top as shown in **FIG 2 : 9**.

2 : 3 Pump removal and dismantling

Early cars:

The pump is under the luggage compartment on the lefthand side. Remove by disconnecting the earth lead from the battery and the supply leads from the pump. Disconnect the inlet, outlet and vent pipe connections. Release the pump bracket from the underside of the floor.

Later cars:

The pump is inside the luggage compartment on the righthand side. To remove it, disconnect the battery earth lead, and from under the car disconnect the inlet and outlet connections, leaving the hoses secured to the pump connections. Lift the compartment floor and remove the drive screws securing the pump bracket to the body. Withdraw the pump and disconnect the earth lead.

Dismantling:

1 Refer to **FIG 2 : 1** and remove terminal parts 30 to 33 and seal 43 if fitted. Take off cover 29. Remove contact blade 22.
2 Remove housing screws 7 and earthing screw 9. Part housing 6 from body 1 or 44 according to type of pump. Unscrew diaphragm 2 anticlockwise, holding the assembly over the bench to catch the eleven brass rollers 3. Do not attempt to remove the diaphragm from its spindle.
3 Remove washer 21 and nut 20. Cut away lead washer 19. Release pedestal 16 (two screws 28). Remove earth tag 13, tip the pedestal and withdraw terminal stud 17 from the terminal tag. Take away the pedestal complete with rocker mechanism.
4 Push out pin 14 to release the rocker mechanism, which cannot be further dismantled.

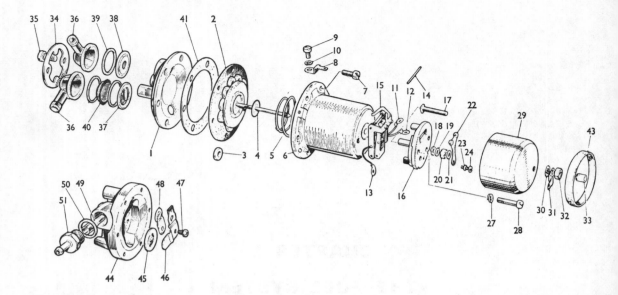

FIG 2:1   Components of SU electric fuel pumps, types SP and AUF.200

Key to Fig. 2:1   1 Pump body (AUF.200 only)   2 Diaphragm and spindle assembly   3 Armature centralizing roller
4 Impact washer   5 Armature spring   6 Coil housing   7 Setscrew   8 Earth connector   9 Setscrew
10 Spring washer   11 Terminal tag   12 Terminal tag   13 Earth tag   14 Rocker pivot pin
15 Rocker mechanism   16 Pedestal   17 Terminal stud   18 Spring washer   19 Lead washer
20 Terminal nut   21 End-cover seal washer   22 Contact blade   23 Washer   24 Contact blade screw
27 Spring washer   28 Screw   29 End-cover   30 Shakeproof washer   31 Connector   32 Nut
33 Insulating sleeve   34 Clamp plate   35 Setscrew   36 Inlet and outlet nozzles   37 Inlet valve
38 Outlet valve   39 Sealing washer   40 Filter   41 Gasket   43 Sealing band   44 Pump body
45 Outlet valve   46 Valve retainer   47 Screw   48 Inlet valve   49 Filter   50 Washer   51 Inlet nozzle
Items 34 to 41, AUF.200 only.   Items 43 to 51, SP only.

5 **On the AUF.200 pump** remove clamp plate 34 (two
 2BA screws). Remove nozzles 36, filter 40 and valves
 37 and 38.

6 **On the SP pump** unscrew inlet nozzle 51 and remove
 filter 49. Take out Phillips screw 47 to release the two
 valve assemblies 45 and 48.

2:4   Examination of pump

Type AUF.200:

1 Clean all the parts and inspect for cracks, damaged
 joint faces and threads. Suck and blow at the valve
 assemblies to check that they are seating properly.
 The narrow retaining tongue on the valve cage should
 allow a valve lift of approximately $\frac{1}{16}$ inch.

2 Look for damage or corrosion in the valve recesses in
 the body. If the valve seating is pitted the body will
 need renewal.

3 Clean the filter with a brush and not with a piece of
 fluffy rag. If it is cracked, renew it. Check all electrical
 leads and tags for damage to insulation and security.

4 If the contact points are badly burned or pitted, renew
 the rocker assembly and blade.

5 Examine the diaphragm for signs of deterioration.
 Be prepared to renew all washers and gaskets,
 remembering that a new lead washer 19 will be
 needed.

Type SP:

Follow the preceding instructions but, as the valves
are different, check the outlet valve 45 for damage and
see that the centre rivet is tight. Check that the lift spring
has not unwound and still holds the valve disc on its
seating. The disc must be free to lift and not be trapped
under the rivet shoulder.

Also examine the inlet valve assembly 48 for kinks or
damage. Slight discolouration of the valve disc is not
important.

2:5   Reassembling pump

1 Fit the rocker assembly to the pedestal as in **FIG 2:2**
 so that the final position is as shown by the inset.
 **Note that the pin is hardened and must only be
 renewed by fitting a genuine SU part.** If the
 rockers are not perfectly free in action, apply a tiny
 drop of oil to the pivots and set the arms with a pair
 of long-nosed pliers if necessary.

2 Fit terminal 17 to the pedestal and then assemble the
 following parts in this order. Fit spring washer 18 and
 then put the terminal stud through the 2BA terminal
 tag. Follow this with the new lead washer 19 and
 coned nut 20 with its coned face to the washer.
 Tighten the nut and lastly add washer 21.

3 Fit the pedestal to the housing with screws 28. The lefthand screw must be threaded through the earthing tag 13 and then the spring washer is fitted, so that the tag is immediately under the head of the screw. When tightening the screw see that the tag does not turn or it may strain the lead. **Do not overtighten or the pedestal will crack. Do not fit the contact blade yet.**

4 Assemble impact washer 4 to the diaphragm spindle and fit spring 5 into the coil housing with the large diameter first. Screw the diaphragm clockwise so that the spindle enters the trunnion in the middle of the rocker assembly. **Do not put jointing compound on the diaphragm.** Screw in the diaphragm until the rocker will not throw-over, but be careful not to confuse this with jamming the armature in the coil housing.

5 Hold the housing vertically with the diaphragm uppermost and fit the eleven brass rollers by turning back the edge of the diaphragm. On later-type rocker mechanisms with adjustable fingers as depicted in **FIG 2 : 6**, fit the contact blade and adjust the finger settings as described under 'Setting modified rocker assemblies' and then remove the blade.

6 Hold the assembly as in **FIG 2 : 3** and push firmly but steadily on the diaphragm. Unscrew it, pressing and releasing the diaphragm until the rocker mechanism just 'throws-over'. Now unscrew the diaphragm to the nearest hole in the edge which aligns with one on the housing flange. From there, turn back or unscrew another four holes, which is equivalent to two-thirds of a complete revolution. Press the centre of the diaphragm and fit the official SU retaining-fork tool behind the trunnion of the rocker assembly. This will keep the diaphragm depressed and prevent the rollers from falling out while the housing is fitted to the body.

Assembling the body, type AUF.200:

1 Inlet and outlet valves are identical. The recess in the body for the inlet valve is deeper to accommodate the filter and an extra washer. With tongue side uppermost, place the outlet valve in the recess marked 'OUTLET', place a joint washer on top and fit the outlet nozzle.

2 With tongue side downwards, fit the inlet valve in the 'INLET' recess, followed by a joint washer, the filter, dome side upwards, another joint washer and the inlet nozzle.

3 Settle the assemblies correctly into their recesses and clamp down with plate 34, first setting the nozzles to point in the desired direction.

Assembling the body, type SP:

1 Do not fit the filter into the body recess, but assemble it into the inlet nozzle 51 and then screw the nozzle into place.

2 Place outlet valve 45 into its recess with the spring downwards, making sure that it seats correctly. Fit inlet valve 48 and retainer 46, making sure that the inlet valve is centralized on its seating.

Attaching body to housing, both types:

1 **Do not put jointing compound on the diaphragm.** With the cast lugs on the coil housing at the bottom, insert the six screws finger tight. Fit the earthing screw and Lucar connector.

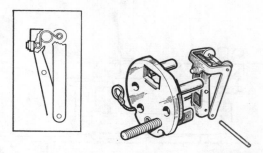

FIG 2 : 2 Fitting rocker assembly to pedestal. Inset shows correct position of toggle spring after assembly

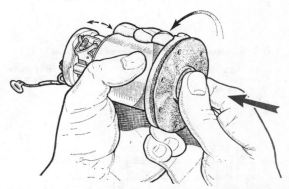

FIG 2 : 3 Unscrewing the diaphragm until the rocker just throws-over

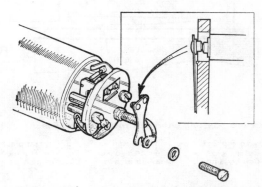

FIG 2 : 4 Inset shows correct relative position of contact points at rest

2 Remove the SU tool which was inserted behind the rocker trunnion and tighten the screws diametrically and evenly. Any further stretching of the diaphragm before final tightening is unnecessary.

Adjusting the contact blade, both types:

1 Fit the contact blade and coil lead to the pedestal with the 5BA screw and washer.

2 The contact points on the blade must be a little above the points on the rocker when closed, as shown in **FIG 2 : 4.** The blade is slotted for adjustment.

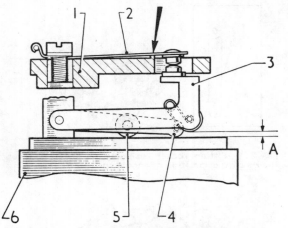

FIG 2:5 Setting early-type rocker assemblies

Key to Fig 2:5
1 Pedestal 2 Contact blade
3 Outer rocker 4 Inner rocker 5 Trunnion
6 Coil housing A=.030 inch

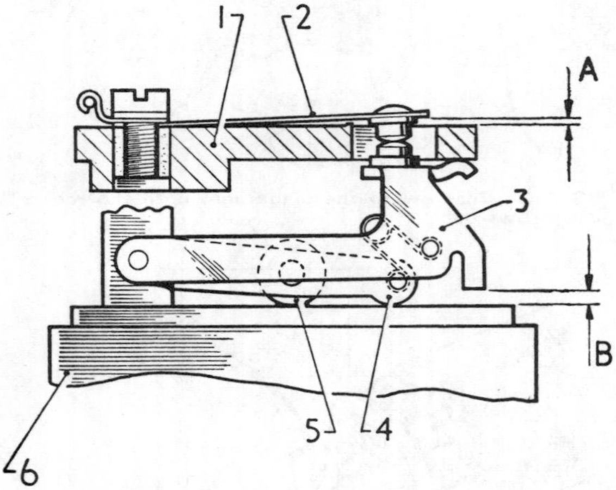

FIG 2:6 Setting later-type rocker assemblies

Key to Fig 2:6
1 Pedestal 2 Contact blade
3 Outer rocker 4 Inner rocker 5 Trunnion
6 Coil housing A=.035 inch B=.070 inch

Contact gap setting, both types:

1 Check that when the outer rocker is pressed back against the coil housing, the contact blade rests on the narrow ridge on the pedestal which is arrowed in **FIG 2:5**. If necessary, swing the blade clear and set it slightly. It must rest lightly on the rib as over-tensioning will restrict rocker travel.

Setting early rocker assemblies:

1 Use **FIG 2:5** as a guide. Press the contact blade against the rib on the pedestal which is indicated by the arrow, but do not deflect the tip. A .030 inch feeler gauge must pass between the fibre rollers and the coil housing face as indicated at **A**.

Setting modified rocker assemblies:

1 Use **FIG 2:6** as a guide. Check dimension **A**. It should be .035±.005 inch and adjustment is made by bending the stop finger just behind the pedestal.
2 Check the gap between the rocker finger and the coil housing face at **B**. If necessary, bend the finger to obtain a gap of .070+.005 inch.

Fitting the end cover, both types:

Fit seal washer 21 to the terminal stud, followed by the cover. Secure with nut 32 and fit the terminal tag or connector. Fit insulating sleeve 33. The pump will now be ready for testing.

2:6 Testing pump, both types

Fit the pump and switch on. If it is suspected that fuel is not reaching the carburetter(s), disconnect the fuel line from the carburetter(s) and switch on. If jets of fuel squirt from the disconnected pipe, check that the needle valve in the carburetter float chamber is not stuck.

If the flow is normal at first but diminishes rapidly, and the pump slows down, check the fuel tank venting by removing the filler cap. Reduced flow can also be caused by blocked fuel lines or by a clogged filter. Remove filter 40 or 49 in **FIG 2:1** and clean with a brush and fuel.

If the pump operates rapidly but does not pump sufficient fuel, check for an air leak on the suction side of the pump, dirt under the valves or faulty valve sealing washers.

If there is no flow, check that current is reaching the pump terminal. If current is there, remove the end cover of the pump to check the contact points. If they are touching, replace the lead on the terminal and short across the contacts with a piece of bared wire. If the pump then makes a stroke the fault is due to dirt, burning or maladjustment of the points.

If an obstructed pipeline is suspected, disconnect the inlet pipe. If the pump then works, there is a restriction in the line from the pump to the tank. Remove the fuel tank filler cap and clear the pipe with compressed air. **Do not pass compressed air through the pump or the valves will be damaged.**

If the preceding operations fail, suspect stiffening of the diaphragm or excessive friction in the rocker mechanism. Remove the coil housing and flex the diaphragm a few times, taking care that the brass rollers do not fall out. When reassembling, apply a little thin oil to the 'throw-over' spring spindles where they pivot in the brass rockers. Follow the original assembly instructions when refitting the coil housing to the body.

If the pump is noisy, suspect an air leak on the suction side. Disconnect the fuel feed to the carburetter(s) and lead it into a container. Switch on and look for continuous air bubbles while the pipe is immersed in fuel. This confirms that there is an air leak. To cure this, check all pipe connections and unions. Also check that the coil housing screws are evenly tightened.

If the pump operates without delivering fuel, check for a serious air leak on the suction side. Another likely cause is dirt under one of the valves, particularly the inlet valve. Remove the valves for cleaning.

2:7 Operation of SU carburetter

A section through the carburetter is shown in **FIG 2:7** and this can be taken as typical of both the HS2 and HS4 types.

The bore through the body is fitted with the usual butterfly valve to be seen on the right. On the air intake side of this valve is a variable choke aperture formed by a piston rising and falling inside a top chamber. This action is automatic, depending on the depression in the intake system arising from the amount of throttle opening and the load on the engine. The varying volume of air will need a varying flow of fuel to give the correct mixture throughout. This is done by using a tapered needle attached to the piston and the needle rises and falls in a fixed size of jet aperture. The smallest diameter of the needle is in the jet aperture when the piston is at the top of its travel and the flow of fuel is then at its greatest. Rapid fluctuations of the piston are damped out by a hydraulic damper, the fluid being contained in oil well 7. Rich mixture for starting is obtained by pulling down the jet to a smaller diameter of the needle. A spring is fitted to assist gravity to return the piston.

2:8 Removing and servicing carburetter

Removing on cars with synchromesh transmission:

Unscrew the wing nut(s) from the top of the air cleaner, remove the cover, extract the element and lift off the cleaner after disconnecting the breather pipe to the rocker cover on cars so fitted.

Disconnect the mixture and throttle cables, the throttle shaft return springs on twin carburetter installations, the distributor suction advance pipe and the fuel pipe. Remove the nuts and spring washers from the carburetter flanges and lift off the carburetters and the cable abutment plate. With twin carburetters, first remove the air cleaner manifold.

Removing from cars with automatic transmission:

Remove the air cleaner and all parts up to the fuel pipe as just detailed. Disconnect the governor control rod fork end from the throttle lever. Remove the securing nuts and spring washers and lift off the carburetter and cable abutment plate.

Refitting, both types:

Reverse the removal instructions but note that the cable abutment plate has a gasket on each side. If these are damaged, clean both plate, carburetter, and manifold flanges, and fit new gaskets.

Dismantling carburetter, both types:

Refer to **FIG 2:8**. Remove the piston and top chamber assembly 6 after marking for correct reassembly. Take special care of these two parts as they are precision machined and will be seriously damaged if dropped. The needle 19 is held in place by screw 7. Unscrew from the float chamber the union nut on the nylon feed pipe to the jet assembly 13. Remove bolt 26 to release the float chamber. Removal of lid 30 will enable the float and the needle valve 32 to be inspected. Remove screw 51 and pull out the jet. Remove nut 18 and spring 17. Undo nut 16 and remove jet bearing 14 with washer 15.

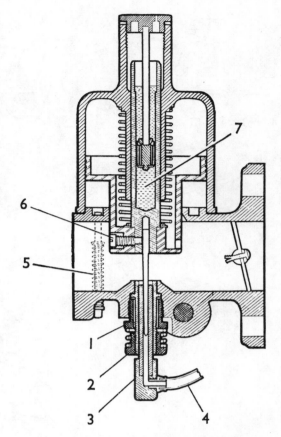

FIG 2:7 A section through the SU carburetter

Key to Fig 2:7   1 Jet locking nut   2 Jet adjusting nut
3 Jet head   4 Nylon fuel pipe   5 Piston lifting pin
6 Needle securing screw   7 Piston damper oil well

If necessary, remove screws 38 to release throttle disc 37 from spindle 36.

Servicing the carburetter, both types:

Remove damper 8, tip out the oil and pull the piston out of the top chamber. Clean very thoroughly and check that the rim of the piston does not touch the inside surface of the chamber at any point. There is slight clearance here and dirt may cause sticking.

If the needle is to be renewed or changed, fit it so that the bottom shoulder is flush with the lower face of the piston. Needle sizes are stamped on the shank. Do not be tempted to stretch spring 10 in an attempt to alter the characteristics of the carburetter. Needle and spring specifications are given in Technical Data.

Clean out all sediment from inside the float chamber and examine the seating on the needle of assembly 32. If there is a noticeable shoulder on the tapered seat, replace the assembly. Checking the float level will be covered in a later section on faults.

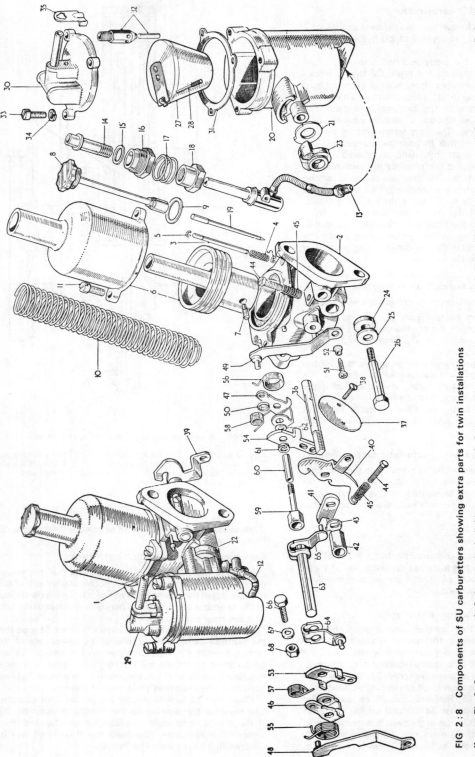

FIG 2:8 Components of SU carburetters showing extra parts for twin installations

Key to Fig 2:8

1 Carburetter body (left)
2 Carburetter body (right)
3 Fibre washer
4 Spring
5 Circlip
6 Piston chamber assembly
7 Screw
8 Cap and damper assembly
9 Piston lifting pin
10 Piston spring
11 Screw
12 Jet assembly (left)
13 Jet assembly (right)
14 Bearing
15 Washer
16 Nut for bearing
17 Spring
18 Adjusting nut
19 Needle
20 Float chamber
21 Support washer
22 Rubber grommet (left)
23 Rubber grommet (right)
24 Washer (rubber)
25 Washer (steel)
26 Bolt
27 Float assembly
28 Lever pin
29 Float chamber lid (left)
30 Float chamber lid (right)
31 Washer
32 Needle and seat assembly
33 Screw
34 Spring washer
35 Baffle plate
36 Throttle spindle
37 Throttle disc
38 Screw
39 Throttle return lever (left)
40 Throttle return lever (right)
41 Lost motion lever
42 Nut
43 Tab washer
44 Throttle screw stop
45 Spring
46 Pickup lever (left)
47 Pickup lever (right)
48 Link (left)
49 Link (right)
50 Washer
51 Screw
52 Bush
53 Cam lever (left)
54 Cam lever (right)
55 Pickup lever spring (left)
56 Pickup lever spring (right)
57 Cam lever spring (left)
58 Cam lever spring (right)
59 Bolt
60 Tube
61 Spring washer
62 Distance washer
63 Jet rod
64 Lever and pin assembly (left)
65 Lever and pin assembly (right)
66 Bolt
67 Washer
68 Nut

Note when reassembling the carburetter in the reverse order, that it will be necessary to centralize the jet with respect to the needle. This operation is covered in the next Section. When reassembling the piston to the chamber, apply a little thin oil to the piston rod and to no other part. When the carburetter is assembled and refitted, fill the damper oil well with 20W engine oil until it is $\frac{1}{2}$ inch above the top of the hollow piston rod as shown in **FIG 2 : 9. Do not use thick oil.**

2 : 9 Centralizing the jet

This operation is always necessary if the jet bearing screw 16 is loosened or removed, or if a new needle is fitted. It is also a possible cure for a sticking piston. If the damper is removed and the piston lifted with a pencil it should fall freely and hit the jet bridge smartly. If it does not, and cleaning of the piston and chamber does not cure the trouble, then centralizing the jet will almost certainly succeed.

1 Remove screw 51 to disconnect rod 49 from the jet head. Unscrew the union holding the nylon feed tube into the float chamber and withdraw tube and jet together (item 13). Remove adjusting nut 18 and spring 17. Replace the adjusting nut without the spring and screw it right home. Replace the jet with the feed tube facing correctly.
2 Slacken off nut 16 so that bearing 14 can be turned with the fingers. Remove damper 8 and press down on the hollow piston rod inside the top chamber. With the piston and needle fully pressed down, tighten locking nut 16.
3 Lift the piston and check that it falls freely, with a soft metallic click when it hits the jet bridge. Fully lower the jet and repeat the test. If the sound of impact is sharper, repeat the centring operation until successful. When satisfied, replace spring 17 above the adjusting nut. It will now be necessary to carry out slow-running adjustments as follows.

2 : 10 Slow-running adjustments

On single-carburetter installations, synchromesh transmission :

This is all the tuning the carburetter should need if the correct needle is fitted. Proceed as follows, referring to **FIG 2 : 10.**

1 Run the engine up to normal temperature. Unscrew throttle stop 1 until it is just clear of the lever and then screw it down one and a half turns.
2 Remove the piston and top chamber, disconnect the mixture control wire and screw jet adjusting nut 7 until the jet is flush with the jet bridge in the bore of the body, or fully up if this position cannot be obtained. Replace the piston and chamber assembly and check that the piston falls freely. Piston lifting pin 5 in **FIG 2 : 7** can be used for this purpose.
3 Turn down adjusting nut 7 two complete turns or 12 flats. Start the engine and adjust the throttle screw until the desired idling speed is indicated by the glowing of the ignition warning light.
4 Keeping the jet pressed upwards, turn the adjusting nut until the fastest idling speed is obtained consistent with even firing. As the mixture is adjusted the engine will probably run faster and the speed must be reduced at the throttle stop screw.

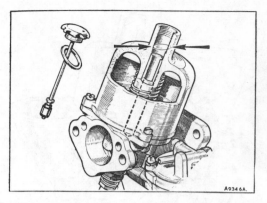

FIG 2 : 9 Damper removed and correct oil level indicated by arrows

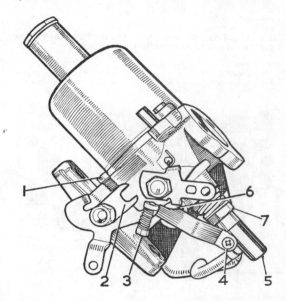

FIG 2 : 10 External controls of the HS2 carburetter

Key to Fig 2 : 10   1 Throttle adjusting screw
2 Butterfly operating fork   3 Fast-idle adjusting screw
4 Jet link securing screw   5 Jet head   6 Float-chamber securing nut   7 Jet adjusting nut

5 Check the mixture strength. Use the lifting pin to raise the piston approximately $\frac{1}{32}$ inch. If engine speed increases and it continues to run faster the mixture is too rich. If engine speed immediately decreases, the mixture is too weak. If engine speed momentarily increases slightly, the mixture is correct. The exhaust note should be regular and even. If it is irregular with a colourless exhaust the mixture is too weak. Heavy rythmical misfiring with black exhaust smoke indicates a rich mixture.
6 When correctly adjusted the carburetter will deliver the right mixture throughout its range. Reconnect the mixture control wire with about $\frac{1}{16}$ inch of free movement before it starts to pull on the cam lever. Set the

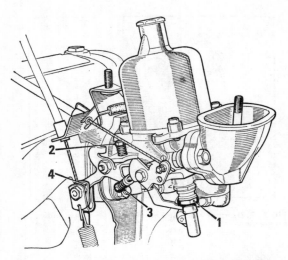

FIG 2:11 External controls of the HS4 carburetter as fitted to cars with automatic transmission

Key to Fig 2:11
1 Jet adjusting nut   2 Throttle adjusting screw
3 Fast-idle adjusting screw   4 Governor control rod

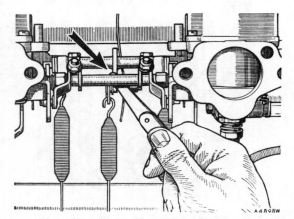

FIG 2:12 Setting throttle levers on twin carburetters. Feeler is between throttle shaft stop and mixture control interconnecting spindle

mixture control knob on the dash to its maximum movement of about $\frac{5}{8}$ inch without moving the carburetter jet, and adjust the fast-idle screw 3 to give an engine speed of around 1000 rev/min hot.

On cars with automatic transmission:

The HS4 carburetter is shown in **FIG 2:11**. All operations are the same as those for the HS2 carburetter covered in the main instructions, with the following exceptions:

When adjusting the slow-running and the jet, connect a tachometer (revolution indicator). Select 'N' on the gear lever quadrant and apply the handbrake. Run the engine up to normal temperature and adjust the jet as described for carburetters on cars with synchromesh

transmission. With the carburetter correctly tuned, adjust throttle screw 2 to give a maximum idling speed of 650 rev/min.

Pull out the mixture control to the maximum fast-idle position. Check and adjust if necessary, to obtain a maximum fast-idle speed of 1050 rev/min. Push in the control and recheck the idling speed. Adjust the governor control rod as detailed in Chapter 6a.

On twin carburetter installations, with synchronization:

1 Complete Operations 1 and 2, making sure to set both jets to the same position when fully up, relative to the jet bridge in the body.
2 Turn down each jet adjusting nut two turns or twelve flats. Start the engine and adjust the throttle screws 1 in **FIG 2:10** an equal amount to give the desired engine idling speed. Listen to the hiss in the air intakes and adjust the screws until the hiss is the same for both carburetters. This will synchronize the throttles.
3 Now adjust the mixture strength by turning adjusting nuts 7 up or down the same amount until the fastest idling speed is obtained consistent with even firing. Keep the jets pressed upwards all the time. As the mixture is adjusted the engine will probably run faster. It will then be necessary to unscrew the throttle stop screws by the same amount each.
4 Check the mixture strength of the lefthand carburetter as in preceding Operation 5. When satisfied, repeat on the righthand carburetter and finally go back to the lefthand carburetter to recheck it, as the tuning is interdependent.

2:11 Twin carburetter linkage

The throttle on each carburetter is operated by a lever and pin, the pin working in a forked lever attached to the throttle spindle. The parts can be seen in **FIG 2:8** and **2:12**. A clearance exists between the pin and fork, and this must be maintained when the throttle is closed and the engine idling. This prevents any load from the accelerator linkage being transferred to the throttle spindle and butterfly.

To set the clearance, slacken the clamping bolts on both throttle shaft levers seen on either side of the arrow in **FIG 2:12**. Put a .012 inch feeler between the throttle shaft stop and the choke control interconnecting rod as shown. Move each lever down in turn until the lever pin rests lightly on the lower arm of the fork in the carburetter throttle lever. Tighten each clamp bolt when the lever is set.

When both levers are correctly set, remove the feeler, which should result in the lever pins having clearance in the forks.

Reconnect the mixture control cable and check that the jet heads return against the lower faces of the adjusting nuts when the control is pushed fully in. Then pull out the control to the maximum extent without moving the jets, which should be about $\frac{5}{8}$ inch. Adjust the fast-idle cam screws 3 in **FIG 2:10** to give an engine speed of 1000 rev/min when hot.

2:12 Carburetter faults

A sticking piston:

This can cause difficult starting and lack of response

to the accelerator pedal. Remove the damper and lift the piston with a pencil, or if the air cleaner is still in place, use the piston lifting pin. The piston should lift freely and fall back smartly. If it does not, remove the piston and top chamber and clean all parts thoroughly. Be prepared for oil to spill from the damper oil well. Only the piston rod makes contact with any other part and this is the only part which must be lightly oiled during reassembly. The piston rim should not touch the inside of the top chamber. If cleaning does not effect a cure, suspect a badly-centred jet and correct this from the instructions in **Section 2 : 9**.

Float chamber flooding :

This is seen when fuel flows from the breather hole in the float chamber lid below the main fuel feed pipe. The usual cause is dirt or grit jamming the float needle in its guide, see items 32 in **FIG 2 : 8**. Remove the lid and clean the needle and guide.

If the needle is jammed shut, then the engine will be starved of fuel. Check this by detaching the main fuel feed pipe from the carburetter and turning it down into a container. Switch on and see whether spurts of fuel come out of the pipe, which will prove that the pump is delivering it. Starvation is then almost certainly due to a needle which is stuck on its seat and cleaning should effect a cure. At the same time clean all pipelines and filters to prevent a recurrence of the trouble.

Level of fuel in float chamber :

This can be checked by referring to **FIG 2 : 13**. Hold the lid assembly upsidedown and place a $\frac{1}{8}$ inch round bar across the centre of the lid as shown. Keep it parallel with the float lever hinge pin. The face of the float lever should just rest on the bar when the needle is on its seating. If this is not so, carefully set the lever at point **C**. Do not curve the lever itself.

2 : 13 Air cleaner

Fit a new element periodically, depending on conditions. Do not unnecessarily disturb the air cleaner cover at any other time or dirt may find its way to the clean side of the intake.

To remove the element unscrew the wing nut(s) from the top of the cleaner, lift off the cover and lift out the element.

During wintry conditions, position the air cleaner intake pipe adjacent to the exhaust manifold to reduce the possibility of carburetter icing. Move it away during warmer weather.

2 : 14 Fault diagnosis

(a) Leakage or insufficient fuel delivered

1 Air vent in tank restricted
2 Fuel pipes blocked
3 Air leaks at pipe connections
4 Pump filter blocked
5 Pump gaskets faulty

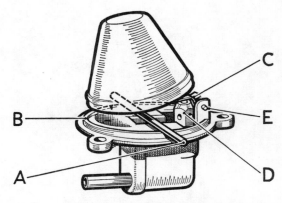

FIG 2 : 13   Checking the position of the float. To adjust, bend at point C

Key to Fig 2 : 13   **A** $\frac{1}{8}$ to $\frac{3}{16}$ inch bar   **B** Machined lip
C Angle of float lever   **D** Float needle and seat assembly
E Lever hinge pin

6 Pump diaphragm defective
7 Pump valves sticking or seating badly
8 Fuel vapourizing in pipelines due to heat

(b) Excessive fuel consumption

1 Carburetter(s) need adjusting
2 Fuel leakage
3 Sticking mixture control
4 Dirty air cleaner
5 Excessive engine temperature
6 Brakes binding
7 Tyres under-inflated
8 Idling speed too high
9 Car overloaded

(c) Idling speed too high

1 Rich fuel mixture
2 Carburetter controls sticking
3 Slow-running screws incorrectly adjusted
4 Worn carburetter butterfly valve

(d) Noisy fuel pump

1 Loose mountings
2 Air leaks on suction side and at diaphragm
3 Obstruction in fuel pipe
4 Clogged pump filter

(e) No fuel delivery

1 Float needle stuck
2 Vent in tank blocked
3 Electrical connections to pump faulty
4 Pump contact points dirty
5 Pipeline obstructed
6 Pump diaphragm stiff or damaged
7 Inlet valve in pump stuck open
8 Bad air leak on suction side of pump

CHAPTER 3

THE IGNITION SYSTEM

3 : 1 Description

All the cars covered by this manual use the Lucas 25D4 distributor which incorporates automatic timing control by centrifugal mechanism and a vacuum operated unit. A micrometer adjustment is provided to enable fine alterations to the ignition point to be made by hand. These alterations can compensate for changes in engine condition or for the use of various grades of fuel.

The weights of the centrifugal device fly out against the tension of small springs as engine speed rises. This movement advances the contact breaker cams relative to the distributor driving shaft to give advanced ignition. The vacuum unit is connected by a small-bore pipe to the inlet manifold. Depression in the manifold operates the vacuum unit, the suction varying with engine load. At small throttle openings, with no load on the engine, there is a high degree of vacuum in the manifold causing the vacuum unit to advance the ignition. When hill-climbing on large throttle openings, the much reduced vacuum ensures that the unit will retard the ignition. The various elements of the two automatic controls can be seen in **FIG 3 : 1** as items 13, 14 and 16.

3 : 2 Routine maintenance

Refer to **FIG 3 : 1** and remove distributor cap 2. Pull rotor 4 squarely off the end of cam spindle 11. Now refer to **FIG 3 : 2** and lubricate the cam spindle at point 5. Add only a few drops of oil to the recess and do not remove the screw. There is clearance provided for the oil to make its way downwards.

Squirt a few drops of oil into gap 4 to lubricate the centrifugal advance mechanism, but take great care to avoid letting oil get onto the contact breaker plate or the points 1. Smear a little grease or engine oil on the cam as shown by the top arrow in **FIG 3 : 3**. Apply the tiniest drop of oil to the contact breaker pivot as indicated by the bottom arrow.

Adjusting the contact breaker points:

Refer to **FIG 3 : 2** and slacken screw 2. Place a screw-driver between notches 3 and turn until the points 1 are set to the correct gap of .014 to .016 inch as measured with a feeler gauge. It will be necessary to turn the engine until one of the cams has opened the points to the fullest extent so that the gap is measured at the position of maximum opening. Do not alter the gap unless it varies considerably from the suggested setting.

Cleaning the contact points:

If the contact points are dirty or pitted they must be cleaned by polishing them with a fine carborundum stone, taking care to keep the faces flat and square. Afterwards wipe away all dust with a cloth moistened in fuel. The contacts may be dismantled to assist cleaning by referring to **Section 3 : 4**. If the moving contact is removed from its pivot, check that it is not sluggish.

If it is tight, polish the pivot pin with a strip of fine emery cloth, clean off all dust and apply a tiny spot of oil to the top of the pin. If a spring testing gauge is available the contact breaker spring should have a tension of 20 to 24 oz. measured at the points.

3 : 3 Ignition faults

If the engine runs unevenly set it to idle at a fast speed. Taking care not to touch any metal part of the sparking plug leads, pull up the insulator sleeves and short each plug in turn, using a screwdriver with an insulated handle. Connect the screwdriver blade between the plug top and the cylinder head. Shorting a plug which is firing properly will make the uneven running more pronounced. Shorting a plug in a cylinder which is not firing will make no difference.

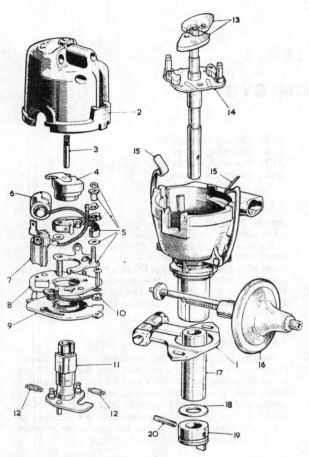

FIG 3 : 1   Components of distributor

Key to Fig 3 : 1   1 Clamping plate   2 Moulded cap
3 Brush and spring   4 Rotor arm   5 Contacts (set)
6 Capacitor   7 Terminal and lead (low-tension)
8 Moving contact breaker plate   9 Contact breaker base plate
10 Earth lead 11 Cam assembly 12 Automatic advance springs
13 Weight assembly   14 Shaft and action plate
15 Cap-retaining clips   16 Vacuum unit   17 Bush
18 Thrust washer   19 Driving dog   20 Pin

Having located the faulty cylinder, stop the engine and remove the plug lead. Start the engine and hold the lead carefullly to avoid shocks so that the metal end is about $\frac{3}{16}$ inch away from the cylinder head. A strong regular spark shows that the fault might lie with the sparking plug. Remove and clean it according to the instructions in **Section 3 : 6**. Alternatively, substitute it with a new plug.

If the spark is weak and irregular, check that the lead is not perished or cracked. If it appears to be defective, renew it and try another test. If there is no improvement, remove the distributor cap and wipe the inside clean and dry. Check the carbon brush 1 in **FIG 3 : 4**. It should protrude from the moulding and be free to move against the pressure of the internal spring. Examine the surface inside the cap for signs of 'tracking', which can be seen as a thin black line between the electrodes or to some metal part in contact with the cap. This is caused by sparking, and the only cure is to fit a new cap.

Testing the low-tension circuit:

Before carrying out electrical tests, confirm that the contact breaker points are clean and correctly set. Then proceed as follows:

1 Disconnect the thin cable from the **CB** terminal on the coil and from the side of the distributor. Connect a test lamp between the two terminals. Turn the engine over slowly. If the lamp lights when the contacts close and goes out when they open, the low-tension circuit is in order. If the lamp fails to light, the contacts are dirty or there is a break or loose connection in the low-tension wiring.

2 If the fault lies in the low-tension circuit, switch on the ignition and turn the crankshaft until the contact points are fully open. Refer to the wiring diagrams in Technical Data and check the circuit with a 0-20 voltmeter. If the circuit is in order the meter should read approximately 12 volts.

3 **Battery to control box terminal B.** Connect the voltmeter between terminal **B** and earth. No reading indicates a faulty cable or loose connection.

4 **Control box.** Connect the meter between the other auxiliary terminal **B** and earth. No reading indicates a broken or loose connection.

5 **Control box auxiliary terminal B to terminal No. 3 on ignition switch.** Connect the meter between terminal No. 3 and earth. No reading indicates a damaged cable or loose connection.

6 **Ignition switch.** Connect the meter between No. 2 switch terminal and earth. Switch on to the ignition position, when no reading indicates a fault in the switch. Now connect the meter to switch terminal No. 1 and earth. Switch to the start position. No reading indicates a fault in the switch.

7 **Ignition switch to fusebox terminal A3.** Connect the meter between **A3** and earth. No reading indicates a damaged cable or loose connections.

8 **Fusebox terminal A3 to ignition coil terminal SW.** Connect the meter between terminal **SW** and earth. No reading indicates a damaged cable or loose connection.

8 **Ignition coil.** Disconnect the cable from terminal **CB** and connect the meter between this terminal and earth. No reading indicates a fault in the primary

winding of the coil and a replacement coil must be fitted. If the reading is correct, remake the connections to the coil.

9 **Ignition coil to distributor.** Disconnect the thin cable from the side terminal on the distributor and connect the meter between the end of this cable and earth. No reading indicates a damaged cable or loose connections.

10 **Contact breaker and capacitor.** Connect the meter across the contact breaker points. No reading indicates a faulty capacitor.

Capacitor:

The best method of testing a capacitor (condenser) is by substitution. Disconnect the original capacitor and connect a new one between the low-tension terminal on the side of the distributor and to earth.

If a new capacitor is needed, fit one complete with bracket, but if necessary unsolder the original bracket and solder it on the new capacitor using as little heat as possible. Capacitor capacity is .18 to .22 microfarad.

3:4 Removing and dismantling distributor

Use **FIG 3:1** for reference. Before removing the distributor turn the crankshaft until the rotor arm 4 is pointing to the brass segment in the cap which is connected to No. 1 cylinder plug lead at the fan end of the engine. This will provide a datum for replacement. Provided the pinch bolt in clamp plate 1 is not loosened, the distributor can be removed and replaced without disturbing the ignition timing. Do not turn the crankshaft after this.

1 Remove cap 2 and disconnect the cable from low-tension terminal 7. Disconnect the suction pipe from vacuum unit 16. Remove the two bolts securing the clamp plate 1 to the housing in the crankcase and withdraw the distributor.

2 Pull off the rotor arm. Remove the nut which holds assembly 5 and lift off the insulating bush, terminal tags, moving contact and spring assembly and the washer. The fixed contact plate can then be lifted off.

3 Remove the two screws securing the base plate 9 and unhook the flexible link coming from the vacuum unit.

4 **Before further dismantling, note the relative positions of the rotor arm driving slot at the top of item 11 and the driving dog 19, which is offset and can only engage its driving spindle in one position.** Then, when the cam assembly is fitted to the centrifugal weights during reassembly, the timing will not be 180 deg. out.

5 Take out the cam retaining screw recessed in the rotor arm housing on the end of the spindle. Remove the springs 12 and lift off the cam. Take out the weights 13.

6 To release the vacuum unit remove the circlip at the adjusting nut end. Unscrew the knurled nut, remove the friction spring and withdraw the unit from the body.

7 Check all parts for wear, and service the cap and contact breaker by following the instructions in **Section 3:2.** If the shaft 14 is slack in the body, drive out parallel pin 20, pull off dog 19 and withdraw the spindle. Press out the old bush 17. Immerse the new bush in thin engine oil for 24 hours and press it into the body.

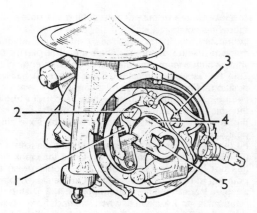

FIG 3:2 Contact breaker adjustment and lubrication

Key to Fig 3:2   1 Contact points   2 Contact plate securing screw   3 Screwdriver adjusting slot
4 Advance mechanism lubrication   5 Cam spindle lubrication

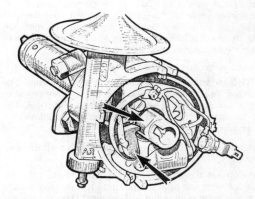

FIG 3:3 Cam and contact pivot lubricating points

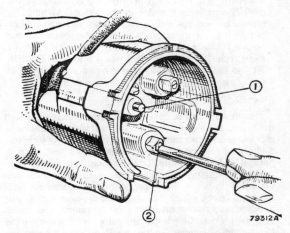

FIG 3:4 Carbon brush 1 and cable-securing screw 2 in distributor cap

Reassembly is the reverse of dismantling but note the following points:

1 Lubricate the parts of the centrifugal advance mechanism, the distributor shaft and that part of the shaft which accepts the cam, with the thin engine oil.

2 Turn the vacuum control adjusting nut to its halfway position. Engage the cam driving pins with the centrifugal weights so that, when seen from above, the small offset of the driving dog is on the right and the driving slot for the rotor arm is at the six o'clock position.

3 Fit the distributor in its housing and turn the rotor arm until the driving dog engages. Provided the crankshaft has not been turned the rotor arm should finish up pointing to No. 1 cylinder segment in the cap. Replace the plug leads in the firing order of 1, 3, 4, 2. Distributor rotation is anticlockwise when viewed from above. If the clamping plate has been moved, resulting in lost timing, refer to the next Section.

3 : 5 Timing the ignition

1 Remove the distributor and the rocker cover. Remove the sparking plugs, engage top gear and move the car until No. 1 piston is at TDC on the compression stroke. The inlet valve of No. 4 cylinder will then be just opening. Turn the crankshaft until the 1/4 mark on the flywheel is in line with the pointer in the aperture in the clutch cover as shown in **FIG 3 : 5**.

On cars with automatic transmission:

FIG 3 : 6 shows the markings on the flywheel. The righthand inset shows where to insert a screwdriver to engage the starter ring gear and turn the flywheel. The hole for inspecting the timing marks is closed with a rubber grommet.

Continue with the timing procedure on all cars as follows:

2 Having set the flywheel to the TDC mark, turn the crankshaft **back** until the pointer indicates the correct ignition setting as given in Technical Data for the car concerned.

3 Ensure that the contact breaker points are correctly set. Insert the distributor into its housing and engage the driving dog with the slot in the driving spindle, by slowly turning the rotor arm. Tighten the clamp plate pinch bolt first, before securing the plate to the housing. Use a torque of 30 lb ft if the bolt is of the fixed type. If the nut is fixed use a torque of 50 lb ft. Fit and tighten the fixing setscrews so that they are in the centre of the elongated holes in the plate.

Electrical setting of timing:

Use this method to obtain an accurate setting. Slacken the clamp plate pinch bolt and turn the distributor anticlockwise until the contact breaker points are fully closed. Switch on the ignition and connect a 12 volt lamp in parallel with the points. One lead will go to the low-tension terminal on the side of the distributor body and the other to earth. Turn the distributor clockwise until the lamp lights, which indicates that the points have just opened. Secure the distributor by tightening the clamp plate pinch bolt. Check that the rotor arm is opposite the No. 1 cylinder segment in the cap. Reconnect the vacuum pipe.

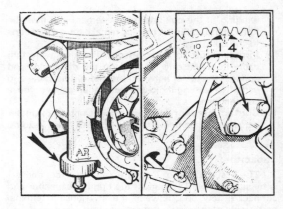

FIG 3 : 5 Micrometer timing adjustment (left), and flywheel timing marks (right). Position shown is TDC

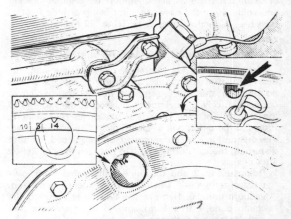

FIG 3 : 6 Timing marks on converter, automatic transmission. Inset on left shows TDC, inset on right shows hole for turning converter with screwdriver

Stroboscopic timing:

With this method do not let engine speed rise above 600 rev/min or the centrifugal advance weights will start to operate. If the vacuum advance pipe is connected direct to the inlet manifold, disconnect it first or the timing will be retarded.

Manual adjustment:

The adjustment nut is indicated in the lefthand view of **FIG 3 : 5**. Turning the nut clockwise from the end of the spindle will retard the ignition or vice-versa. Each graduation on the barrel represents an approximate range of 5 deg., and this is equal to 55 clicks on the knurled nut. This will enable fine adjustments to be made, particularly if there is a change in the fuel octane rating.

3 : 6 Sparking plugs

Inspect, clean and adjust sparking plugs regularly. The inspection of the deposits on the electrodes is particularly useful because the type and colour of the deposit gives a clue to conditions inside the combustion chamber, and is therefore most helpful when tuning.

Remove the sparking plugs by loosening them a couple of turns and then blowing away loose dirt from the plug recesses with compressed air or a tyre pump. Store them in the order of removal.

Examine the gaskets. If they are about half their original thickness they may be used again.

Examine the firing end of the plugs to note the type of deposit. Normally, it should be powdery, and range from brown to greyish tan in colour. There will also be slight wear of the electrodes, and the general effect is one which comes from mixed periods of high-speed and low-speed driving. Cleaning and resetting the gap is all that will be required. If the deposits are white or yellowish they indicate long periods of constant-speed driving or much low-speed city driving. Again, the treatment is straightforward.

Black, wet deposits are caused by oil entering the combustion chamber past worn pistons, rings or down valve stems. Sparking plugs of a type which run hotter may help to alleviate the problem, but the cure is an engine overhaul.

Dry, black, fluffy deposits are usually the result of running with a rich mixture. Incomplete combustion may also be a cause and this might be traced to defective ignition or excessive idling.

Overheated sparking plugs have a white, blistered look about the centre electrode and the side electrode may be badly eroded. This may be caused by poor cooling, wrong ignition, or sustained high speeds with heavy loads.

Have the sparking plugs cleaned on an abrasive-blasting machine and tested under pressure after attention to the electrodes. File these until they are clean, bright, and parallel. Set the electrode gap to .025 inch. **Do not try to bend the centre electrode.**

Before replacing the plugs clean the threads with a wire brush. Do not use a wire brush on the electrodes. If it is found that the plugs cannot be screwed in by hand, run a tap down the threads in the cylinder head. Failing a tap, use an old sparking plug with crosscuts down the threads. Finally tighten the plugs to a torque of 30 lb ft. If a torque wrench is not available, tighten with a normal box spanner through half a turn.

Sparking plug leads:

Fit new leads in the manner shown in **FIG 3 : 4**. Undo screw 2, insert the cable after smearing the socket with silicone grease to prevent water from entering. Push the lead right home and then secure it with the screw. To fit the high-tension cable to the ignition coil, slip the knurled terminal nut over the cable first. Then bare about 1/4 inch of the wires and thread them through the brass washer removed from the old cable. Fan out the wires over the face of the washer to hold it in place. Screwing the terminal nut into the coil socket will hold the cable firmly.

3 : 7 The distributor driving spindle

If, for any reason, the driving spindle has been removed from its housing in the crankcase, it must be correctly meshed with the camshaft gear or it will be impossible to set the ignition timing. The operation is covered in **Section 1 : 7** in the Engine Chapter.

3 : 8 Fault diagnosis

(a) Engine will not fire

1 Battery discharged
2 Distributor contact points dirty, pitted or maladjusted
3 Distributor cap dirty, cracked or 'tracking'
4 Carbon brush inside distributor cap not touching rotor
5 Faulty cable or loose connection in low-tension circuit
6 Distributor rotor arm cracked
7 Faulty coil
8 Broken contact breaker spring
9 Contact points stuck open

(b) Engine misfires

1 Check 2, 3, 5 and 7 in (a)
2 Weak contact breaker spring
3 High-tension plug and coil leads cracked or perished
4 Sparking plug(s) loose
5 Sparking plug insulation cracked
6 Sparking plug gap incorrectly set
7 Ignition timing too far advanced

CHAPTER 4

THE COOLING SYSTEM

4 : 1   Description

All the cars which are being covered in this manual have the same type of pressurized cooling system. The natural thermo-syphon action of the water is augmented by a centrifugal impeller mounted at the cylinder block end of the fan spindle. The impeller receives water from the bottom tank of the radiator and passes it through the cylinder block. From here it rises into the cylinder head until it reaches a thermostat valve which prevents cold water from passing to the top tank of the radiator. The water is then recirculated through the engine until it is hot enough to open the thermostat valve, thus giving a quick warm-up. The hot water in the top tank of the radiator falls through the finned core, where it is cooled. The passage of cooling air past the core is assisted by the action of the fan.

A spring-loaded valve in an expansion tank filler cap pressurizes the system and so increases the temperature at which the water boils. The expansion tank is connected to the radiator top tank by hose 25 in **FIG 4 : 1**. As the water in the cooling system expands, the excess will pass down this hose into the expansion tank. When the temperature of the coolant drops, a partial vacuum is created in the radiator top tank and the spillage returns to it. With this system, if it is filled with antifreeze of the ethylene-glycol type there should be no reason to top up the coolant level for at least two years.

4 : 2   Protective maintenance

There is only one lubrication point and this is a plug in the water pump casing which can be seen to the left of the letter **A** in **FIG 4 : 6**. At approximately every 12,000 miles remove the plug and introduce some recommended grease. Do not force the lubricant in under pressure or it may pass through the bearings and get onto the pump seal, impairing the efficiency of the seal.

The cooling system should be drained, flushed through and refilled at regular intervals. Antifreeze may be used for two years, so it may be collected for reuse during that period.

Draining:

The radiator drain plug is shown in **FIG 4 : 2** and the one for the cylinder block in **FIG 4 : 3**. Remove the radiator filler cap, both drain plugs and open the heater tap to drain the system completely.

Flushing:

Introduce water from a hose into the top tank of the radiator and let it continue to run through the system and out through the drain plug holes until it runs clear. If the radiator is blocked, remove it, turn it upsidedown and let the water run through in the reverse direction.

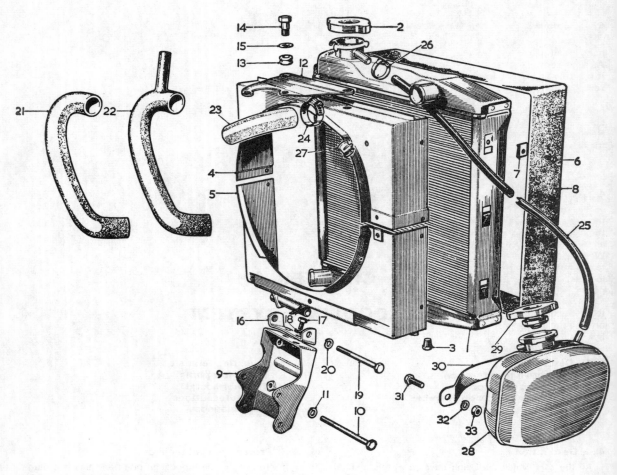

FIG 4:1 Components of radiator system

Key to Fig 4:1   1 Radiator assembly   2 Filler cap (radiator)   3 Drain plug   4 Top cowl
5 Bottom cowl   6 Screw   7 Nut   8 Cowl surround (rubber)   9 Radiator mounting bracket
10 Bolt   11 Spring washer   12 Radiator upper support bracket   13 Support bracket grommet   14 Screw
15 Plain washer   16 Radiator lower support bracket   17 Screw   18 Shakeproof washer   19 Bolt
20 Spring washer   21 Radiator hose to pump   22 Radiator hose to pump (heater)   23 Radiator outlet hose
24 Hose clip   25 Radiator to expansion tank hose   26 Hose clip   27 Radiator cowl hose clip
28 Expansion tank   29 Expansion tank cap   30 Expansion tank strap   31 Screw   32 Spring washer   33 Nut

Filling:

Close the heater tap and disconnect the heater hose. Fill the system through a funnel inserted in the heater hose until the radiator is full to the top of the filler neck. The level of coolant in the expansion tank should be approximately $2\frac{1}{4}$ inch from the bottom. The location of the expansion tank is shown in **FIG 4:4**.

Reconnect the hose and open the heater tap. Refit the radiator and expansion tank caps and run the engine up to normal working temperature. Switch off and allow the system to cool. **Do not remove either filler cap when the system is hot.** Finally, check the level in the radiator and top-up if necessary.

4:3 Removing the radiator

1 Remove the cowling upper support bracket 12, as shown in **FIG 4:1**. Release the lower support bracket 16 (one bolt 19). Release the clips and pull top hose 23 from the radiator inlet pipe. Do the same to the bottom hose from the water pump and disconnect the heater hose, if fitted.

2 Remove the expansion hose 25 from the radiator top tank and the hose clip 27 from the radiator cowling.

3 Extract the screws securing the radiator to the cowling, remove the top half of the cowling 4 and lift the radiator away.

Refitting is a reversal of the removal procedure.

4:4 Removing the expansion chamber

Normally, the expansion chamber needs no maintenance and tampering with it is to be discouraged. **As high temperatures are reached in the chamber, it is likely to lead to injury if the pressurized cap is removed when the system is hot.**

To remove the tank, disconnect and remove the spill hose from its connection on the radiator top tank. Disconnect the spill hose clip from the radiator cowling. Remove the setscrews securing the bracket and lift away the chamber complete with bracket and spill hose.

Refit in the reverse order of dismantling.

4:5 Adjusting and removing the fan belt

Slacken the two generator pivot bolts and the bolt on the slotted adjusting link. Lift the generator by hand until the belt tension is correct. Do not overdo the tension as an undue load will be placed on the generator bearings. When the bolts have been retightened, check the belt tension by moving the belt laterally in the middle of the longest run. About 1 inch of movement should be about right.

On cars fitted with an alternator, as shown in **FIG 4 : 5,** the deflection of the belt should be about $\frac{1}{2}$ inch. Pull only on the alternator end bracket 3 when tensioning the belt.

To remove the belt, slacken the three generator bolts and push the generator right down. Release the belt from the crankshaft pulley and manoeuvre it between the top of each fan blade and the radiator cowling, where enough clearance has been provided to let the belt pass between the blades and the righthand top of the cowling flange.

4:6 The water pump

This is shown in **FIG 4 : 6,** where the water impeller is on the lefthand end of the spindle and the flange for the fan on the right. The bearing assembly can be seen and also the seal pressing against the inner face of the impeller boss. The carbon face of the seal is moulded into a spring-loaded rubber housing.

Removing the water pump:

1 Drain the cooling system as explained in **Section 4 : 2.** Remove the radiator as instructed in **Section 4 : 3.**
2 Remove the hose from the water pump inlet connection and slacken the top clip of the thermostat bypass hose. Remove the generator.
3 Release the fan blades from the hub (4 setscrews) and remove blades, pulley and belt.
4 Remove the setscrews holding the pump to the cylinder block and lift away the pump and bypass hose.

Dismantling the water pump:

1 Pull out the bearing locating wire from the hole in the top of the pump body. Use a puller to remove the fan hub. Gently tap the spindle rearwards until the bearing is clear of its housing.
2 With a suitable extractor, withdraw the impeller from the end of the spindle, which will enable the seal to be lifted off.

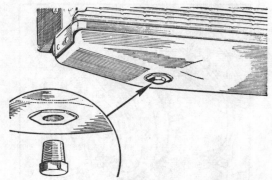

FIG 4 : 2 The radiator drain plug is under the front of the car

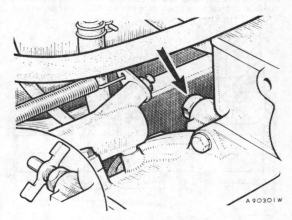

FIG 4 : 3 Either a drain plug or a tap may be found at the rear end of the cylinder block

FIG 4 : 4 The arrow is pointing to the expansion chamber filler cap

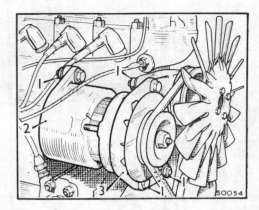

FIG 4 : 5 Slacken bolts 1 to adjust the belt. Pull up on alternator 2 by the end bracket 3. The adjustment is made in the same way on cars with the normal generator

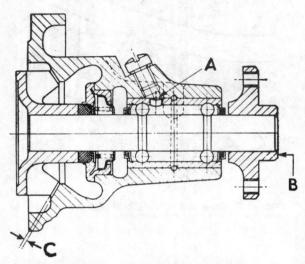

FIG 4 : 6 The water pump in section. Lubricating hole 'A' must coincide with tapped hole in body. Face of hub 'B' must be flush with end of spindle. Clearance 'C' must be .020 to .030 inch

The bearing and spindle assembly cannot be dismantled and is serviced as an assembly. If the bearings are rough or the seals at the ends are defective the bearing and spindle must be renewed. Also renew the impeller seal assembly if it is worn or damaged, or if water leakage has been troublesome.

Reassembling the water pump:

This is a reversal of the dismantling procedure. When pressing the bearing into the body, line up the hole in the outer sleeve with the lubricating hole **A** in the illustration.

The fan hub is an interference fit on the spindle. If this fit is impaired, due to removal from the spindle, a new hub must be fitted. Note the dimension **C** in FIG 4 : 6. This is the clearance of .020 to .030 inch by which the

tips of the impeller vanes must clear the body. Note also that the fan hub must be pressed on until its face is flush with the end of the spindle.

4 : 7 The thermostat

To remove the thermostat, drain the cooling system and remove the cowling upper support bracket. Refer to **FIG 1 : 4** in the Engine Chapter and remove the housing 48 (three nuts and spring washers). Remove joint washer 49 and lift out the thermostat 52.

The thermostat can be tested by immersing it in water so that it does not touch the sides or bottom of the container. The temperature of the water is raised until the thermostat valve starts to open at the temperature given in Technical Data. If the valve does not open, or sticks in the fully open position, renew it. It is impossible to repair a defective thermostat.

Fit the thermostat with the threaded stem uppermost. Fit a new paper joint washer if the original one is damaged.

4 : 8 Frost precautions

When a heater is fitted antifreeze must be used, as draining the cooling system does not drain the heater.

To add antifreeze mixture the cooling system should first be drained and flushed through with water until it runs out clean. Pour in the antifreeze first followed by the water. To prevent the $\frac{1}{2}$ pint of water in the expansion chamber freezing add $\frac{1}{4}$ pint of pure antifreeze. Ensure that the cap with the pressure valve is fitted to the expansion chamber, and that both caps are securely locked in position.

Use only antifreeze of the ethylene-glycol type which conforms to Specification BS.3151 or BS.3152. The mixture can remain in the system for two years provided that the Specific Gravity is checked periodically and fresh antifreeze added as required. After the second winter drain the system, flush out the water and refill with new solution.

Do not use antifreeze in the windscreen washer container. The recommended quantities of antifreeze for different degrees of frost are:

Antifreeze	Starts freezing at	Absolute safe limit
$1\frac{3}{4}$ pints	—9°C or 16°F	—19°C or —3°F
2 pints	—13°C or 9°F	—26°C or —15°F
$2\frac{1}{4}$ pints	—16°C or 3°F	—33°C or —28°F

4 : 9 Fault diagnosis

(a) Internal water leakage

1 Cracked cylinder wall
2 Loose cylinder head nuts
3 Cracked cylinder head
4 Faulty head gasket
5 Cracked tappet chest wall

(b) Poor circulation

1 Radiator core blocked
2 Engine water passages restricted
3 Low water level
4 Loose fan belt
5 Defective thermostat
6 Perished or collapsed radiator hoses

(c) Corrosion

1 Impurities in the water
2 Infrequent draining and flushing

(d) Overheating

1 Check (b)
2 Sludge in crankcase
3 Faulty ignition timing
4 Low oil level in sump
5 Tight engine
6 Choked exhaust system
7 Binding brakes
8 Slipping clutch
9 Incorrect valve timing
10 Retarded ignition
11 Mixture too weak

CHAPTER 5

THE CLUTCH

5 : 1 Description

The clutch is a single-plate dry-disc type operating on the inner face of the flywheel. **FIG 5 : 1** shows the clutch in section, but note that it is the earlier one which is fitted with coil springs 4. The later type of clutch shown in **FIG 5 : 4** uses a diaphragm spring 22. When the clutch is fully engaged the pressure springs exert a powerful pull on pressure plate 19 through lugs and setscrews 14. This pressure nips the driven plate 20, by its friction linings, between the inner faces of the flywheel and the pressure plate. When the engine is running this means that the driven plate is revolving with the flywheel and carries round with it the primary gear 22, to which the plate is splined. The primary gear transmits the drive to the transmission. To disengage the clutch, a lever which is hydraulically connected to the clutch pedal causes a release bearing to press on the thrust plate 8 which moves the pressure plate away from the driven plate and so disconnects the drive. The driven plate and primary gear are then free to revolve on the crankshaft or come to a stop without transmitting any drive even though the crankshaft may continue to turn.

5 : 2 Removing and dismantling clutch

Use **FIG 5 : 2** to identify the parts mentioned. Note that these instructions concern the clutch fitted with coil springs. There will be later reference to the diaphragm spring type in **Section 5 : 4**.

1 Remove the flywheel and clutch assembly as instructed in **Chapter 1. The clutch to flywheel driving straps 10 are laminated so that two are fitted to each of the three driving points. Mark all components including straps and driving pins before dismantling so that they can be refitted in their original positions.**

2 To compress the pressure springs 16, set up Service Tool 18G.304M as shown in **FIG 5 : 3**. Insert the three screws of the tool through the three recessed holes in the spring housing 18. Screw them right home into the flywheel and then fit the three nuts finger tight.

3 Proceed to tighten the three nuts a turn at a time until all the load is taken off the pressure plate screws 20. These are called driving pins in **FIG 5 : 1**. Remove the screws and gradually turn back the nuts until the springs are released from compression.

4 Examine all parts for wear, taking particular note of the holes in the spring housing for the driving setscrews. These holes must not be elongated, and setscrews 12 and 20 must not be worn or ridged. **All setscrews and driving straps must be renewed as sets of three and not individually.**

5 Renew the flywheel and pressure plate if the friction faces are pitted or deeply scored. The friction linings should stand well proud of the rivets and have a light colour, with a polished glaze through which the grain of the material should be clearly visible. A dark, glazed deposit is generally caused by oil getting on to the linings. Any signs of oil in the clutch will call for attention to the seal in the flywheel. Renew release bearing 30 if it feels rough.

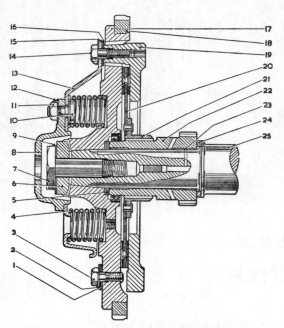

FIG 5 : 1 The coil spring clutch in section

Key to Fig 5 : 1

1 Driving strap		2 Lockwasher
3 Driving pin	4 Pressure spring	5 Circlip
6 Keyed washer	7 Flywheel screw	8 Thrust plate
9 Locking washer	10 Pressure spring guides	11 Guide nut
12 Lockwasher	13 Pressure spring housing	14 Driving pin
15 Lockwasher	16 Driving strap	17 Flywheel
18 Starter ring	19 Pressure plate	20 Driven plate
21 Driven plate hub		22 Crankshaft primary gear
23 Primary gear bearing	24 Thrust washer	25 Crankshaft

5 : 3 Reassembling and refitting clutch

1 Follow the dismantling instructions in reverse. The hub of the driven plate must be centralized with the hub of the flywheel during reassembly and Service Tool 18G.684 is available for this purpose. Insert the tool through the hub of the driven plate and the bore of the flywheel and secure it in place against the flywheel boss with the screw and retaining plate.

2 Locate the thrust plate screws 17 correctly in the slotted holes in the spring housing. Assemble the springs and housing, making certain that all parts are returned to their marked positions. Use Service Tool 18G.304M to compress the springs and to ensure that the holes in the housing and the driving straps are lined up with the tapped holes in the pressure plate lugs. If the holes are not aligned there may be difficulty in inserting the shouldered setscrews. Screw up tight, making sure that the shoulders pass through the driving straps and then turn up the locking washers. **It is important to check that two driving straps are fitted to each of the three driving points and that each set is returned to its original position.**

3 Refit the clutch and flywheel as instructed in **Chapter 1.**

5 : 4 The diaphragm spring clutch

FIG 5 : 4 shows this type of clutch in section. It is the clutch fitted to later cars and the components which differ radically in design are numbered 21 to 26 in **FIG 5 : 2**. Note that instead of the coiled compression springs 16 which were originally fitted, there is a dished diaphragm spring 23. Note also that the release bearing presses on a separate thrust plate 25 which is held in place by a retaining spring 26.

This clutch is serviced by following the instructions for the earlier type as covered in **Sections 5 : 2** and **5 : 3**. It is not, however, necessary to use the recommended Service Tools to dismantle this clutch.

When refitting the clutch, if the original cover has been reassembled, align the mark 'A' with the 1/4 mark on the flywheel to preserve the balance.

5 : 5 Adjusting the operating lever

Refer to **FIG 5 : 5**. It is important that clearance should be present between the clutch release bearing and the thrust plate. As the clutch linings wear this clearance will diminish, and if adjustment is neglected clutch slip will result.

An adjustable stop is provided on the transmission casing just forward of the clutch operating lever. Clearance between the stop and the lever is indicated by the right-hand arrow. Pull the lever outwards until all free movement is taken up and then check with a feeler gauge that there is a clearance of .020 inch between the lever stop and the head of the adjusting bolt, as shown in the inset. Obtain the correct clearance by unlocking and turning the bolt.

5 : 6 Servicing the hydraulic system

The clutch is operated hydraulically, the clutch pedal being connected to pushrod 1 in **FIG 5 : 6**. The pushrod will press piston 11 down the master cylinder bore when the pedal is depressed. Fluid in front of the piston will then be forced along pipes until it reaches the slave cylinder shown in **FIG 5 : 7**. Here, piston 4 will move down the bore in body 5, pushing rod 8 in front of it. This rod is connected to the clutch operating lever to be seen in **FIG 5 : 5**. Fluid leakage past the pistons is prevented by rubber seals or cups 13 and 3 in the two illustrations respectively. When the master cylinder piston is fully retracted a small hole in the cylinder is uncovered. This communicates with supply tank 4 and provides replenishing fluid to the system if there has been any loss. The hole is covered as soon as the piston starts to move.

Servicing operations must be carried out in conditions of great cleanliness as dirt will score the highly-finished bores and prevent the rubber cups from sealing properly.

Removing the master cylinder:

Withdraw the clevis pin connecting the clutch pedal lever to the master cylinder pushrod. Disconnect the pressure pipe union from the cylinder, remove the two bolts securing the cylinder to the bulkhead and withdraw the assembly.

Dismantling the master cylinder:

Refer to **FIG 5 : 6**. Drain the fluid from the supply tank.

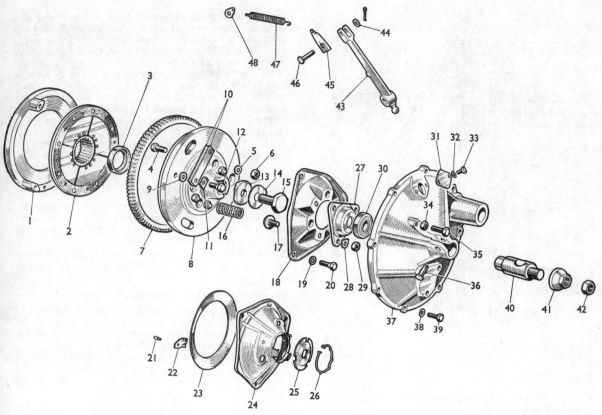

FIG 5 : 2   The clutch components. Items 21 to 26 are for the later clutch with diaphragm spring

Key to Fig 5 : 2

1 Pressure plate	2 Clutch driven plate	3 Flywheel oil seal	4 Hub screw
5 Lockwasher	6 Nut	7 Starter ring	8 Flywheel assembly	9 Washer	10 Driving strap
11 Lockwasher	12 Strap screw	13 Key	14 Lockwasher	15 Flywheel screw	16 Pressure spring
17 Thrust plate screw	18 Spring housing (coil spring clutch)	19 Washer	20 Pressure plate screw
21 Rivet dowel	22 Retaining clip	23 Diaphragm spring	24 Spring housing	25 Thrust plate
26 Plate retaining spring	27 Clutch thrust plate	28 Lockwasher	29 Nut	30 Release bearing
31 Cover plate	32 Washer	33 Screw	34 Locknut	35 Screw	36 Lever pin
37 Clutch cover	38 Washer	39 Cover screw	40 Throw-out plunger	41 Throw-out stop
42 Stop locknut	43 Clutch operating lever	44 Washer	45 Spring anchor (lever)	46 Pushrod pin
47 Lever pull-off spring	48 Spring anchor (cylinder)		

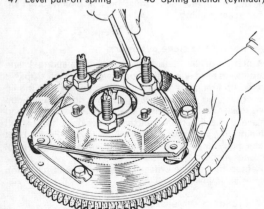

FIG 5 : 3   Coil spring clutch. Compressing the springs, using Service Tools 18G.304M and 18G.684

Pull back rubber boot 2 and remove circlip 8. Withdraw pushrod 1 with dished washer 9. Extract all the internal parts. Gentle air pressure at end plug 7 may be used to blow out the parts, but use extra care. Remove secondary cup 10 by stretching it over the piston flange using only the fingers.

Reassembling the master cylinder:

Clean all the rubber parts in the correct grade of hydraulic fluid. Any solvents such as petrol, paraffin or trichlorethylene which may be used to clean the metal parts must be dried off completely before reassembling. Examine the rubber cups for damage or distortion, particularly to the knife-edges. The cups are available in kits of replacement parts and if they have seen considerable service it is wise to renew them even though they may seem to be satisfactory. Do not turn the cups inside out.

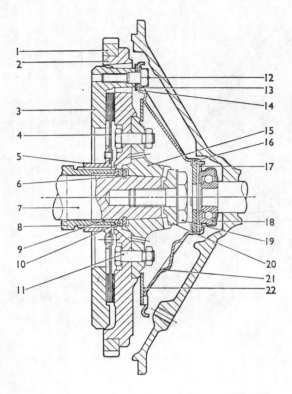

FIG 5:4 Section of later clutch with diaphragm spring

Key to Fig 5:4   1 Starter ring   2 Flywheel
3 Pressure plate   4 Driven plate   5 Driven plate hub
6 Circlip   7 Crankshaft   8 Crankshaft primary gear
9 Primary gear bearing 10 Thrust washer 11 Flywheel hub bolt
12 Driving pin   13 Lockwasher   14 Driving strap
15 Flywheel hub   16 Thrust plate   17 Plate retaining spring
18 Thrust bearing   19 Flywheel screw   20 Keyed washer
21 Cover   22 Diaphragm spring

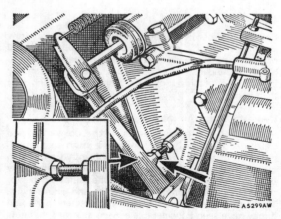

FIG 5:5 There must be a clearance of .020 inch between the operating lever and the adjustable stop

Start by dipping all internal parts in brake fluid and assemble them wet. Stretch the secondary cup over the piston flange and work it about with the fingers until it is correctly seated. Insert spring 15, large end first, making sure that retainer 14 is in place at the small end. Insert the main cup 13 lip first, taking great care not to damage or turn back the lip. Press it down the bore onto the spring retainer. Fit washer 12, followed by the piston. Refit the pushrod and circlip, followed by the rubber boot.

Before refitting the assembly to the car, test it by filling the supply tank with Lockheed Disc Brake Fluid (Series 11). Push the piston down the bore and let it return. After one or two strokes, fluid should flow from outlet 7.

Refitting the master cylinder:

Fit the master cylinder to the bulkhead crossmember (two bolts). Connect the pressure pipeline to the outlet from the cylinder. Line up the pushrod yoke with the end of the pedal lever and connect up with the clevis pin. Check the level of the fluid in the supply tank and bleed the system as instructed in **Section 5:7**.

Removing the slave cylinder:

Fit a length of rubber tube to the nipple on the body of the slave cylinder and open the nipple screw three-quarters of a turn. Pump the clutch pedal until all the fluid has been transferred into a clean container.

Unscrew the pressure pipe from the cylinder, release the cylinder body from the clutch housing (two bolts) and remove the clevis pin to free the pushrod from the operating lever.

Dismantling the slave cylinder:

Clean the exterior thoroughly. Withdraw the pushrod 8 in **FIG 5:7** and remove rubber boot 7, using only the fingers to displace the boot retaining ring. Extract circlip 6 and withdraw parts 1 to 4 or blow them out with gentle air pressure.

Clean the internal parts with brake fluid and assemble them wet. It is always a good plan to renew all the rubber parts, particularly sealing cup 3. Any solvents used for cleaning the metal parts must be completely dried off before reassembling.

Assembling the slave cylinder:

Attach cup filler 2 to the small end of spring 1 and insert the assembly into the bore, large end first. Cup 3 is entered lip first, taking special care to ensure that the lip is not damaged or turned back. Press it down to the cup filler. Push the piston down the bore, flat end first, and replace circlip 6. Check that the rubber boot has a small retaining ring in position on the inner flange. Fit the boot to the body and secure it with the large retaining ring. Replace pushrod 8.

Refit in the reverse order of dismantling and bleed the system as follows.

5:7 Bleeding the system

Fill the master cylinder supply tank with Lockheed Disc Brake Fluid (Series 11). Attach a rubber tube to the

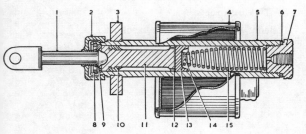

FIG 5:6 The clutch master cylinder in section

Key to Fig 5:6   1 Pushrod   2 Rubber boot
3 Mounting flange   4 Supply tank   5 Body
6 Washer   7 End plug   8 Circlip   9 Stop washer
10 Secondary cup   11 Piston   12 Piston washer
13 Main cup   14 Spring retainer   15 Return spring

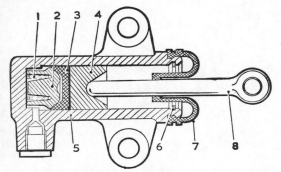

FIG 5:7 A section through the clutch slave cylinder

Key to Fig 5:7   1 Spring   2 Cup filler   3 Cup
4 Piston   5 Body   6 Circlip   7 Rubber boot
8 Pushrod

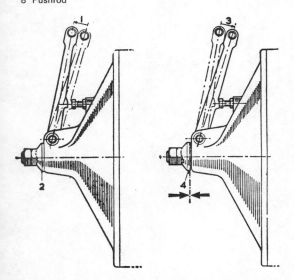

FIG 5:8 Adjusting the clutch throw-out stop 2. On left, clutch fully released 1 and stop is touching cover boss. On right, clutch engaged 3 and stop screwed .002 to .005 inch nearer the boss at 4

bleed screw nipple on the slave cylinder. Immerse the open end of the tube in a small amount of the same brake fluid in a clean container. A second operator is needed to pump the clutch pedal after the bleed screw has been opened about three-quarters of a turn. At the end of each down stroke of the pedal close the bleed screw and let the pedal return to the 'off' position. At first, air bubbles will emerge from the immersed end of the tube. When clear fluid free from bubbles is delivered into the container, tighten the bleed screw on a down stroke of the pedal.

The operation of bleeding the system is necessary whenever the pipelines are disconnected or when the fluid in the supply tank has fallen so low that air has entered the system.

It is not advisable to use again fluid which has been collected in the container unless it is clean beyond all doubt. Even then it must be allowed to stand for twenty-four hours to become de-aerated.

5:8 Clutch throw-out stop

This is item 2 in **FIG 5:8**. It is set and locked in the correct position during initial assembly and should not be disturbed during normal servicing. The only adjustment is then to the lever stop screw as covered in **Section 5:5**.

If it is necessary to remove the throw-out plunger 40 in **FIG 5:2**, the stop 41 must be reset as follows:

Screw the stop and the locknut as far away from the clutch cover boss as the limit of travel. Depress the clutch pedal fully to release the clutch. Hold it in this position and screw the stop back against the cover boss. Now release the clutch pedal so that the clutch becomes fully engaged and screw the stop a further .002 to .005 inch nearer the boss. This is equivalent to approximately one flat on the hexagon. Tighten the locknut.

Finally, check the clearance at the lever stop screw and adjust as in **Section 5:5**.

5:9 Fault diagnosis

(a) Drag or spin

1 Oil or grease on driven plate linings
2 Leaking master cylinder, slave cylinder or piping
3 Driven plate hub binding on splines
4 Distorted driven plate
5 Warped or damaged pressure plate
6 Broken driven plate linings
7 Air in the clutch hydraulic system

(b) Fierceness or snatch

1 Check 1, 2, 4 and 5 in (a)
2 Worn clutch linings

(c) Slip

1 Check 1 in (a) and 2 in (b)
2 Weak pressure spring(s)
3 Seized piston in clutch slave cylinder
4 Operating lever stop has no clearance

(d) Judder

1 Check 1 and 4 (a)
2 Pressure plate incorrectly fitted to spring housing
3 Contact area of driven plate linings not evenly distributed
4 Faulty rubber mountings

(e) Tick or knock

1 Badly worn driven plate hub splines
2 Worn release bearing
3 Faulty drive pinion on starter
4 Elongated holes in spring housing
5 Defective drive straps

CHAPTER 6

SYNCHROMESH TRANSMISSION

6 : 1 Description

All 1098cc Mk I models have synchromesh gear engagement on second, third and top gears.

The layout of the components in the transmission casing is shown in **FIG 6 : 1** as seen from the rear. The drive from the clutch is through primary gear 40 to idler gear 43. This in turn drives first motion shaft gear 45 which is splined to the righthand end of shaft 61. The smaller gear on this shaft engages the largest gear on layshaft gear 54. Third motion shaft 65 carries the gear and synchromesh assemblies **68 to 85**, its righthand end running freely in roller bearing 62 in the end of the first motion shaft 61, the other end being supported in bearing 66. Splined to the lefthand end of the shaft is final drive pinion 90 which meshes with drive gear 3 in **FIG 6 : 7** which in turn drives the shafts coupled to the front wheels.

6 : 2 Dismantling the transmission

1 Remove the transmission casing from the crankcase as instructed in **Section 1 : 10** of the Engine Chapter. Remove idler gear 43 from the crankcase, noting thrust washers 44. A special extractor is needed for the idler gear bearings 20, the tool number being 18G.581.

2 Remove the differential assembly as detailed in

Section 6 : 5. Remove plug 135 and extract spring 134 and plunger 133. Remove selector operating lever 122 and withdraw shaft 120, taking care not to damage seal 121 with key 123. Remove speedometer pinion and housing 93 to 99. Remove end plate and speedometer gear 100 to 104.

3 Remove the radiator, cowling, mounting bracket and spacer. Remove front cover 137. Remove oil suction pipe 33 (screws 31 and 37). Withdraw the pipe from strainer 26. Note paper washer 34.

4 Lock up two gears and remove nut 91, washer 92 and pinion 90 from the end of third motion shaft 65. From the centre web of the casing remove bearing retainer 86, noting shims 89.

5 Remove the circlip and roller bearing from the righthand end of first motion shaft 61, knock up locking washer 47, unscrew nut 46 and pull off gear 45. Remove the layshaft and reverse gear shaft locating plate 55 and push the layshaft out of the casing. Remove laygear 54 and thrust washers 59 and 60.

6 Remove the screwed plugs 117 from the outside of the casing and extract the selector rod interlocking plungers and springs 115 and 116. Extract circlip 64 and use an impulse extractor such as Tool 18G.284 with adaptor 18G.284B screwed onto the first motion shaft thread to draw out the shaft with bearing 63

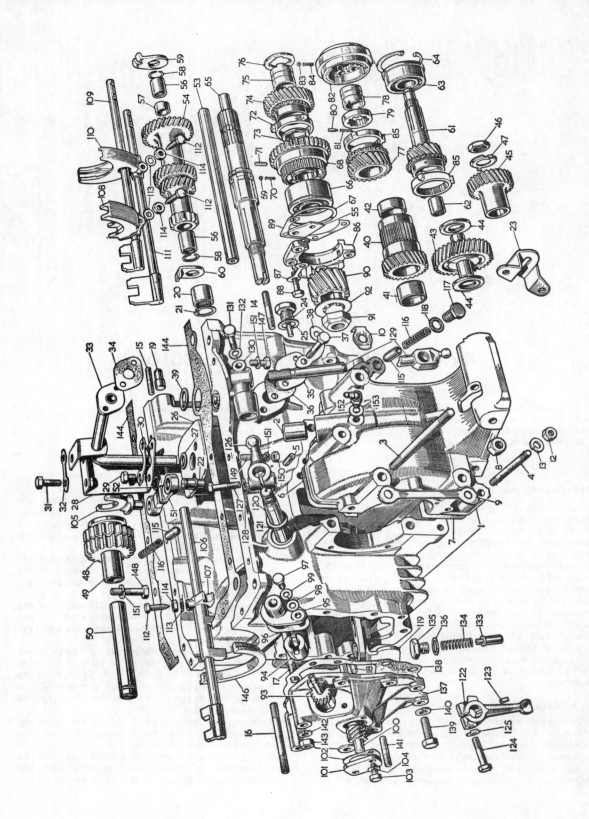

FIG 6:1 Transmission components seen from the rear

Key to Fig 6:1

1 Transmission case
2 Control shaft bush
3 Differential cover bush
4 Differential cover stud
5 Differential cover dowel
6 Differential cover joint washer (upper)
7 Differential cover joint washer (lower)
8 Nut
9 Washer
10 Washer
11 Washer
12 Nut
13 Washer
14 Flywheel housing stud
15 Flywheel housing stud
16 Front cover stud (lower)
17 Front cover stud (long)
18 Front cover dowel
19 Flywheel housing dowel
20 Idler gear bearing
21 Bearing circlip
22 Operating lever pin
23 Exhaust pipe bracket
24 Drain plug
25 Plug washer
26 Oil suction pipe
27 Oil strainer
28 Strainer bracket
29 Screw to strainer
30 Washer
31 Screw to casing
32 Washer
33 Oil suction pipe
34 Joint washer
35 Pipe flange
36 Joint washer
37 Pipe screw
38 Washer
39 Sealing ring
40 Primary gear
41 Gear bush (front)
42 Gear bush (rear)
43 Idler gear
44 Idler gear thrust washer
45 First motion shaft gear
46 Nut
47 Lockwasher
48 Reverse shaft
49 Bush
50 Reverse shaft
51 Reverse operating lever
52 Pivot pin circlip
53 Layshaft
54 Laygear
55 Locating plate
56 Bearing
57 Distance piece
58 Retaining ring
59 Thrust washer (rear)
60 Thrust washer (front)
61 First motion shaft
62 First motion shaft roller bearing
63 First motion ball bearing
64 Circlip
65 Third motion shaft
66 Third motion shaft bearing
67 Circlip
68 First speed gear
69 Synchronizer ball
70 Spring
71 Second speed synchronizer plunger
72 Baulk ring
73 Second speed gear thrust washer
74 Second speed gear
75 Bush
76 Interlocking ring
77 Third speed gear
78 Bush
79 Third motion shaft thrust washer
80 Thrust washer peg
81 Spring
82 Third/top synchronizer
83 Ball
84 Spring
85 Baulk ring
86 Bearing retainer
87 Lockwasher
88 Screw
89 Bearing shim
90 Final drive pinion
91 Nut
92 Washer
93 Speedometer pinion
94 Bush
95 Bush assembly
96 Joint washer
97 Bush screw
98 Washer
99 Washer
100 Speedometer spindle and gear
101 End plate
102 Plate joint
103 Screw
104 Washer
105 Reverse fork
106 Reverse fork rod
107 Fork rod selector
108 First and second speed fork
109 First and second speed fork rod
110 Third and fourth speed fork
111 Third and fourth speed fork rod
112 Selector screw
113 Washer
114 Locknut
115 Plunger, fork end
116 Plunger spring
117 Plug
118 Plug washer
119 Changespeed gate
120 Gearchange shaft
121 Oil seal
122 Operating lever
123 Key
124 Lever screw
125 Washer
126 Reverse check plunger
127 Lever screw
128 Washer
129 Remote control shaft
130 Shaft lever
131 Lever screw
132 Washer
133 Reverse check plunger
134 Plunger spring
135 Spring plug
136 Plug washer
137 Front cover
138 Cover joint
139 Cover screw
140 Washer
141 Mounting adaptor strip
142 Washer
143 Nut
144 Crankcase joint washer (righthand)
145 Crankcase joint washer (lefthand)
146 Bearing cap oil seal
147 Transmission to crankcase screw
148 Transmission to crankcase screw (long)
149 Transmission to crankcase stud
150 Nut
151 Washer
152 Lubricator
153 Washer

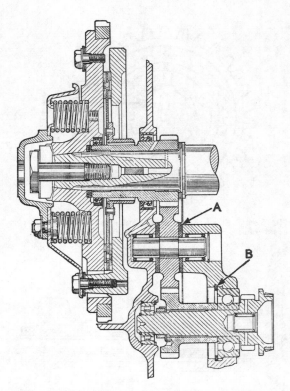

FIG 6:2 Section through primary, idler and first motion shaft gears. Thrust washers 'A' adjust idler gear end float. Measure at 'B' for thickness of circlip

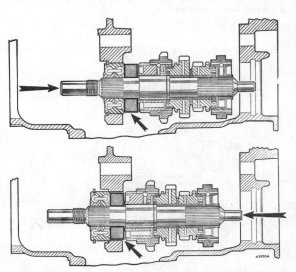

FIG 6:3 Using Service Tool 18G.613 to remove the third motion shaft bearing. Collar indicated by lower arrow

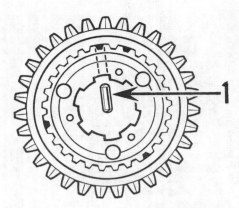

FIG 6:4 First and second speed gear correctly assembled on hub, with plunger arrowed at 1

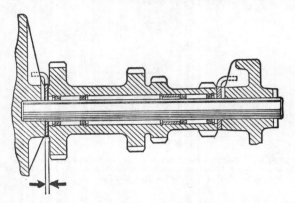

FIG 6:5 Section through laygear and thrust washers. Measure where indicated to determine thickness of thrust washer required

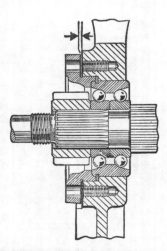

FIG 6:6 Section through third motion shaft bearing and retainer. Measure gap indicated to determine thickness of shims required

7 Remove selector screw 112 and withdraw fork rod 109. Lift out fork 108. Refer to·**FIG 6:3** and drive the third motion shaft 65 carefully in the direction of the lefthand arrow in the top view until Tool 18G.613 can be inserted between the bearing and the first speed gear hub 68 as indicated. The recessed face of the tool must be towards the bearing. Drift the shaft carefully out of the casing until the bearing is almost free, then gently lever it off the shaft and out of its housing. **This operation must be done with care so that the selector forks are not damaged.** With the bearing withdrawn the third motion shaft can be removed.

8 Remove oil strainer bracket 28 complete with strainer. **Release fork 110 from its rod 111.** Withdraw both rod and fork. Remove reverse gear shaft 50, gear 48 and selector fork 105. Extract detent spring 116 and plunger 115. Remove circlip 52 and lift off reverse operating lever 51.

6:3 Servicing third motion shaft

To service a shaft with three synchromesh assemblies, proceed as follows:

1 Remove the first speed gear and hub 68 from the rear of the shaft 65. If the gear is pressed off the hub, be prepared to catch the three sets of balls and springs 69 and 70 by wrapping the assembly in a cloth. Withdraw the third/top gear hub and synchronizer 82 from the righthand end of the shaft, noting that the plain side of the hub faces to the left. Remove baulk ring 85.

2 Press down locating plunger 80 with a piece of wire and turn washer 79 until its splines register with those on the shaft and it can be withdrawn. Pull off third speed gear 77. Remove the plunger and spring. Pull off bush 78, interlocking ring 76, second speed gear 74 and bush 75. Remove rear thrust washer 73.

Reassembling third motion shaft:

1 Reverse the dismantling procedure. Fit rear thrust washer 73 and prepare to fit a new bush 75. Both this and bush 78 must always be renewed as the interference fit is destroyed on removal. Heat the new bushes to 180-200°C or 356-392°F so that they càn be fitted without force. Follow bush 75 with interlocking ring 76 after lubricating gear 74 and sliding it into place. Fit bush 78, engaging the dogs with the ring. Position gear 77 with plain side to the left and insert the spring and plunger. Depress the plunger and slide washer 79 over it. Turn the washer until the plunger engages a spline.

2 Check the end float of the second and third speed gears. This must be between .0035 and .0055 inch. Renew the thrust washers if end float is excessive. Fit assembly 82 with its plain face to the washer 79.

3 Fit assembly 68 and baulk ring 72. The cone side of the hub must be to the right, and also the plain ends of the first gear teeth. If the assembly has been dismantled, refer to **FIG 6:4** which shows the correct position of the gear on the hub. The plunger 1 must align with the cutaway tooth in the gear or selection of first gear will be impossible.

Refit the assembly as follows:

6 : 4 Reassembling transmission

1 If it was removed, press the reverse lever pivot pin 22 into its hole in the casing. Fit the operating lever 51 and secure with circlip 52. Position the reverse gear and fork to engage the operating lever and push shaft 50 through the centre web of the casing, plain end first. Fit the interlock spring and plunger. Push rod 106 into the casing to pick up fork 107 on the way. Position fork 110 and push rod 111 into place, picking up the fork as it goes. Tighten and lock the fork retaining screws.

2 Fit the oil strainer and insert the fixing screws through the strainer bracket and the casing lug, leaving the nuts slack. Smear a little grease on sealing ring 27.

3 Fit the third motion shaft assembly into the casing with the slotted end passing through the centre web and the sliding hubs engaging the selector forks.

4 Fit the ballrace to the first motion shaft and insert the assembly into the casing. Position the third motion shaft bearing in the casing web, line up both shafts and carefully drift the bearings into place. Service Tool 18G.579, with its distance collar, is used to drift the third motion shaft bearing into the centre web. Place the collar in the recess on the end of the tool so that the outer race will be driven into the casing at the same time as the inner race is driven onto the third motion shaft. Use the same tool to drift the first motion shaft bearing into the casing, without the distance collar. Fit bearing retaining circlip 64. **FIG 6 : 2** shows this circlip at **B**. There are two thicknesses of circlip available and either is used according to the measurement between the bearing face and the register. There is a gauge for taking this measurement and the number is 18G.569. If the measurement at **B** is .096 to .098 inch, use circlip No. 2A.3710. If the measurement is .099 to .100 inch, use circlip No. 2A.3711.

5 Fit fork 108 and rod 109. Lock into place. Refit the first and second, third and top selector rod detent plungers and springs. Each plug must be fitted with a sealing washer. Fit the drive pinion 90 to the third motion shaft, tightening and locking the nut. Refit gear 45 to the first motion shaft with the pegs on the locking washer engaged in the holes in the gear. Tighten the nut and bend up the washer.

6 Refit the laygear, putting a thrust washer at each end and the shaft with its slotted end to the left. Use a dummy layshaft such as Tool 18G.471 to hold the washers in place while the shaft is fitted. End float must be between .002 and .006 inch and thrust washers are available in a range of sizes from .121 to .132 inch in thickness to enable this figure to be obtained. **FIG 6 : 5** shows the layshaft and gear cluster in section. When the gap indicated is .125 to .127 inch, use thrust washer No. 22A.48. When it is .128 to .130 inch, use washer No. 22A.49. When it is .131 to .133 inch, use washer No. 22A.50, and when it is .134 inch, use washer No. 22A.52. Turn the layshaft and reverse gear shaft till the slots in the ends face each other and fit locating plate 55 after checking for the thickness of shims 89 required under retainer 86. **The locating plate goes on top of the shims.**

FIG 6 : 6 shows the gap to be measured to determine the thickness of shims required. When the gap is .005 to .006 inch, use shims totalling .005 inch. When .006 to .008 inch, use shims to .007 inch. When .008 to .010 inch, use shims to .009 inch. When .010 to .012 inch, use shims to .011 inch. When .012 to .014 inch, use shims to .013 inch. When .014 to .015 inch, use shims totalling .015 inch. Secure the retainer (four setscrews and lock plates).

7 Remove the righthand screw of the two holding the strainer bracket. Lightly grease the end of pipe 33 and insert in the strainer, taking care not to displace seal 27. Fit paper gaskets 34 and 36, flange 35 and fit and tighten screws 37. Tighten and lock the bracket screws.

8 Fit changespeed gate 119 and cover 137 with a new gasket 138. Insert speedometer gear 100 to engage the slot in the end of the third motion shaft. Fit coverplate and gasket 101 and 102 (two setscrews and spring washers). Fit parts 93 to 99. Renew oil seal 121 if necessary, using Tool 18G.573 to drive the new one into place. Fit shaft 120, key 123 into the bottom end and position lever 122 with its end engaging in the interlocking arm. Push the shaft through the lever boss and into its lower bearing in the casing. Line up the recess in the shaft, then insert, tighten and lock setscrew 124. Fit parts 133 to 136. Refit the differential assembly as in **Section 6 : 5**.

9 If the idler gear bearing in the flywheel housing needs renewal, give adequate support to the casing boss during the pressing-in operation. Service Tool 18G.582 will fit either of the idler gear bearings. The collar supplied with the tool controls the depth to which the bearing is pressed into the flywheel housing. **If the bearing is pressed fully home it will blank off the oil supply hole.** This collar is not needed when fitting an idler gear bearing into the transmission casing. Refit the roller bearing to the end of the first motion shaft.

10 Before refitting the transmission assembly check the end float of the idler gear as follows:

Clean the casing joint faces and fit a new flywheel housing gasket to the transmission casing. Fit the idler gear with the chamfered bore of the thrust washers against the gear face. Smear the first motion shaft bearing rollers with high-melting point grease to stop them tilting and fit the flywheel housing. If there is resistance, withdraw the housing and find the cause. Do not use force. Tighten the stud nuts to 18 lb ft and check the idler gear end float. This should be between .003 and .008 inch and thrust washers are available in thicknesses from .132 to .139 inch to arrive at the correct float. Remove the housing and gasket and refit the transmission casing to the crankcase as instructed in **Section 1 : 10** of the Engine Chapter. **Do not fit the housing gasket used for checking idler gear end float. A new gasket must be fitted on final assembly.**

6 : 5 Servicing differential assembly

The component parts are shown in **FIG 6 : 7**, and a section is given in **FIG 6 : 8**. Remove as follows:

1 Remove the engine and transmission as instructed in the Engine Chapter. Remove the pivot pin and bell-

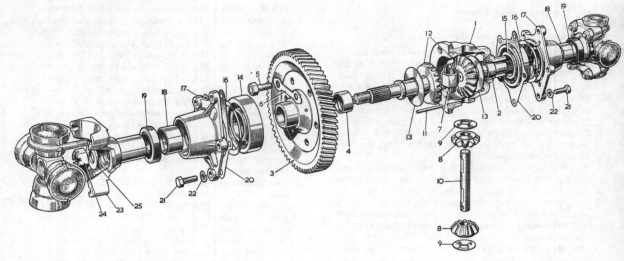

FIG 6 : 7   Components of differential assembly

Key to Fig 6 : 7

	1 Differential case	2 Case bush	3 Drive gear	4 Gear bush	5 Gear bolt
6 Lockwasher	7 Thrust block	8 Differential pinion	9 Pinion thrust washer		10 Centre pin
11 Pin peg	12 Differential gear	13 Gear thrust washer	14 Drive gear bearing		15 Case bearing
16 Bearing shim	17 End-cover	18 Cover bush	19 Oil seal	20 Cover joint	21 End-cover screw
22 Washer	23 Driving flange	24 Flange nut	25 Washer		

crank lever from the lower rear part of casing 1 in **FIG 6 : 1.** Remove lever 130 and withdraw remote control shaft 129. Remove the nylon seating and tension spring from both the remote control shaft and the shaft lever.

2 Remove the splitpins from nuts 24 in **FIG 6 : 7,** hold the flanges 23 with Service Tool 18G.669 and unscrew the nuts. **Never use the transmission casing as a stop or leverage point when removing the flange nuts or any other components of the transmission or serious damage to the casing may result.**

3 Remove the two end covers 17 (five setscrews each). Note the number of shims 16 between the bearings and housings. Remove the differential housing stud nuts, withdraw the housing from the transmission casing and remove the differential assembly.

Dismantling the differential assembly:

1 Use Service Tool 18G.2 to withdraw the two bearings 14. Unlock and remove the six setbolts 5. Mark the gear and differential case before separating them so that they can be reassembled in the original positions. Withdraw the differential gear 12 with thrust washer 13.

2 Tap out taper pin 11. This operation can only be done after the drive gear and case are parted. Remove centre pin 10, thrust block 7, pinions 8 and thrust washers 9.

Reassembling:

This is the reverse of the dismantling procedure. Make sure that the gear thrust washers 13 are replaced with their slightly chamfered bores against the machined faces of the differential gears 12. Replace all parts in their original

positions. Tighten the drive gear to differential case bolts to a torque of 55 to 60 lb ft.

Refitting:

1 Place the differential assembly in the transmission casing with a slight bias in the direction of the flywheel end of the engine. Fit the differential housing and joint washers, tightening the nuts just enough to hold the bearings firmly and yet allow the assembly to be displaced by the fitting of the righthand final drive end cover.

2 Refit the righthand end cover and joint washer. Line up the holes carefully and insert the setscrews, tightening them evenly and a little at a time to ensure maximum contact with the outer race of the drive gear bearing. As the screws are tightened the differential assembly will be displaced away from the flywheel end of the engine. Fit the other end cover without a gasket.

3 Be careful during the next operation, as the cover may be distorted by overtightening. Keeping the cover square all the time, tighten the cover screws until the register just nips the bearing outer race. Refer to **FIG 6 : 8** and measure the gap at point **A** with a feeler gauge. Take the measurement at several points round the flange. Any variation will prove that the screws have not been tightened evenly. **Adjust the tightness of the screws accordingly but be very careful not to put excessive strain on the cover flange.** Check the measurement again. If the feeler gauge cannot be inserted, fit shims to the value of .008 inch between the bearing outer race and the end cover register.

4 **The required preload on the bearings is .001 to .002 inch.** The compressed thickness of the cover joint washer is .007 inch. The correct gap is therefore

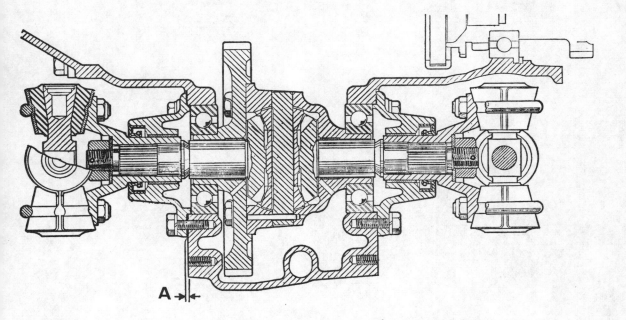

FIG 6:8 Measure gap at 'A' to determine thickness of shims to give required bearing preload on differential assembly

.008 to .009 inch. Any deviation from this figure must be made up by shims. For example, if the gap is .005 inch a shim .003 inch thick must be fitted between the outer race of the bearing and the register on the end cover. Remove the cover, fit the necessary shims into the bearing recess, fit the joint washer and end cover and tighten the setscrews to a torque of 18 lb ft.

5 Tighten the differential housing nuts, refit the driving flanges and tighten the slotted nuts to a torque of 70 lb ft. **Do not slacken to align a splitpin hole but tighten further.** Use a new splitpin. Now check that the drive shafts require equal effort to turn them. Tightness on one side more than the other will affect the steering, making it pull in one direction.

6 Fit the operating lever to the splined end of the gearchange operating shaft. Make certain that the recess in the shaft lines up with the hole through the lever boss before inserting the setscrew. Position the remote control shaft lever on the ball end of the operating lever, insert the remote control shaft into the gearchange extension from the bottom and engage it with the splined bore of the lever. Make sure that the recess in the splined end of the shaft lines up with the hole through the lever boss before inserting the setscrew. Refit the bellcrank lever.

6:6 Lubrication

There is a grease nipple 152 in **FIG 6:1** which needs attention at major overhauls only. It lubricates the gearchange shaft. Use only grease.

6:7 Fault diagnosis

(a) Jumping out of gear

1 Broken spring behind selector rod locating plunger
2 Excessively worn groove in selector rod
3 Worn synchromesh coupling dogs
4 Fork to selector rod securing screw loose

(b) Noisy transmission

1 Insufficient oil
2 Excessive end float of laygear
3 Incorrect end float of idler gear
4 Incorrect preload on differential bearings
5 Worn or damaged bearings
6 Worn bushes on third motion shaft
7 Worn or damaged gear teeth

(c) Difficulty in engaging gear

1 Incorrect clutch pedal adjustment
2 Worn synchromesh cones
3 First and second gear incorrectly assembled on hub

(d) Oil leaks

1 Damaged joint washers
2 Worn or damaged oil seals
3 Faulty joint faces on covers
4 Ineffective oil seal on gearchange operating shaft

64

CHAPTER 6a

AUTOMATIC TRANSMISSION

6a : 1   Description

This transmission system uses a fluid torque converter in place of the normal flywheel and clutch. From the converter, torque is transmitted through an idler gear to an input gear coupled to a bevel gear train which provides four forward gears and reverse. All these parts can be seen diagrammatically in **FIGS 6a : 2** to **6a : 7**, the sequence of operations in each gear being clearly shown. Refer to **FIG 6a : 1** for a perspective view of the gear train and hydraulic control arrangements.

The final drive is from pinion 12 in **FIG 6a : 2** to a conventional differential unit 13 which is connected to the front wheels by the drive shafts. The complete gear assembly in **FIG 6a : 1**, together with the differential unit, is housed below the crankshaft in a casing which also forms the engine sump.

Gear selection is by a lever on the floor of the car. Reverse, neutral and drive positions are for normal automatic driving. First, second, third and fourth positions are for manual operation or override as required. When used as an automatic fourspeed transmission, it is possible to go from rest to maximum speed with the gears changing automatically according to throttle position and load. To select a lower gear for rapid acceleration, the accelerator pedal is 'kicked-down' to full throttle position and this immediately produces the change.

Manual control of the selector lever will provide rapid changes of all four forward gears, but it is important to make downward changes at the correct road speeds or serious damage to the automatic transmission unit may result. There is engine braking in second, third and top gears whether driving automatically or manually. In first gear there is freewheeling during deceleration. Manual selection of third or second gear gives engine braking, and the driver can stay in the lower gear to suit road conditions or to descend steep hills.

The main oil pump 2 in **FIG 6a : 1** provides oil under pressure to the engine and also to the transmission system. Valve block 4 routes the oil to the converter by pipe 6, to the engine by pipe 5 and to the servos 13 which apply brake bands for gear selection. There are two multi-disc clutches 10 and 12 which are operated hydraulically. Clutch 10 is for top and reverse and clutch 12 is engaged for all forward motion. The governor 11 is of the orthodox bob-weight type and it is connected to a valve in block 4 by a linkage. Low pressure valve 8 prevents the converter draining when the engine is stopped. This stops the converter from being noisy and inefficient when restarting. There is an auxiliary pump 15 which is of low capacity. It is responsive to road speed only and operates when tow-starting the engine. As soon as the engine starts the main pump takes over.

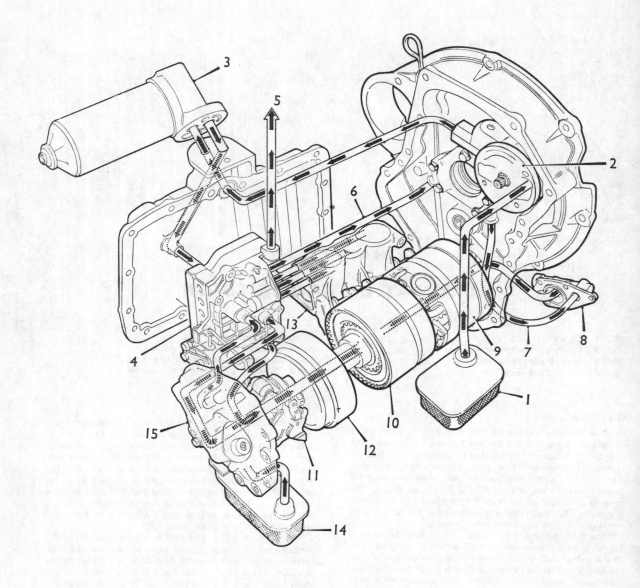

FIG 6a : 1 Layout of automatic transmission system with arrows to indicate 'power flow' of oil to the various components

Key to Fig 6a : 1   1 Main oil strainer   2 Oil pump   3 Oil filter assembly   4 Valve block
5 Engine oil feed   6 Converter feed pipe   7 Converter to low pressure valve feed   8 Low pressure valve
9 Gear train   10 Top and reverse clutch   11 Governor   12 Forward clutch   13 Servo unit
14 Auxiliary pump oil strainer   15 Auxiliary pump

6a : 2 Power flow (mechanical)

Diagrams **6a : 2, 3, 4, 5, 6** and **7** show how the various ratios are obtained. Note that the key to all the diagrams is given once only, below **FIG 6a : 2**. Four speeds and reverse are provided and these are brought into operation by friction bands 7, 8 and 9, and by clutches 10 and 11. Crankshaft 1 drives the outer casing of the converter on the extreme left. This is filled with oil and also contains an inner member which is connected to output gear 2. The inner member can be induced to revolve within the outer casing by the action of vanes on the oil, so that eventually both parts of the converter may turn almost as one unit in the manner of a normal clutch. The drive down to the gear train is by way of idler gear 3 and input gear 4.

6a : 3 Faulty performance

Those tests and adjustments which can be made by a reasonably competent owner are given, always assuming that a tachometer (revolution indicator) and a pressure gauge calibrated up to 280 lb/sq in. are available. **Serious trouble which can only be cured by extensive dismantling must be countered by giving the work to a properly equipped Service Station. Appreciation of the problems involved in servicing the transmission will be realized when it is known that 24 Special Tools are required.**

Road test procedure:

All suspected faults must be checked by road testing. In cases of slip or poor acceleration, carry out a converter stall speed test as in **Section 6a : 4.**

Change speed chart:

Check performance in all seven selector positions as follows. **Note that the first column of speeds is for the early type of automatic transmission with a final drive ratio of 3.48 : 1. Use it for this type only.**

Selector	Throttle	Gear shift	mile/hr (early)	mile/hr (later)
'D'	Light	1 to 2	9 to 13	10 to 14
		2 to 3	14 to 18	15 to 19
		3 to 4	19 to 23	20 to 24
'D'	Kick-down	1 to 2	24 to 32	27 to 34
		2 to 3	38 to 46	41 to 49
		3 to 4	50 to 58	51 to 61
'D'	Kick-down	4 to 3	47 to 39	50 to 42
		3 to 2	39 to 31	41 to 33
		2 to 1	26 to 18	27 to 19
'D'	Nil (roll out)	4 to 3	20 to 16	21 to 17
		3 to 2	14 to 10	15 to 11
		2 to 1	8 to 4	9 to 5

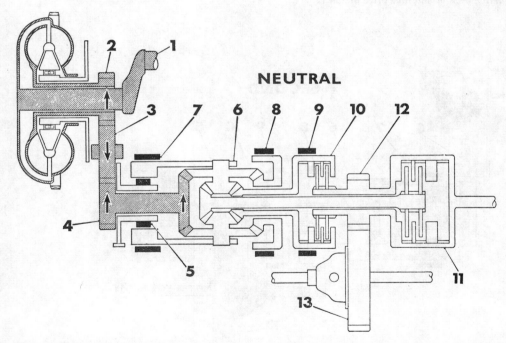

NEUTRAL

FIG 6a : 2 Mechanical power flow in neutral. All gear bands and clutches are disengaged and there is no drive to the final drive pinion. Note that the key is applicable to FIGS 6a : 3, 4, 5, 6 and 7

Key to Fig 6a : 2   1 Crankshaft   2 Converter output gear   3 Idler gear   4 Input gear
5 One-way clutch   6 Gear carrier   7 Reverse band   8 Third gear band   9 Second gear band
10 Top and reverse clutch   11 Forward clutch   12 Final drive pinion   13 Final drive gear

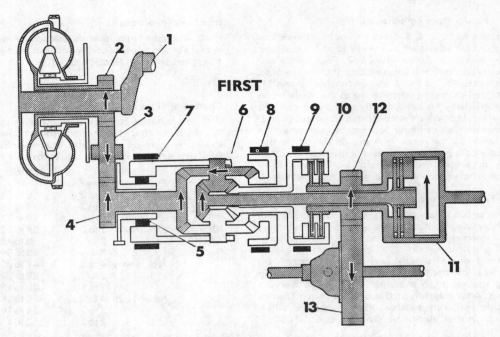

FIG 6a:3 Power flow in first speed. Forward clutch applied, one-way clutch 5 operating and carrier stationary. Input bevel drives planet wheels, planet pinions drive the forward output pinion and shaft. Power thus transferred to mainshaft, forward clutch 11 and final drive pinion 12

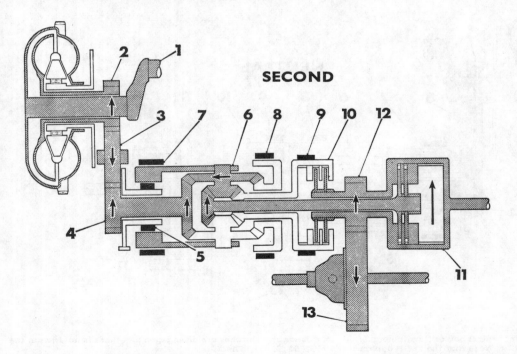

FIG 6a:4 Power flow in second speed. Forward clutch 11 engaged and second gear band 9 applied. Planet cluster orbits round reverse drive bevel pinion so power is transmitted from input bevel through planets to mainshaft, forward clutch and final drive

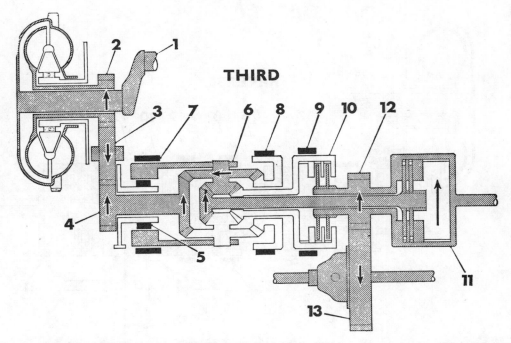

FIG 6a : 5 Power flow in third speed. Third speed bevel gear held by band 8. Planet clusters orbit round this gear and power is transmitted from input bevel through planets to mainshaft, forward clutch and final drive

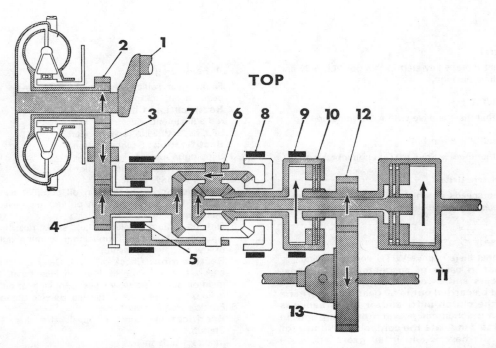

FIG 6a : 6 Power flow in top speed. Clutches 10 and 11 engaged. This locks all bevel gears and the assembly rotates as one unit to give direct drive

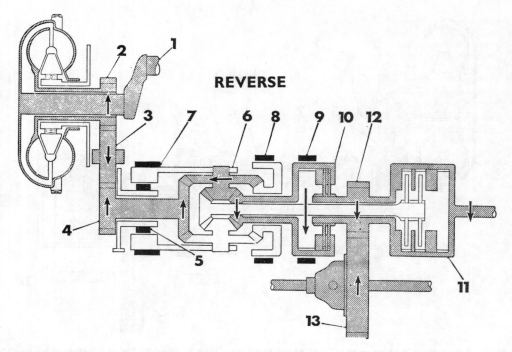

REVERSE

FIG 6a : 7   Power flow in reverse. Reverse band 7 applied and top and reverse clutch 10 engaged. Input bevel drives planet wheel and planet pinion drives reverse gear. Drive is through planet assemblies to top and reverse clutch and so to the final drive

Test 'neutral':

Check that there is key start in this position only and not in the drive position.

Test manual '1':

Confirm that there is drive with **NO** engine braking.

Test manual '2', '3' and '4':

Confirm that there is drive **WITH** engine braking.

Test automatic drive:

Check the speeds at which all up-shifts and down-shifts are changing as detailed in the preceding 'Change-speed chart'.

Test reverse:

Confirm that there is drive **WITH** engine braking.

Note that in cases of suspected faulty transmission gears and/or clutch units, a stall speed test should be carried out in all gears to determine which of the clutch units and/or brake bands is faulty. The mechanical power flow diagrams in FIGS 6a : 2 to 7 indicate the components in use for each gear. If there is slip in all gears a low oil pressure is indicated. Confirm this with a pressure check as in Section 6a : 5.

6a : 4 Fault diagnosis

1 Faulty gear selection, possibly with tie-up in 'D' position on kick-down.
   Rectification: Check gearchange cable and selector rod adjustment.
2 Slip, or no drive in forward gears.
   Rectification: Service Station.
3 Slipping in reverse.
   Rectification: Service Station.
4 Slip or no drive in all gears.
   Rectification: Check main oil pump, flow valve, supply, feed pipe and main oil strainer seals. After this, Service Station.
5 Difficult or bumpy selection and shifts, possibly with squawk on selection, lubricating warning light on, or low oil gauge pressure.
   Rectification: Check oil level. Carry out pressure check. Check O-ring seals in oil filter head. Check main oil pump and flow valve; supply, feed pipe and main oil strainer seals. After this, Service Station.
6 Erratic automatic shifts.
   Rectification: Check oil level. After this, Service Station.
7 Incorrect shift speeds.
   Rectification: Check governor control rod adjustment.

8 Excessive creep or engine stalls when selecting gear.
 Rectification: Check carburetter adjustment for incorrect idling speed.
9 Unable to tow start.
 Rectification: Service Station.
10 Gear whine consistent with road speed but not in top gear.
 Rectification: Service Station.
11 Continual whine consistent with engine speed.
 Rectification: Check converter housing bush, see Engine Chapter.
12 No drive in '1', automatic and manual first gear.
 Rectification: Service Station.
13 Slip or no drive in '2', automatic and manual second gear.
 Rectification: Service Station.
14 No drive in '2', '3' or '4' positions manual, but drives on automatic 'D'.
 Rectification: Service Station.
15 No drives in '2', '3' or '4' in automatic position 'D', but drives on manual selection.
 Rectification: Service Station.
16 Poor acceleration.
 Rectification: Carry out stall speed check.
17 Reduced maximum speed in all gears with severe converter overheating.
 Rectification: Change the torque converter unit.

6a : 5 Adjustments

Inhibitor switch:

This is located on the rear of the gear selector housing as shown in **FIG 6a : 8**. Two of the four terminals are connected through the ignition/starter circuit and are marked 2 and 4. Thus the engine will start only when the gearlever is at 'N'. Terminals 1 and 3 are reversing light connections, if fitted. Before adjusting the switch check the gearchange cable and the selector rod adjustment as detailed later.

To adjust, select 'N'. Disconnect the electrical cables. Slacken the locknut and unscrew the switch as far as possible. Connect a test lamp or meter across terminals 2 and 4. Screw in the switch until the circuit is made and mark the switch body. Continue turning and note the number of turns required to break the circuit. Remove the test equipment and unscrew the switch, half the number of turns counted. Tighten the locknut and refit the cables.

Verify that the starter operates only when the gearlever is at 'N'. Also check that the reversing light, when fitted, operates only when 'R' is selected. **If the switch cannot be adjusted to operate properly it must be renewed.**

Gearchange and selector rod:

Refer to **FIG 6a : 9** and pull back the rubber boots. Disconnect yokes 3 and 4. **Do not start the engine with the selector rod disconnected.**

Check that the selector rod is screwed in tightly and pushed into the transmission casing as far as it will go. Fit the clevis pin into the selector yoke and check dimension 'A', which should be $\frac{25}{32}$ inch. If necessary adjust by slackening the locknut and turning the fork. The top datum is the centre line of the pin. When satisfied, connect up the rod to the bellcrank lever.

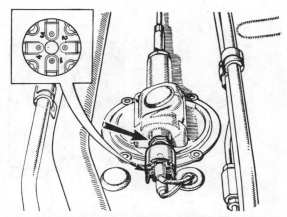

FIG 6a : 8 Inhibitor switch on gearchange lever housing with locknut arrowed. Inset shows connections

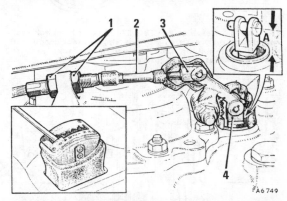

FIG 6a : 9 Gearchange cable and selector rod. Insets show lever at 'D' and dimension 'A' which should be $\frac{25}{32}$ inch
Key to Fig 6a : 9   1 Cable adjusting nuts   2 Cable
3 Cable yoke   4 Selector rod yoke

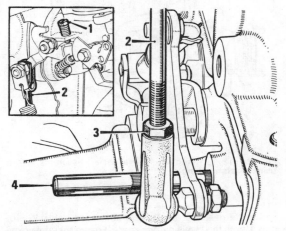

FIG 6a : 10 Governor control rod adjustment
Key to Fig 6a : 10   1 Throttle adjustment screw
2 Governor control rod   3 Locknut   4 $\frac{1}{4}$ inch dia. rod

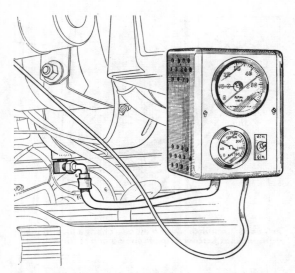

FIG 6a:11 Service Tool 18G.677 is used to check stall speeds and oil pressures. For speeds, connect green lead to 'CB' terminal on coil and red and black leads to battery positive and negative

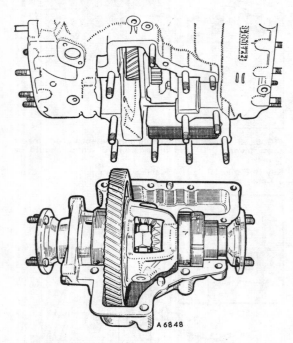

FIG 6a:12 Removing differential assembly from transmission casing

Set the gearlever at 'D' and adjust the cable 2 with nuts 1 until the clevis pin fits easily. Ensure that the yokes are square with the bellcrank before finally fitting the clevis pins.

Check the adjustment with the gearlever in 'R' and the selector rod pulled out to its fullest extent. The check will also verify the condition of the cable, the clevis pins and the yokes.

Governor control rod adjustment:

Run the engine up to normal working temperature. Disconnect the governor control rod at the carburetter (see FIG 6a:10). With the carburetter correctly tuned, adjust the throttle screw 1 to give a tickover of 650 rev/min on a tachometer. Insert a $\frac{1}{4}$ inch dia. rod 4 through the hole in the control rod bellcrank lever and into the hole in the transmission casing as shown. Slacken locknut 3 and adjust the rod to suit the carburetter linkage in the tickover position. Connect the rod, tighten the locknut and remove the checking rod.

Stall speed check:

For this test it is necessary to provide a tachometer to register engine rev/min. Run the engine up to working temperature and check the oil level. Apply the foot and handbrakes, select any gear except 'N' or '1' and give maximum throttle opening for not more than ten seconds. Compare the tachometer reading with the following chart:

Rev/min	Condition	Rectification
1700–1800	Satisfactory	Nil
Under 1000	Stator freewheel slip	Change torque converter
Over 1900	Transmission slip	Check transmission unit (see Road Test note at end of Section 6a:3)
1100–1600	Engine down for power	Check engine

Pressure check:

For this test a pressure gauge reading to 280 lb/sq in. will be needed. Remove the pressure point plug from the head of the engine oil filter and connect the gauge. FIG 6a:11 shows the BMC Service Tool 18G.677 in use.

Run the engine up to normal working temperature and check the oil level. Start up and check for the following approximate pressures:

1 In all gear positions except 'R' a pressure of 100 lb/sq in.
2 In 'R' a pressure of 150 lb/sq in.

If these approximate pressures are not obtainable see Section 6a:3.

6a:6 Removing transmission unit

Remove the engine and transmission from the car as instructed in Chapter 1. Remove the transmission from the engine as detailed but only if it is necessary to fit a replacement engine, transmission casing, or to remove the main oil strainer pickup pipe and seals.

6a:7 Servicing the differential assembly

Removal:

1 Remove the engine and transmission from the car as instructed in Chapter 1. Drain the oil from the unit. Hold the driving flanges with Service Tool 18G.1100, remove the centre securing bolts and pull the flanges off the splined shafts.

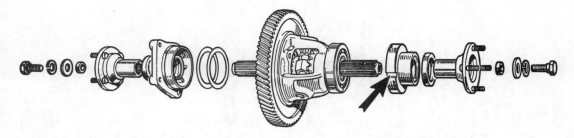

FIG 6a : 13   Differential components. Arrow indicates alignment slot in spacer

2 Knock back the lockwashers and remove the nuts from
the final drive housing. Remove the securing screws
and pull the kick-down linkage assembly clear of the
transmission casing.

3 Remove the two setscrews securing the end cover to
the transmission and remove the final drive assembly
as in **FIG 6a : 12.** Remove the remaining bolts from
the end cover and remove both cover and adjustment
shims.   These parts can be seen to the left of the
driving gear.

Dismantling :

1 Remove the differential assembly from the housing.
Withdraw the oil seal housing and pull off the bearings
with Service Tool 18G.2.

2 Unlock and remove the bolts securing the drive gear to
the differential case after marking both parts for correct
reassembly. Remove the differential gear and thrust
washer from the drive gear.

3 Tap out the roll pin, drive out the centre pin and remove
the pinions, thrust washers, pinion spacer and the other
differential gear with its thrust washer.

Inspection :

Clean the parts and renew any which are worn. If any
component has been so worn that swarf has entered the
lubricating system, the automatic transmission must be
removed and dismantled by a Service Station. This also
applies when fitting a replacement drive gear pinion into
the transmission unit. **At all times, absolute cleanliness is essential.**

Reassembling :

This is a reversal of the dismantling procedure. Make
sure that the differential gear thrust washers are fitted with
their chamfered bores against the machined faces of the
differential gears. Refit all components in their original
positions. Use a torque of 55 to 60 lb ft when tightening
the drive gear bolts.

Refitting :

1 Fit the assembly to the transmission casing and push it
in the direction of the converter. Align the slot arrowed
in **FIG 6a : 13** with the dowel in the casing.

2 Fit a new joint washer coated with Hylomar compound.
Make sure the oil seal is pressed squarely against the
face of the spacer and refit the differential housing,
fit new locking plates and lightly tighten the securing
nuts.

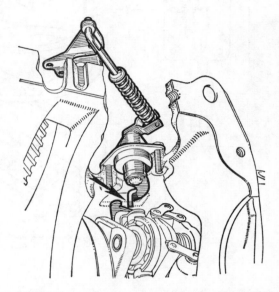

FIG 6a : 14   Correct position for kick-down rod assembly

3 To adjust the assembly, refit the end cover without a
joint washer but with the original shims. Tighten the
cover bolts evenly and just enough for the cover
register to nip the outer race of the bearing. **Overtightening will distort the flange.**

4 Take feeler gauge measurements at various points
between the cover flange and the housing. Variations
in the measurement will indicate that the bolts are
unevenly tightened. Adjust the tension on the bolts
until the same measurements are obtained at every
point but beware of overtightening the bolts.

5 The compressed thickness of a new joint washer is
.007 inch. The required preload on the bearings is
.002 inch. Therefore the correct gap under the cover
flange must be .009 inch, and any deviation from this
figure must be adjusted by adding or subtracting
shims. For example, if the feeler gauge measurement
is .005 inch add a shim .004 inch thick between the
bearing and the end cover.

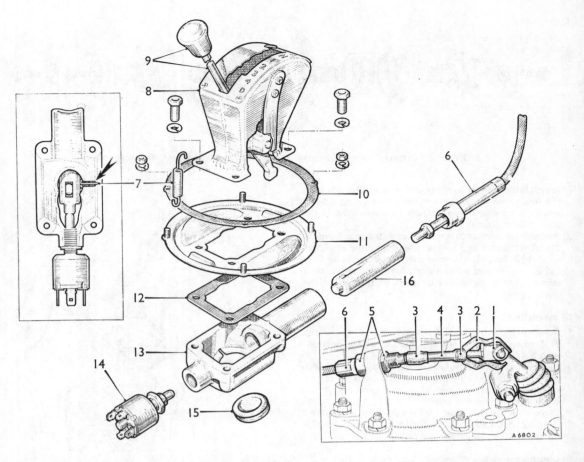

FIG 6a : 15 Gearchange housing and cable components. Left inset shows reverse return spring location. Right inset shows cable connections

Key to Fig 6a : 15

1 Yoke	2 Rubber sleeve	3 Rubber ferrules	4 Cable sleeve
5 Cable adjusting nuts	6 Cable	7 Reverse return spring	8 Quadrant	9 Gear selector lever
10 Joint washer—base plate	11 Base plate	12 Joint washer—housing	13 Gearchange housing
14 Inhibitor switch	15 Rubber grommet—housing	16 Lever plunger	

6 Remove the cover, fit the shims and refit the cover with a new joint washer coated in Hylomar compound. Tighten the housing nuts and end cover bolts to a torque of 18 lb ft. Tap up all locking plate tabs except the one under the nut which takes the exhaust pipe bracket, as this will need fixing when the unit is back in the car.

7 Lubricate the driving flange oil seals. Fit the flanges, making sure that the split collets are correctly located inside them. Fit new rubber seals to the central securing bolts, hold the flanges with Tool 18G.1100 and tighten the bolts to a torque of 40 to 45 lb ft.

8 Using a new washer, refit the governor control linkage to the transmission casing. See that the lever is correctly positioned relative to the governor as shown in **FIG 6a : 14.** Refit the engine and transmission unit as detailed in **Chapter 1.**

6a : 8 Servicing gearchange cable

Removal :

1 Refer to **FIG 6a : 15** and pull back sleeve 2. Remove the clevis pin from yoke 1, slacken the locknut and unscrew the yoke. Remove the nut, sleeve 2, rubber ferrules 3 and sleeve 4. Remove the front adjusting nut of pair 5 and pull the cable clear of the housing lug.

2 Release the cable clip from the floor panel and remove the front floor covering.

3 Disconnect the electrical cables from the inhibitor switch (see **FIG 6a : 8).** Remove the gearchange housing plate from the floor panel (four nuts) and remove the housing and cable assembly.

Dismantling:

Hold the assembly in a vice and remove the setscrews securing the quadrant to the housing. Release the reverse return spring from the base of the housing and remove the quadrant and lever assembly. Unscrew the cable securing nut from the front of the housing and release it from the gearchange lever plunger. Clean all parts and renew any which are worn.

Reassembly:

Lubricate all moving parts with grease and then reassemble in the reverse order of dismantling.

Refitting:

This is also a reverse process. Fit a new joint washer to the housing plate if necessary. Adjust the inhibitor switch and the gearchange cable and selector rod as in **Section 6a : 5.**

CHAPTER 7

DRIVE SHAFTS AND SUSPENSION

7 : 1 Drive shaft description

The assembly of the shaft can be seen in **FIG 7 : 5** as item 74. At the outer end the constant-velocity bell joint is protected by rubber boot 75. The inner end, which is splined to flange 76 is protected by seal 77.

The components of the constant-velocity joint can be seen in **FIGS 7 : 1** and **7 : 2**. The inner and outer members of the joint have partly-spherical surfaces, each provided with six grooves machined in line with the shaft axis. A cage carrying six balls is interposed. The balls engage the grooves in both members to key them together and yet allow them to hinge freely upon each other.

7 : 2 Maintenance of drive shafts

Periodically examine the rubber boots and replace them if there is any sign of damage or deterioration. If a boot is faulty, lubricant will be lost and road grit will enter the joint. It will then be necessary to dismantle and inspect the components of the joint.

If a rubber boot has been damaged in the workshop and no dirt has entered the joint, a new boot may be fitted as described in **Section 7 : 3.** This is done without dismantling the joint but the drive shaft must be removed from the car.

The joint must be packed with Duckham's MB grease (BMC pack AKF.1457).

7 : 3 Servicing bell joints

Each joint may be removed for replacement as a unit or to have a Service kit fitted. **Never replace individual components in a bell joint assembly.** Remove the drive shaft as described in **Section 7 : 14,** then clean the shaft of road dirt and grease and mount it centrally in a vice equipped with soft jaws. To pull back the boots, cut the iron binding wire or on later models prise off the clips shown in **FIG 7 : 4.** Hold the shaft as in **FIG 7 : 1** and give the edge of the outer race a sharp tap with a soft-faced hammer. This should contract the round-section spring ring located in a deep groove in the extreme end of the shaft and enable the joint to be drawn off. It should not be necessary to use heavy blows for this operation.

Dismantling:

The joint should be dismantled only if it is believed to be still serviceable.

1 The components were originally mated and have been working together, so that they must be reassembled in the same relationship. Before dismantling therefore, mark the relative positions with something like paint which will not wash off during cleaning.

2 With the shaft withdrawn the inner race can swivel freely. Refer to the first illustration in **FIG 7 : 2** and tilt the inner race to remove one ball. Continue to ease out each ball in turn, using a pointed tool if the parts are sticky with grease.

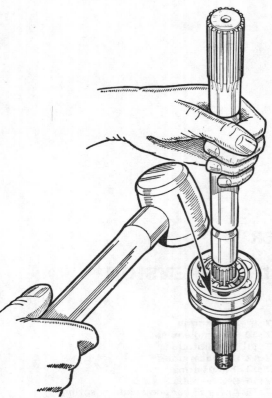

FIG 7:1 Drive the bell joint from the shaft at the point indicated

3 Turn the cage as in the second illustration in **FIG 7:2** so that two opposite elongated windows coincide with two lands of the outer member. One land will drop into a window and allow the cage and inner race to be lifted out.

4 Swivel the inner race at right angles to the cage as in the third view in **FIG 7:2**. Turn it until two of the lands between the inner race tracks are opposite elongated windows in the cage. One land will drop into a window to allow the inner race to be extracted.

5 Clean all parts and dry off. Normal wear will be distributed evenly over the components and the joint will be serviceable until end float exceeds a maximum of .025 inch. If the six balls are worn, rust-pitted or have flats on them, the joint must be renewed. The inner and outer races will be marked where the balls roll, but the marking should be consistent and free from indentations. The contact surfaces of the cage and the inner and outer races must be polished but free from signs of 'picking up'. If the edges of the cage windows show wear towards the outer side this may cause knocking when the joint is operated at high angles of deflection.

6 Examine the shaft for cracks and ensure that the square-section circlip shown in **FIG 7:3** is firmly in its groove.

Renewing the ball cage:

Use a Service kit to renew a ball cage which is worn. The majority of cages are of a standard size, but there are also three non-standard sizes. A joint will only accept a new cage of the same size as the original. The size of the original cage is checked with Service Ring Gauge 18G.1012. As it is difficult to measure the inside of the cage, the outside of the race which fits inside it is measured instead.

The larger bore of the gauge will accept a standard-sized cage, but will reject an oversize one. Similarly, the smaller bore will accept only a standard-sized race.

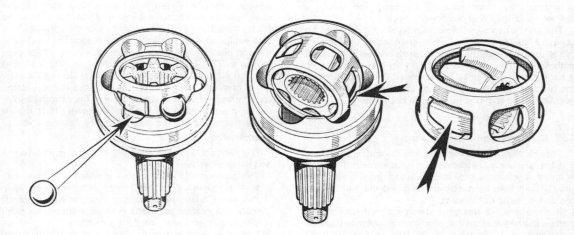

FIG 7:2 Dismantling the bell joint. Left, tilting the inner race to remove or replace balls. Centre, removing cage and inner race. Right, removing the inner race from the cage

1 If both cage and inner race pass through their respective bores, then the cage is of standard size.
2 If the cage passes through the larger bore but the race will not pass through the smaller, then the cage is .004 inch oversize on the inside.
3 If the cage will not pass through the larger bore but the race passes through the smaller bore, then the cage is .010 inch oversize on the outside.
4 If neither the cage nor the race will pass through the gauge then the joint is of a very early type for which no kit is available. Renew the joints as units. Kits are available as follows:

Early models	Colour code	Part No.
Standard	Green	18G.8075
.004 inch oversize on inside	Yellow	18G.8077
.010 inch oversize on outside	Black	18G.8076
Later models		
Standard	Green	18G.8175
.010 inch oversize	Black	18G.8176

Reassembling:

This is an exact reversal of the dismantling procedure. Lubricate all parts lightly with Duckham's MB grease (BMC pack AKF.1457). The parts should assemble easily and without force.
1 Insert the inner race into the cage and these two into the outer member of the joint by following the sequence in **FIG 7 : 2** from right to left. The three parts can then be turned freely in relation to each other.
2 Line up the marks on the cage and inner race which were made before dismantling. Tilt the cage until one ball can be inserted in a window, and repeat for the remaining five. Check that the inner race and cage articulate freely in the outer race, but take care not to release the balls.
3 Fill the joint with the remainder of the grease in the pack before inserting the shaft.

Refitting:

1 Fit a new rubber boot if necessary, smearing the inside with Duckham's MB grease. Be careful when easing the boot over the shaft circlip. Renew the round-section spring ring whether a new or an original shaft is being fitted.
2 Hold the shaft in a vice and locate the inner race on it. Press the joint assembly against the spring ring, locating the ring centrally and compressing it so that it enters the chamfer in the inner race. A sharp tap on the stub axle shaft with a soft-faced hammer will close the ring and allow the assembly to be tapped home. Make sure that the inner race is hard up against the square-section circlip and that the spring ring has expanded inside the joint.
3 Slide the rubber boot over the bell joint until the radiused rib registers in the locating groove. Use Service Tool 18G.1099 to clinch the large clip as shown in **FIG 7 : 4**. The clip must be fitted with the tab pulled through away from the direction of forward rotation. Locate the other end of the boot in the groove in the drive shaft and secure it with the small clip.

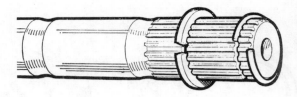

FIG 7 : 3   Bell joint end of drive shaft showing circlip and round-section spring ring

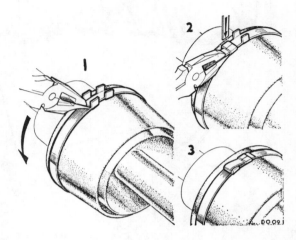

FIG 7 : 4   Fitting the clinching clips with Service Tool 18G.1099

Key to Fig 7 : 4   1 Pull free end tightly between tabs   2 Hold and secure with front tabs   3 Fold clip back over front tabs and secure with rear tabs

7 : 4 The sliding joint

Refer to **FIG 7 : 5** and remove the wire or clips from seal 77. Slide off the seal and remove flange 76. Reassemble by lubricating the two sets of splines and sliding the seal into place on the shaft. Fill the cavity in the flange with $\frac{3}{4}$ oz. of Duckham's MB grease and fit the flange to the shaft. Locate the seal and push the shaft to the bottom of the flange so that the grease is driven back into the seal. Hold the outer lip of the seal open so that air and surplus grease can escape. The outside diameter of the bellows must not exceed 1.75 inch. Secure the seal with clips clinched with Tool 18G.1099.

7 : 5 The 'Hydrolastic' suspension

Components of the suspension units are shown in **FIGS 7 : 5, 7 : 6** and **7 : 7**. The fluid coupling of the displacer units is shown in **FIG 7 : 8**.

The system is designed to give less pitching and rolling, with a smooth flat ride which also gives the best handling characteristics. It consists of two front and two rear displacers as shown in section in **FIG 7 : 7**. These are

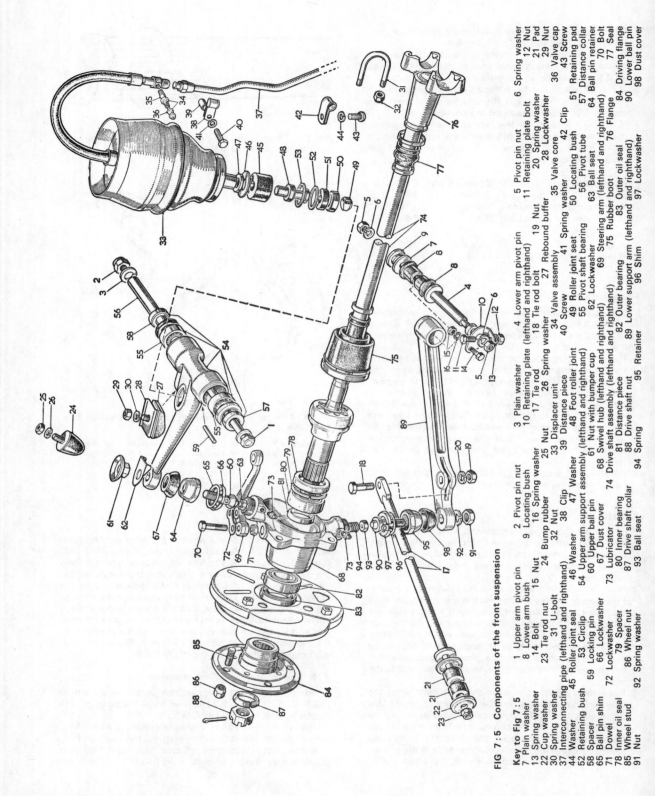

FIG 7:5 Components of the front suspension

Key to Fig 7:5

1 Upper arm pivot pin	2 Pivot pin nut	3 Plain washer	4 Lower arm pivot pin	5 Pivot pin nut	6 Spring washer
7 Plain washer	8 Lower arm bush	9 Locating bush	10 Retaining plate (lefthand and righthand)	11 Retaining plate bolt	12 Nut
13 Spring washer	14 Bolt	15 Nut	16 Spring washer	17 Tie rod	18 Tie rod bolt	19 Nut	20 Spring washer	21 Pad
22 Cup washer	23 Tie rod nut	24 Bump rubber	25 Nut	26 Spring washer	27 Rebound buffer	28 Lockwasher	29 Nut
30 Spring washer	31 U-bolt	32 Nut	33 Displacer unit	34 Valve assembly	35 Valve core	36 Valve cap
37 Interconnecting pipe (lefthand and righthand)	38 Clip	39 Distance piece	40 Screw	41 Spring washer	42 Clip	43 Screw
44 Washer	45 Roller joint seal	46 Washer	47 Washer	48 Foot roller joint	49 Roller joint seat	50 Locating bush	51 Retaining pad
52 Retaining bush	53 Circlip	54 Upper arm support assembly (lefthand and righthand)	55 Pivot tube	56 Pivot shaft bearing	57 Distance collar
58 Spacer	59 Locking pin	60 Upper ball pin	61 Nut with bumper cup	62 Lockwasher	63 Ball seat	64 Ball pin retainer
65 Ball pin shim	66 Lockwasher	67 Dust cover	68 Drive shaft assembly (lefthand and righthand)	69 Steering arm (lefthand and righthand)	70 Bolt
71 Dowel	72 Lubricator	73 Lubricator	74 Drive shaft assembly	75 Rubber boot	76 Flange	77 Seal
78 Inner oil seal	79 Spacer	80 Inner bearing	81 Distance piece	82 Outer bearing	83 Outer oil seal	84 Driving flange
85 Wheel stud	86 Wheel nut	87 Drive shaft collar	88 Drive shaft nut	89 Lower support arm (lefthand and righthand)	90 Lower ball pin
91 Nut	92 Ball seat	93 Ball seat	94 Spring	95 Retainer	96 Shim	98 Dust cover

80

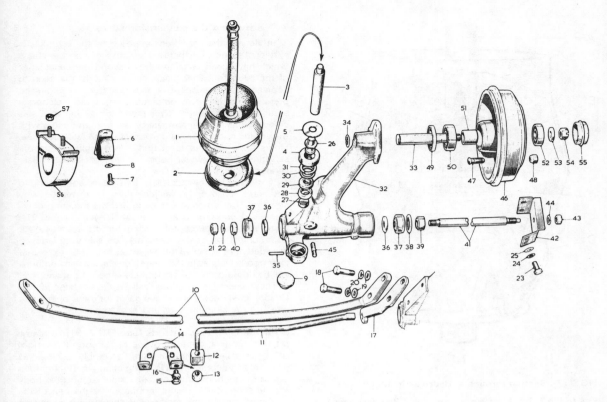

FIG 7:6 Components of rear suspension

Key to Fig 7:6
1 Displacer unit 2 Piston sleeve 3 Displacer strut 4 Seal 5 Washer
6 Bump rubber 7 Screw 8 Spring washer 9 Rebound buffer 10 Anti-roll bar (earlier models)
11 Auxiliary spring (lefthand and righthand), (earlier models) 12 Bearing 13 Nut 14 Bracket 15 Screw
16 Nut 17 Bracket (lefthand and righthand) 18 Bolt 19 Plain washer 20 Spring washer 21 Nut
22 Spring washer 23 Screw 24 Shakeproof washer 25 Plain washer 26 Roller joint foot
27 Roller joint seat 28 Locating bush 29 Retaining pad 30 Retainer 31 Circlip
32 Radius arm (lefthand and righthand) 33 Stub shaft (lefthand and righthand) 34 Circlip 35 Locking pin
36 Oil seal 37 Pivot shaft bearing 38 Dust seal 39 Outer spacer 40 Inner spacer 41 Pivot shaft
42 Retaining plate (lefthand and righthand) 43 Nut 44 Spring washer 45 Stud 46 Brake drum hub assembly
47 Wheel stud 48 Wheel nut 49 Oil seal 50 Inner bearing 51 Spacer 52 Outer bearing
53 Washer 54 Nut (lefthand and righthand) 55 Grease-retaining cap 56 Arch spring (later models)

coupled by pipes **A.** Each unit contains a piston **E** pressing on a diaphragm **H.** Upper and lower fluid chambers are separated by member **G.** The spring is a cone of compressed rubber **B.**

An upward movement of a front wheel deflects the diaphragm, and increasing pressure forces fluid up into the top chamber. The increased pressure and fluid displacement deflects the rubber spring and the resultant pressure increase forces fluid along the interconnecting pipe and into the rear displacer unit where the diaphragm is pressed down against the piston and the car body position at the rear is raised. These events are virtually simultaneous and the car rides obstructions without pitching. The action is the same in reverse when the rear wheels negotiate bumps, as shown in **FIG 7:8.**

The fluid is a mixture of water and alcohol with an anti-corrosive additive.

The front suspension uses arms of unequal length as seen by parts 54 and 89 in **FIG 7:5.** These pivot on bearings located in the sidemembers of the front subframe and the outer ends are ball jointed to the swivel hubs 68. The rear suspension shown in **FIG 7:6** consists of the two Hydrolastic units, independent trailing radius arms 32, auxiliary springs 11 and an anti-roll bar 10. Rubber arch springs 56 replace parts 10 and 11 on later models.

7:6 Suspension lubrication

Jack up the front of the car to take the load off the swivel joints. Clean all round the nipples 73 in **FIG 7:5** and make sure they are not blocked with dirt. If the joints are already full of grease it will be found that very little can be forced in.

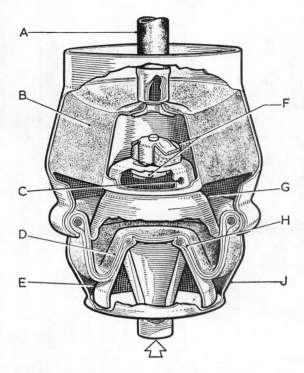

FIG 7:7 Section through a 'Hydrolastic' unit

Key to Fig 7:7   **A** Interconnecting pipe   **B** Rubber spring
C Damper bleed   **D** Butyl liner   **E** Tapered piston
F Damper valves   **G** Fluid-separating member   **H** Rubber
diaphragm (nylon reinforced)   **J** Tapered cylinder

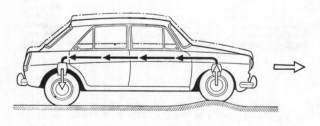

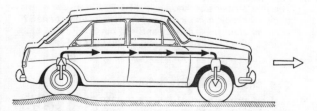

FIG 7:8   Action of 'Hydrolastic' system. Top, tail rises
in response to upward movement of front wheels.
Bottom, nose rises in response to upward movement of
rear wheels

7:7 Servicing the suspension system

In view of the conditions imposed by the Hydrolastic
system of suspension there are several servicing operations
which have been considered as beyond the capabilities
of the average owner/mechanic in view of the need to
depressurize the suspension before starting work and to
pressurize again on completion, for which elaborate
equipment is required. Operations which fall into this
category include the removal of the front subframe with
the engine and transmission assembly, the rear subframe,
radius arms and displacer units. Also included are the
servicing of the swivel hubs, anti-roll bar and auxiliary
springs.

If the home operator feels that he is competent to
undertake these or similar jobs there is no reason why
he should not do so after having had the system profes-
sionally depressurized at his local Service Station. The
journey home after depressurizing, and the journey back
after completion of the work, may be safely undertaken
provided that a speed of 30 miles/hr is not exceeded
over good roads as in this condition the suspension arms
will be riding on the bump rubbers at both front and rear.

The relevant instructions will be found later in this
Chapter after details have been given for those operations
which do not require qualified assistance.

Subframes and mountings (see FIG 7:9): To renew
the mountings at the front of the car, support the weight
of the engine and transmission assembly as near as
possible to the one which is being changed. If more than
one is to be changed at the same time, support the body
on the sling. Either of the mountings at the rear of the
rear subframe can be renewed in the same way as that
used for the front mountings. To remove and fit mountings
at the front of the rear subframe it is necessary to remove
the subframe assembly, which entails depressurizing the
system.

7:8 Servicing hubs

Removing, front:

Place a piece of wood between the jack head and the
transmission casing and lift the front of the car. Remove
the road wheel and disconnect the brake caliper assembly
as detailed in **Chapter 9**. Do not let the weight of the
caliper hang on the hydraulic hose but tie it out of the way.
Remove nut 88 in **FIG 7:5** and pull off the hub flange
and disc assembly using Service Tool 18G.304 with
adaptor 18G.304B.

Refitting, front:

Pack the bearings with grease and refit in the reverse
order of dismantling. Make sure that the bearings, when
inserted into the swivel hub are fitted with the sides
marked 'THRUST' adjacent to the bearing spacer or
distance piece 81. Tighten the nut to a torque of 150 lb ft
and align to the next splitpin hole.

Removing, rear:

Raise the car with a jack placed under the rear frame
crossmember. Remove the road wheel and grease-
retaining cap 55 in **FIG 7:6**. Remove nut 54 and washer
53. Pull off the hub and drum assembly 46 using Service
Tool 18G.304 with adaptor 18G.304B.

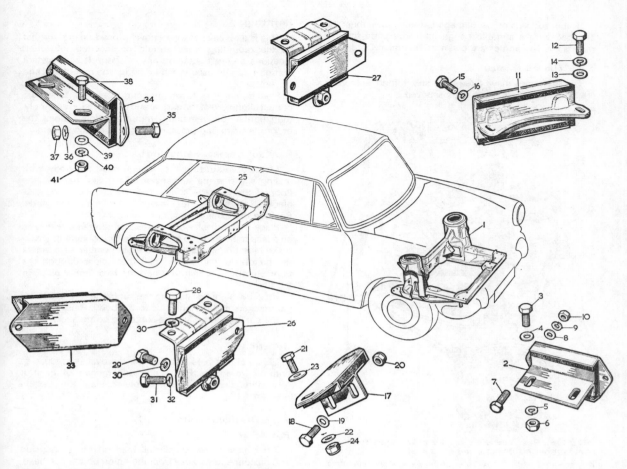

FIG 7 : 9 Front and rear subframes and mountings

Key to Fig 7 : 9   1 Front subframe assembly   2 Front subframe front mounting   3 Screw   4 Plain washer
5 Spring washer   6 Nut   7 Screw   8 Plain washer   9 Spring washer   10 Nut
11 Rear upper subframe mounting   12 Screw   13 Plain washer   14 Spring washer   15 Screw
16 Spring washer   17 Rear lower front subframe mounting   18 Screw   19 Plain washer   20 Nut
21 Screw   22 Plain washer   23 Washer   24 Nut   25 Rear subframe assembly
26 Front righthand rear subframe mounting   27 Front lefthand rear subframe mounting   28 Screw (long)
29 Screw (short)   30 Spring washer   31 Screw   32 Spring washer   33 Rear righthand rear subframe mounting
34 Rear lefthand rear subframe mounting   35 Screw   36 Spring washer   37 Nut   38 Screw   39 Plain washer
40 Spring washer   41 Nut

Refitting, rear:

Pack both bearings with grease until there is a slight
protrusion of grease on either side of each one. Pack the
cavity between the inner bearing and the oil seal 49 with
grease too. Do not fill the cavity between the bearings
with grease nor put any in the grease retaining cap, but
lightly smear the spacer 51. When refitting in the reverse
order to dismantling, ensure that the bearings are fitted
with the sides marked 'THRUST' adjacent to the spacer.
Fit washer 53 with its inner chamfered edge towards the
bearing. Tighten the nut to a torque of 60 lb ft. Do not
slacken to align a splitpin hole but tighten further to the
next slot.

7 : 9 Arch spring

This part, which is item 56 in **FIG 7 : 6** is in permanent

contact with the rear radius arm on each side and replaces
the original anti-roll bar and auxiliary springs. To remove
one raise the rear of the car and take off the road wheel.
Remove the luggage floor and release the two nuts
securing the arch spring from inside the boot. When
refitting an arch spring note that it is marked 'FRONT'.

7 : 10 Steering angles

The castor and camber angles, the swivel hub
inclination and wheel alignment of the front suspension,
together with the camber and wheel alignment of the
rear suspension are design settings that have a very
important effect on the handling of the car. With the
exception of the front wheel tracking, all the settings are
determined during manufacture and no adjustment is
provided.

If the suspension is damaged, the angles must be checked with a suitable gauge and new parts fitted if necessary. The angles are given in Technical Data.

7:11 The subframes

The subframes may be removed and refitted as follows after the system has been depressurized.

Front (see FIG 7:10):

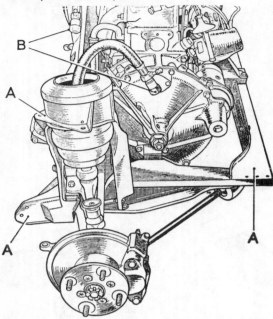

FIG 7:10 Rear end view of the power unit removed complete with subframe and drive shaft

Key to Fig 7:10   A Three of the six subframe mounting points   B Displacer hose ends sealed against dirt

Place a block of wood under the transmission casing and raise the car sufficiently to take all the load off the suspension. Remove the road wheels. Disconnect the battery. Remove the bonnet. Disconnect all electrical connections to the engine. Remove the horn. Remove the carburetters. Release the exhaust pipe from the manifold, from the transmission casing and from the two mountings on the rear subframe.

Release the speedometer cable. Drain the cooling system. Disconnect the heater hoses and release the cables from the water control valve.

Release the clutch slave cylinder and wire it out of the way. Remove the gearbox extension. Disconnect the displacer hoses at the bulkhead and plug them to prevent the entry of any dirt. Disconnect brake hoses and steering tie rods.

Take the weight of the body on slings under the front wings. Remove the two bolts at each front and each rear corner of the subframe which secure it to the body brackets. Remove the two nuts securing each tower holding the displacer units. Remove the bolts securing the mounting brackets to the body and lift out the brackets.

Lower the jack, lift the body with a sling and wheel the engine and transmission assembly clear.

Refitting:

This is a reversal of the removal procedure, noting that all the mounting bolts should be inserted into their locations before tightening any of them. It is important that no force be used when lining up the mountings and the bolts.

First tighten the tower mounting brackets to ensure correct alignment of the engine and transmission assembly, then tighten the remaining mounting bolts. Bleed the braking system and pressurize the suspension system.

Rear subframes. Removing:

After depressurizing the system, raise the body with a sling and free the suspension of all load. Remove the floor of the luggage compartment and release the displacer unit hoses, not forgetting to plug the ends. Remove the exhaust pipe and silencer.

Place a length of wood under the subframe and raise on a jack to remove the road wheels. Disconnect the main brake pressure pipe at the front crossmember, disconnect the handbrake cables and pull them clear through the floor. Remove the rear seat and the two rubber plugs in the floor.

Unscrew all bolts securing the subframe to the mounting brackets and the brackets to the body. Raise the rear of the car and withdraw the subframe on the jack.

Refitting:

This again is a reversal of the removal procedure as with the front units. Ensure correct alignment of the strut foot and displacer units before having the system pressurized.

7:12 Displacer units

Front:

After depressurizing take all load off the suspension and disconnect the hose from the union on the bulkhead. Unscrew the nut and remove the outer end of the upper suspension arm from the knuckle. Remove the upper arm pivot bolt and remove the upper arm complete with the displacer strut foot. Withdraw the displacer.

Reverse the above procedure when refitting.

Rear:

Raise the rear of the car and remove the appropriate road wheel, disconnect the displacer unit hose at the union inside the boot. Remove the displacer strut and the displacer unit.

Reverse the above to refit.

7:13 Radius arms

Early models. It is first necessary to remove the subframe assembly as described in **Section 7:11**, then to disconnect the hydraulic brake hose not forgetting to plug the ends.

Withdraw the splitpin and clevis pin and disconnect the handbrake cable from the lever on the backplate.

Unscrew the nut and washer from the handbrake cable sector pivot and lift off the sector. The handbrake cable may now be released from its bracket by unscrewing the ferrule and sliding the cable through the slot in the bracket.

Remove the anti-roll bar and auxiliary springs, then remove the nut from each end of the radius arm pivot and the four setscrews from the outer support bracket. The radius arm may now be lifted out with the displacer unit.

Dismantling is quite straightforward, but it will be necessary to use the Service Tool to remove the bearing cups.

Reassembly:

First press the fixed length collar on the outer end of the pivot shaft so that the flat face of the collar is flush with the stepped face of the shaft, then fit the mounting bracket taking care that it does not interfere with the collar on the shaft.

Using a suitable mandrel, press the bearing cups into the radius arm, pack with molybdenized grease and fit the bearings into the radius arm. Note that the dust shield fits flush with the outer end face.

The pivot shaft is then slid through the bearings from the outer end and a .301 inch spacer fitted. Then fit a suitable distance piece on the inner end of the shaft to butt against the stepped face of the pivot shaft. Fit and lightly tighten the nuts and spring washers and check that the spacer is not too thick and so subject the bearings to excessive strain when fully tightened, If in order, tighten the nuts.

Now check the torque required to rotate the shaft. This should be between 5 and 10 lb inch and a suitable spacer from the range of nine available should be chosen to obtain this condition.

It is important to rotate the bearings while the variable width spacer is being fitted and to ensure that the inner race assembly rotates with the shaft (not on it) when the preload is measured.

When replacing the displacer unit strut ensure that the foot is correctly located in the radius arm and that the thrust washer has its relieved face towards the bearing.

Later models:

It is not necessary on later models to remove the complete rear subframe to replace a radius arm, but depressurizing on the appropriate side is required.

Raise the rear of the vehicle and remove the road wheel. Release the handbrake, slacken the adjuster and remove the clevis pin from the lever on the brake backplate. Remove the handbrake cable swivel sector from its pivot under the radius arm. Disconnect the brake hose from the union on the subframe.

Undo the radius arm shaft inner pivot nut, remove the outer support bracket and the displacer strut and ease the radius arm assembly from the car.

Refitting is the reverse of the above ensuring that the displacer unit and strut are correctly seated before re-pressurizing. Readjust the handbrake.

7:14 Swivel hubs

After depressurizing, jack up the car and remove the road wheel. Remove the brake caliper and support it carefully. Remove the stub shaft nut and withdraw the wheel hub. Disconnect the tie rod ball end from the steering lever and the drive shaft at the flexible coupling marking the driving flange and the flexible joint for later refitting.

Disconnect the upper and lower suspension arms from the swivel hub ballpins and withdraw the hub assembly and drive shaft.

Before refitting, thoroughly clean all parts and replace the ball seat, pin and ball housing without the packing shims, locking washer or lower ball joint seat spring. Screw down the ball housing until there is no free movement between the ball and its seating, then measure with a feeler gauge the gap between the housing and the swivel hub (see **FIG 7:11**).

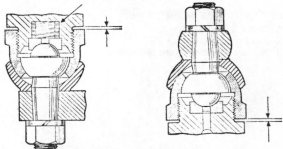

FIG 7:11 Section through swivel hub ball joint. Feeler gauge measurements to be taken where indicated

Remove the housing and ballpin, refit the spring under the lower joint ball seat, repack the assembly with grease, adding shims to the value of the measurement just taken minus the thickness of the locking washer .036 inch. When finally assembled there must be an end float of zero to .003 inch and a further shim must be added to produce this condition.

Replace the locking washer and refit the assembly to the swivel hub. Any excessive end float or tightness must be rectified by adjusting the thickness of the housing shims as necessary.

Tighten the ballpin retainer with Service Tools 18G.372 and 587 to a torque of 70 lb ft. Tap up the locking washer. Replace the dust seal and the suspension arm and tighten the ballpin nut to a torque of 25 lb ft. Reconnect the tie rod yoke to the lower arm. Refit the road wheel and lower the car. Pressurize the system.

7:15 Anti-roll bar and auxiliary springs

First remove the subframe assembly as described in **Section 7:11** and then move the radius arm to full bump and take out the special setscrews securing the anti-roll bar and auxiliary springs to the inside face of the radius arm. Remove the nuts holding the auxiliary spring and lift off the two assemblies.

Refitting:

The clearance between the inside face of the auxiliary spring bracket and the underside of the rear subframe should be .125 inch, but small trimming adjustments may be made if required. The maximum gap permissible is .25 inch.

To increase the height of the rear end, slacken off the two auxiliary spring bar-nuts. Release the locknuts on the two adjuster screws and turn the screws as required.

To decrease the height of the rear end, apply a load to the rear end so as to produce a 'full bump' effect. This will reduce the load on the spring bars. Then turn the screws as necessary to increase the gap.

7:16 Fault diagnosis

(a) Wheel wobble

1 Incorrect tracking
2 Worn hub bearings
3 Defective suspension units
4 Worn swivel hub joints
5 Loose wheel fixings

(b) 'Bottoming' of suspension

1 Check 3 in (a)
2 Incorrect pressurizing
3 Rebound rubbers worn or missing

(c) Heavy steering

1 Neglected swivel hub lubrication
2 Wrong suspension geometry

(d) Excessive tyre wear

1 Check 1 in (a) and 2 in (c)

(e) Rattles

1 Check 1 in (c)
2 Radius arm mounting defective

(f) Excessive rolling

1 Check 3 in (a) and 2 in (b)
2 Anti-roll bar broken or fixings loose

CHAPTER 8

STEERING

8 : 1 Description

The rack-and-pinion steering gear is shown in component form in **FIG 8 : 1**. Rack housing 1 is secured to the engine bulkhead and carries a pinion 13 which engages with rack 5. The top end of the pinion shaft is splined to steering column 43. The outer ends of the rack are ball-jointed to tie rods 23 which carry ball joints 31. These in turn are secured to the steering arms on the swivel hubs. Pinion end play is eliminated by shimming end cover 18. Damper yoke 6 controls the backlash between the pinion and the rack.

If, during maintenance, the front wheels are lifted clear of the ground do not move them forcefully from lock to lock or serious damage to the steering mechanism may result.

8 : 2 Lubrication

No grease nipple is provided for periodical lubrication. Replenishment is needed only when oil has been lost from the rack housing or the rubber gaiters. If the leakage can be rectified without removing the rack assembly from the car, proceed to recharge with lubricant as follows:

Remove retaining clip 29 from the gaiter at the right-hand end of the rack housing and pull the gaiter from the housing. Do the opposite end on lefthand drive cars. Move the rack to the straight-ahead position. Insert an oil nozzle into the end of the housing and inject not more than one third of a pint of Extreme Pressure SAE.90 oil.

Reconnect the gaiter and move the rack from side to side to distribute the oil.

8 : 3 Removing steering wheel

Lever out the horn push-control. Remove retaining nut 56 and use a suitable extractor to pull off the wheel. When refitting the wheel, tighten the nut to a torque of 50 lb ft.

8 : 4 The steering column

Removing:

Disconnect the direction indicator and horn control wires at the snap connectors under the parcel shelf. Pull back the rubber shroud at the bottom end of the column and remove bolt 49. Remove the two screws securing the column support bracket to the underside of the facia, pull the column assembly upwards to disengage it from the pinion shaft splines and lift it from the car.

Inspection:

Heavy steering can often be traced to a bent inner column. To check this replace the inner column on the pinion shaft without the outer column. Jack up the car beneath the front subframe and turn the wheels gently from lock to lock. If the top bearing surface runs out by more than a total of $\frac{1}{8}$ inch the column must be removed, straightened and rechecked.

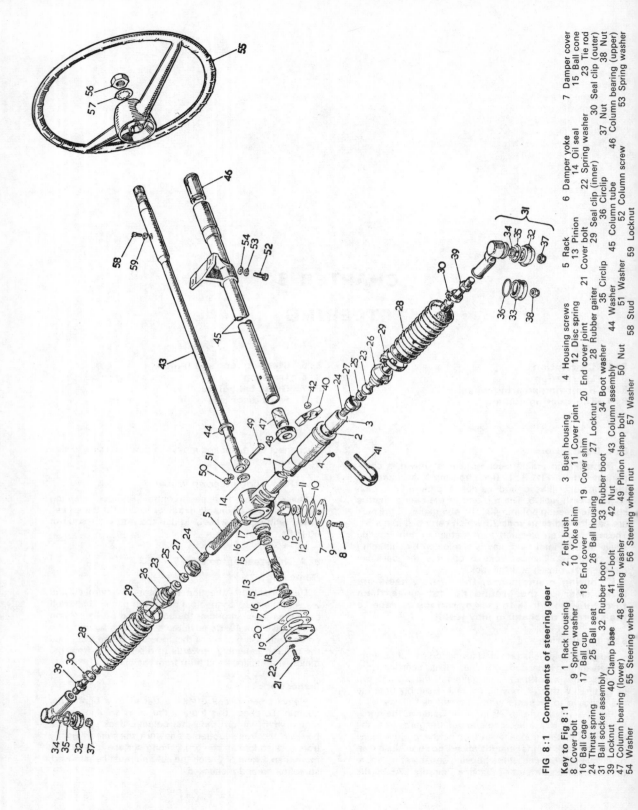

FIG 8:1 Components of steering gear

Key to Fig 8:1

1 Rack housing 2 Felt bush 3 Bush housing 4 Housing screws 5 Rack 6 Damper yoke 7 Damper cover
8 Cover bolt 9 Spring washer 10 End cover 11 Cover joint 12 Disc spring 13 Pinion 14 Oil seal 15 Ball cone
16 Ball cage 17 Ball cup 18 End cover 19 Cover shim 20 End cover joint 21 Cover bolt 22 Spring washer 23 Tie rod
24 Thrust spring 25 Ball seat 26 Ball housing 27 Locknut 28 Rubber gaiter 29 Seal clip (inner) 30 Seal clip (outer)
31 Ball socket assembly 32 Rubber boot 33 Ball housing 34 Boot washer 35 Washer 36 Circlip 37 Nut 38 Nut
39 Locknut 40 Clamp base 41 U-bolt 42 Nut 43 Column assembly 44 Washer 45 Column tube 46 Column bearing (upper)
47 Column bearing (lower) 48 Sealing washer 49 Pinion clamp bolt 50 Nut 51 Washer 52 Column screw 53 Spring washer
54 Washer 55 Steering wheel 56 Steering wheel nut 57 Washer 58 Stud 59 Locknut

88

Refitting:

Reverse the sequence of removal. Make sure that the slot in the clamp at the bottom of the inner column is correctly located with the road wheels in the straight-ahead position. On righthand drive models the clamp must be under the column with the bolt hole horizontal, so that the cancelling lug for the direction indicator is correctly placed. On lefthand drive models, or where the switch is moved to the left side of the column the clamp must be positioned with the slot uppermost.

Tighten the steering column pinch bolt 49 to a torque of 8 to 9 lb ft.

8 : 5 Steering rack and pinion

Removing:

1 Remove the steering column as just described. Jack up beneath the front subframe and remove the front wheels. Disconnect the steering tie rod ball joints 31.

2 Support the engine from above or below according to the equipment available. Remove the setscrews and bolts from the six subframe mounting points (see **FIG 7 : 9** in the preceding chapter).

3 From inside the car remove the nuts from U-bolts 41. Lower the engine just far enough for the rack assembly to be released from the toeboard and withdrawn from the car on the driver's side. **The operation of lowering the engine must be carried out with great care.** The suspension displacer hoses, hydraulic hoses and controls are not disconnected, so avoid damaging them and lower the engine only the minimum amount.

Dismantling:

1 Unlock nuts 39 and remove ball joints 31. Release gaiter clips 29 and 30. Drain the oil from the housing and pull off the rubber gaiters 28.

2 Remove damper cover 7 (two bolts and spring washers), take care of shims 11 and extract the damper yoke 6 with disc springs 12.

3 Remove pinion end cover 18 (two bolts and spring washers). Collect shims 19 and extract the lower ball bearing parts 16 and 17. Pull out pinion 13. The top bearing parts will be trapped behind the rack and can only be removed after the rack is withdrawn. Extract oil seal 14.

4 Using the Special peg spanners 18G.707, unlock and remove the ball joint housings as follows. Punch the indentations in the lockwasher clear of the slots in the locking ring and the ball housing 26. On later models there is no locking washer, so punch or prise up the indentations in the locknut clear of the slots in the rack and the ball housing. Slacken the locknut and unscrew the housing to release the tie rods 23, ball seats 25 and thrust springs 24.

5 Withdraw the rack from the pinion end of the housing to avoid damage to the felt or 'Vulkellan' bush 2 fitted in the other end. Remove housing screw 4 and extract the bush from its housing 3.

Inspection:

Clean and examine all parts for wear and fractures. Any cracks, hollows or roughness of the gear teeth will make the rack or the pinion unserviceable.

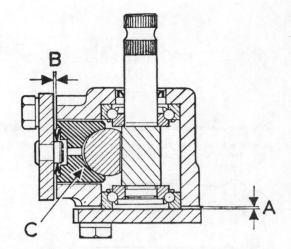

FIG 8 : 2 Early pinion and rack damper. Pinion end play adjusted at 'A'. Shimming for damper yoke 'C' is fitted at 'B'

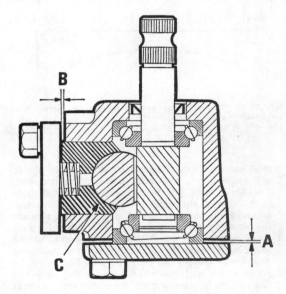

FIG 8 : 3 Later pinion and rack damper. Pinion end play adjusted at 'A'. Shimming for damper yoke 'C' is fitted at 'B'

If the rubber gaiters show the slightest signs of deterioration they must be renewed. Also check the tie rod ball joint surfaces for evidence of wear. The outer ball joint assemblies 31 cannot be dismantled and must be renewed if worn. If the original joints are to be refitted make sure the rubber boots are in perfect condition.

Reassembling:

1 Use the new type 'Vulkellan' plastic bush as a replacement for felt bush 2. The plastic bush has a steel sleeve and a spacer. Insert the spacer plain end first into the

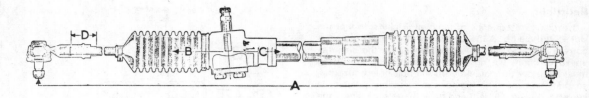

FIG 8:4   Dimensions for setting steering rack assembly

Key to Fig 8:4   **A** The assembled length between the ball pins 45.34 inch   **B** Rack travel from the central position, 2.5 inch
C Rack travel from the central position, 2.5 inch   **D** The threaded length of the tie rod

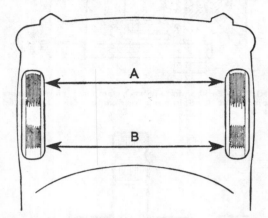

FIG 8:5   Tracking of front wheels is such that dimension 'A' is $\frac{1}{16}$ inch greater than 'B'

rack housing, fit the plastic bush into the steel sleeve and insert it into the rack housing plain end first. The flats on the plastic bush must be positioned offset to the hole for the retaining screw. When the spacer and bush are correctly placed, drill the bush, through the retaining screw hole, with a $\frac{7}{64}$ inch drill. Remove swarf, coat the screw with jointing compound and refit to secure the bush. Check that the point of the screw does not project into the bore of the bush.

2 Fit the pinion shaft seal and the top bearing. Insert the rack into the housing and refit the pinion and the lower bearing. Replace cover 18 without the shims, but do not overtighten the screws. Check the clearance at 'A' in either **FIG 8:2** or **8:3** according to type. Subtract .001 to .003 inch from the feeler gauge measurement and fit shims of the thickness thus obtained. This will preload the pinion bearings. Refit the cover, using shellac on the joint faces to prevent leakage of oil.

3 Always use new locknuts 27. Fit to the rack and replace the tie rod complete with thrust spring and ball seat. Tighten down the ball housing until the tie rod is pinched. Screw the locknut back to meet the ball housing and check that the tie rod is still pinched. Slacken back the ball housing by $\frac{1}{8}$ of a turn to allow full articulation of the ball joint. Relock the housing by tightening the locknut to a torque of 33 to 37 lb ft, at the same time making sure that the ball housing does

not turn. If adjustment is correct the preload on tie rod ball joints will be such that a torque of 32 to 52 lb in will be required to produce articulation. A 4 to 6.5 lb pull with a spring balance attached to the steering ball joint end will give this figure. Lock by punching the lips of the locknut into the slots in the ball housing and the rack.

4 **Damper adjustment, early type**: Refer to **FIG 8:2** and fit the yoke with springs but without shims. Tighten the cover bolts until it is just possible to turn the pinion shaft from the straight-ahead position with the bearing preload gauge set to 15 lb in. Use feeler gauges to take measurement 'B'. Subtract .001 to .003 inch from this measurement and use cover shims to the thickness obtained. Coat the joint faces with shellac and refit the cover with the selected shims. The torque required to start movement of the pinion after assembly must not exceed 25 lb in.

5 **Damper adjustment, later type**: Refer to **FIG 8:3** and fit yoke 'C' without spring or shims. Set the rack in the straight-ahead position and tighten the cover bolts until it is just possible to turn the pinion shaft with a bearing preload gauge set to 15 lb in. Take a feeler gauge measurement at 'B', which is the clearance between the cover and its rack housing seating. The thickness of shims required will be the feeler gauge measurement plus .002 to .005 inch. Coat the joint faces with shellac and refit the cover with the necessary shims. After tightening the cover bolts the torque required to turn the pinion shaft must not exceed 35 lb in.

6 Continue with the assembly of the rack housing by fitting the rubber gaiters. Before finally securing the clip round the gaiter and tie rod at the pinion end, stand the assembly upright and pour in about one third of a pint of Extreme Pressure SAE.90 oil through the end of the gaiter. Fit and tighten the clip.

7 Centralize the rack and mark the pinion so that the position of the rack can be verified when the assembly is back on the car. The full travel of the rack from stop to stop is 5 inch, that is $2\frac{1}{2}$ inch on either side of the central position. Full travel is equivalent to three and one third turns of the pinion.

8 Fit the locknuts and outer ball joints, screwing them on an equal amount at both ends. Check the distance between the two ball pins as shown in **FIG 8:4**, where 'A' is 45.34 inch. Tighten the locknuts just enough to hold the joints while the assembly is being fitted to the car.

Refitting:

This is a reversal of the removal procedure, but leave the support nuts slack until the steering column clamp bolt has been tightened to a torque of 8 to 9 lb ft. Then tighten the column bracket nuts and finally the steering rack U-bolts. Check and adjust the front wheel tracking as follows.

8 : 6 Tracking

When correctly adjusted the front wheels must toe-out a total of $\frac{1}{16}$ inch as shown in **FIG 8 : 5.** This can be checked with the car standing unladen on level ground with the tyres inflated to the recommended pressure.

Turn the wheels to the straight-ahead position. Measure between the tyres at a height of $10\frac{1}{4}$ inch above the ground surface and on a diameter of $16\frac{3}{4}$ inch on the side walls of the tyres. Mark the tyres at this point with chalk then roll the car forward half a revolution of the wheels. Measure between the chalk marks at the rear. The difference should be such that the front dimension is $\frac{1}{16}$ inch greater than the rear.

If the alignment is incorrect slacken the locknuts for the outer ball joints, and the small clips securing the gaiters to the tie rods. Then turn each tie rod equally in the desired direction, noting that both rods have righthand threads. For the steering .geometry to be correct and for the steering rack to be in the central position it is important that the tie rods are adjusted to exactly equal lengths. Lastly, tighten the locknuts.

8 : 7 Outer ball joints

As these joints have nylon seats and are sealed, they do not need periodical lubrication. Dirt is excluded by rubber boots and if these are found to be damaged or perished the whole joint and boot must be renewed. If the boot is damaged during overhaul and no dirt has entered the joint it is only necessary to renew the faulty boot. Before fitting it smear the area adjacent to the joint with a little Dextagrease Super GP.

8 : 8 Fault diagnosis

(a) Wheel wobble

1 Unbalanced wheels and tyres
2 Slack steering ball joints
3 Incorrect steering geometry
4 Excessive play in steering gear
5 Faulty suspension
6 Worn hub bearings

(b) Wander

1 Check 2, 3 and 4 in (a)
2 Uneven tyre pressures
3 Uneven tyre wear

(c) Heavy steering

1 Check 3 in (a)
2 Very low tyre pressures
3 Neglected lubrication
4 Wheels out of track
6 Rack damper too tight
7 Excessive pinion bearing preload
8 Inner steering column bent
9 Column bushes tight

(d) Lost motion

1 Loose steering wheel, worn splines
2 Worn rack and pinion teeth
3 Worn ball joints
4 Worn swivel hub joints
5 Slack pinion bearings

CHAPTER 9

THE BRAKING SYSTEM

9:1 Description

Disc brakes are fitted to the front wheels and drum brakes to the rear. All four are hydraulically operated by the brake pedal and the handbrake lever operates the rear brakes only, through a mechanical linkage which normally requires no separate adjustment.

The front brakes on all Mk I models are of the rotating disc and rigidly mounted caliper type, each caliper comprising two friction assemblies between which the disc rotates. The friction pads are applied by two pistons operated by hydraulic pressure from the master cylinder. They are automatically retracted when pedal pressure is released. Wear is taken up automatically and no adjustment is provided. Both pistons operate simultaneously to exert equal pressure on the friction pads. This type of assembly is shown in **FIG 9:1**.

The rear brakes are of the internal expanding type with one leading and one trailing shoe to each brake. A double-ended cylinder expands both shoes into contact with the drum under hydraulic pressure from the master cylinder. When pedal pressure is released the shoes are retracted by springs. A valve is fitted in the hydraulic fluid line to limit the pressure on the rear brakes. This controls the tendency for the rear wheels to lock under heavy braking due to weight transfer to the front wheels.

The brake pedal is directly coupled to the hydraulic master cylinder, where pressure on the fluid is generated. This is transmitted to the brakes by a system of metal and flexible pipes.

9:2 Maintenance

Periodically look at the level of fluid in the supply tank of the brake master cylinder shown in **FIG 9:2**. Note that the brake tank is deeper than the one for the clutch system. The fluid level should be $\frac{1}{4}$ inch below the bottom of the filler neck. If frequent topping up is necessary there must be a leak in the system which should have immediate attention. Wipe dirt from round the cap before unscrewing it. Use the recommended fluid, which is Lockheed Disc Brake Fluid Series II.

Adjust the rear brake shoes when pedal travel becomes excessive. The adjuster is arrowed in **FIG 9:3**. Jack-up each rear wheel in turn after chocking the front wheels and releasing the handbrake. Turn the adjuster clockwise until the drum is locked then slacken off about a quarter of a turn or until the drum can be revolved without binding. This adjustment automatically sets the handbrake.

Preventive maintenance:

Regularly examine friction pads, rear brake linings and all pipes, unions and hoses. If one front friction pad is worn more than the other, change them over.

Change all the brake fluid every 18 months or 24,000 miles. Every three years or 40,000 miles check all flexible hoses and fluid seals in the system and renew if necessary. The bores of all cylinders should be highly polished and without signs of pitting or corrosion.

Never use anything but the recommended fluid.

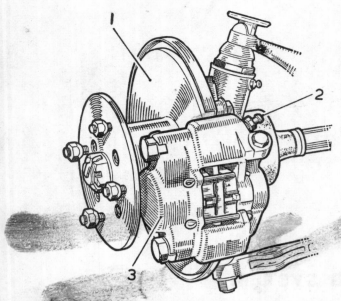

FIG 9:1 Fixed caliper disc brake showing disc 1, bleeder screw 2 and caliper 3

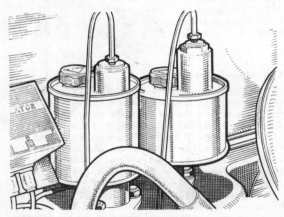

FIG 9:2 Master cylinder supply tank on left (righthand drive)

Do not leave it in unsealed containers as it will absorb moisture which can be dangerous. It is best to discard fluid drained from the system or after bleeding.

Observe absolute cleanliness when working on all parts of the hydraulic system.

9:3 Fixed caliper front brakes
Renewing friction pads:

1 Jack-up the car and remove the road wheel. Refer to **FIG 9:4**, depress retaining spring 2 and withdraw splitpins 3.

2 Remove the spring and withdraw friction pads 1 and anti-squeak shims 11. Use a pair of pointed-nose pliers for this operation.

3 Clean the exposed face of each piston 6 and ensure the recesses in the caliper for the friction pad assemblies are free from dirt and rust. Press each piston back into the caliper. This will lead to a rise in the fluid level in the master cylinder supply tank. It may be necessary to syphon off some fluid to prevent overflowing.

4 Check that the relieved face of each piston is correctly positioned and then fit the new friction pad assemblies. Fit the anti-squeak shims between each piston and pad. Check that the pad assemblies move freely in the caliper recesses. Any high-spots on the pad pressure plate can then be removed by judicious filing.

5 Refit the retaining spring, press it down and insert the splitpins. Fit new springs if the original ones have lost tension or have been damaged.

6 After fitting new pads operate the brake pedal several times to adjust the brake and top up the master cylinder tank if necessary.

Removing and dismantling a fixed-type caliper:

1 Disconnect the brake fluid supply hose as instructed in **Section 9:7**. Refer to **FIG 9:5**. Remove the two bolts securing the caliper to the hub and lift it away. Depress retaining spring 16 and remove the splitpins. Remove the friction pads and anti-squeak shims. Clean the outside of the caliper and dry off all traces of cleaning fluid.

2 Reconnect the fluid supply hose and support the caliper so that the hose is not strained. Clamp the piston in the mounting half of the caliper, which is the part with the fixing lugs. Gently apply the brake pedal which will force the unclamped piston outwards. Remove the piston by hand when it has emerged enough. Catch the draining fluid in a clean container.

3 Use a blunt-nosed tool to remove the fluid seal 13 from its groove in the bore, being particularly careful not to damage either the bore or the groove. The retainer of seal 14 can be levered out with a screwdriver and the rubber seal detached.

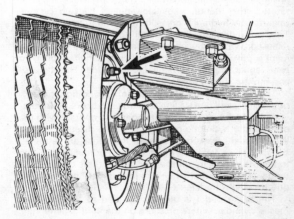

FIG 9:3 Arrow indicates square-headed adjuster for rear brake

4 Remove the clamp. To remove the remaining piston it
will be necessary to refit the first one and fit it with a
clamp, repeating the preceding instructions.

5 **To clean the internal parts of the caliper use only
methylated spirits or the correct grade of
Lockheed brake fluid. Never use any other fluid
on the rubber seals. All parts must be spotlessly
clean.**

Reassembling a fixed-type caliper:

1 Renew all rubber seals, which are obtainable in kit form.
Never replace old seals if there has been the slightest
sign of leakage. Take a perfectly dry inner seal and coat
it with Lockheed Disc Brake Lubricant. Use the
fingers to ease it into its groove and seat it properly.
Slacken bleeder screw 18 one complete turn.

2 Coat a piston with the same fluid Lubricant and locate
it squarely in the mouth of the bore with the cutaway
part of the piston face positioned uppermost. Press in
the piston until about $\frac{5}{16}$ inch protrudes, taking care
that it does not tilt. If the outer seal and retainer were
removed, dry a new seal thoroughly and coat it with
the Lubricant. Fit it in the retainer and slip the assembly
over the piston with the rubber seal innermost. Keep
the seal square and press both piston and seal inwards
with a clamp. Retighten the bleeder screw.

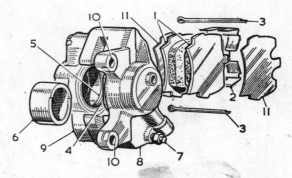

FIG 9:4   Components of fixed-type front brake caliper

Key to Fig 9:4   1 Friction pads   2 Pad retaining spring
3 Retaining pin   4 Piston dust seal   5 Piston fluid seal
6 Piston   7 Bleeder screw   8 Caliper (mounting half)
9 Caliper (rim half)   10 Caliper mounting point
11 Anti-squeak shims

3 Deal with the mounting-half piston in the same way,
but disconnect the flexible hose to enable the clamp
to be used and again slacken the bleeder screw.

4 When the pistons and seals are assembled, reconnect
the hose and bolt the caliper to the hub. Do not depress

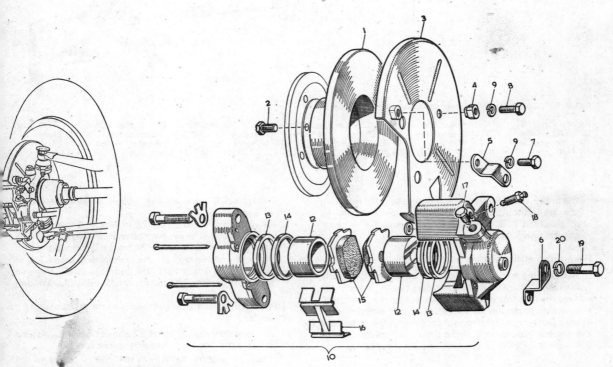

FIG 9:5   Components of fixed-type front brake

Key to Fig 9:5   1 Brake disc   2 Flange bolt   3 Dust cover   4 Nut   5 Dust cover bracket—R.H. top, L.H. bottom
6 Dust cover bracket—L.H. top, R.H. bottom   7 Cover bolt   8 Cover bolt   9 Washer   10 Caliper assembly
12 Piston   13 Seal (inner)   14 Seal   15 Pad assembly   16 Spring   17 Plug   18 Bleeder screw
19 Caliper bolt   20 Spring washer

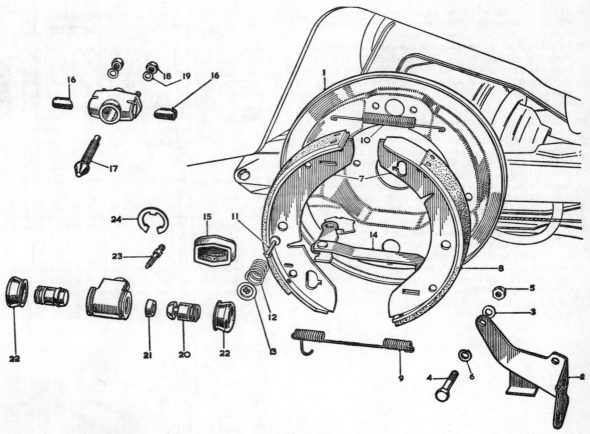

FIG 9:6   Components of rear drum brake

Key to Fig 9:6   1 Brakeplate   2 Cable and hose bracket   3 Washer   4 Plate screw   5 Nut
6 Spring washer   7 Shoe assembly   8 Lining   9 Shoe return spring   10 Shoe return spring   11 Steady pin
12 Steady spring   13 Washer   14 Handbrake lever   15 Cylinder boot   16 Adjuster tappet   17 Wedge
18 Nut   19 Washer   20 Cylinder piston   21 Seal   22 Boot   23 Bleed screw   24 Cylinder clip

the brake pedal. Replace the friction pads, the retaining springs and splitpins and bleed the system as described in **Section 9:5.** After bleeding, operate the pedal several times to adjust the brake.

Removing and refitting a brake disc:

Remove the hub as instructed in **Section 7:8** of the Suspension Chapter. Remove flange bolts 2 which will release the disc from the hub. When refitting a disc check the maximum runout of the faces at the outside edge, using a dial gauge. If the runout exceeds .006 inch remove the disc and reposition it on the drive shaft splines. Check the mating surfaces of disc and hub for dirt and burrs.

9:4 Rear brakes

Removing the wheel cylinder:

1 Jack-up the car under the rear subframe, remove the road wheel and thoroughly clean behind the brake

backplate. Disconnect the flexible hose as described in **Section 9:7.**

2 Unscrew the bleed screw 23 in **FIG 9:6** from behind the backplate. The cylinder boss protrudes through the backplate. Remove circlip 24 from it. Remove the hub cap and nut and pull off the brake drum and hub unit with Service Tools 18G.304 and 18G.304B. Remove the shoes as described later and take away the cylinder.

Dismantling and reassembling a rear wheel cylinder:

1 Remove dust seal or boots 22 and extract both pistons 20. Use the fingers to remove rubber seals 21.

2 Clean all internal parts with methylated spirits or the correct Lockheed brake fluid. If other solvents such as petrol are used to clean metal parts, every trace must be dried off before reassembly.

3 Renew the rubber seals at every overhaul, or if there is any sign of leakage. Inspect the pistons and cylinder

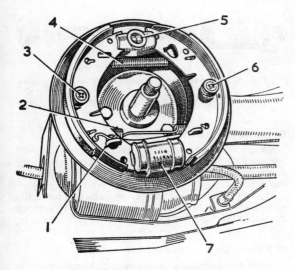

FIG 9:7 Righthand rear brake assembly

Key to Fig 9:7   1 Handbrake lever   2 Shoe pull-off spring
3 Steady spring   4 Shoe pull-off spring   5 Adjuster assembly
6 Steady spring   7 Hydraulic cylinder

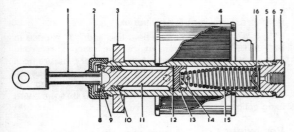

FIG 9:8   Brake master cylinder in section

Key to Fig 9:8   1 Pushrod   2 Rubber boot
3 Mounting flange   4 Supply tank   5 Cylinder body
6 Washer   7 End plug   8 Circlip   9 Stop washer
10 Secondary cup   11 Piston   12 Piston washer
13 Main cup   14 Spring retainer   15 Return spring
16 Valve assembly

bore and renew parts which are worn or pitted with
corrosion.
4 Fit the new seals using the fingers only. Assemble all
internal parts after wetting with the brake fluid. Refit the
cylinder to the backplate in the reverse order of dismantling. Upon completion the brake shoes must be
adjusted as in **Section 9 : 2** after the system has been
bled according to the instructions in **Section 9 : 5**.

Removing rear brake shoes:

1 Chock the front wheels and release the handbrake.
Jack-up the car under the rear subframe and remove the
road wheel.

2 Remove the hub cap and nut and pull off the drum and
hub unit with Service Tools 18G.304 and 18G.304B.
3 Disconnect steady springs 3 and 6 in **FIG 9:7** by
pressing and turning the slotted washers. Make a note
of the positions of the return springs 2 and 4. Pull one
shoe outwards away from the cylinder and adjuster
and then release the tension on the pull-off springs.
This will release the second shoe. **Do not press the
brake pedal while the shoes are off.**
It is a good idea to put wire or rubber bands round the
two pistons to prevent ejection and if the car is to be left
without rear shoes for a long time a notice should be
hung on the brake pedal to warn against depressing the
pedal.

Relining rear brake shoes:

If the linings are worn down to the rivets, renewal is
necessary. It is not recommended that owners should
reline brake shoes themselves. It is important that the
linings should be perfectly bedded down on the shoes
and then ground to perfect concentricity with the brake
drums. For this reason it is best to obtain sets of replacement shoes already lined. The correct lining material is
given in Technical Data. Do not fit odd shoes and do not
mix materials or unbalanced braking will result.
**Do not allow grease or paint to contact friction
linings.** If the original linings are contaminated with oil
or grease do not attempt to clean them with solvents as
nothing useful can be done.

Refitting rear brake shoes:

This is a reversal of the dismantling procedure. Make
sure that the pull-off springs are correctly fitted to the
holes in the webs and that the shoes register correctly
in the slotted ends of the pistons and adjusters. Before
trying to fit the drum and hub, slacken off the brake
adjuster completely, by turning it anticlockwise as seen
from behind the backplate. Also fully release the handbrake. Readjust the shoes when assembly is completed.
This will also set the handbrake correctly.

9:5 Bleeding the system

This is not routine maintenance and is only necessary
if air has entered the hydraulic system because parts have
been dismantled or because the fluid level in the master
cylinder supply tank has dropped so low that air has been
drawn in through the hole in the cylinder bore mentioned
in **Section 9:6**.
1 Fill the master cylinder supply tank with Lockheed Disc
Brake Fluid, Series II. During the bleeding operation
fluid will be used and constant topping up of the supply
tank will be needed. If this is not done it is possible
for air to enter the master cylinder, which will nullify
the operation and necessitate a fresh start.
2 Attach a length of rubber or plastic tube to the bleeder
screw in a rear wheel cylinder, or to the screw on the
caliper in the case of the front brakes. Immerse the free
end of the tube in a small volume of brake fluid in a
clean jar.
3 Open the bleed screw one turn and get a second
operator to press down slowly on the brake pedal.
After a full stroke let the pedal return without assistance,
pause a moment and repeat the down stroke. At first

there will be air bubbles issuing from the bleed tube, but when fluid alone is ejected, hold the pedal firmly down to the floorboards and tighten the bleeder screw. Repeat this on both rear brakes and then do both the front.

4 On completion, top up the fluid in the supply tank to the correct level. **Discard all dirty fluid. If the fluid is perfectly clean, let it stand for 24 hours to become clear of air bubbles before using it again.**

9:6 The master cylinder

This is shown in section in **FIG 9:8**. Pushrod 1 is connected to the brake pedal. When the pedal is depressed the pushrod moves piston 11 down the bore of cylinder 5, forcing fluid through end plug 7 into the pipelines connected to the brake cylinders. Rubber cup 13 prevents fluid from passing the piston in the reverse direction. When the piston returns fully to the 'OFF' position the lip of the rubber cup uncovers a hole in the cylinder bore which communicates directly with supply tank 4. The fluid in the tank is then available to replenish any which has been lost in the pipes and cylinders. The hole is immediately closed when the piston starts to move down the bore. Valve 16 operates only when the system is being bled. It prevents fluid which has been pumped out of the master cylinder from returning, to ensure that a fresh charge is delivered at each stroke of the pedal.

Removing master cylinder:

Remove the circlip and clevis pin securing the pushrod to the pedal lever. Disconnect the pipe union from the end plug of the cylinder, remove the two flange bolts and lift the assembly away.

Dismantling master cylinder:

Drain the fluid from the tank. Pull back dust cover or boot 2, remove circlip 8 with a pair of long-nosed pliers and remove pushrod 1 together with washer 9. Withdraw all the internal parts. Using the fingers only, stretch secondary cup 10 over the piston flanges to remove it.

Reassembling the master cylinder:

1 Clean all rubber parts in methylated spirits or correct hydraulic fluid. Any solvents used to clean metal parts must be completely dried off.
2 Renew all rubber seals when reassembling, particularly if there has been leakage. Assemble the internal parts after wetting them with brake fluid.
3 Stretch the secondary cup over the end flange of the piston so that the lip of the cup faces towards the opposite end of the piston and will enter the bore first. Gently work the cup into the groove with the fingers.
4 Fit valve 16 to the spring and make sure that retainer 14 is in place when fitting the spring large end first. Insert the main cup 13 lip first. Take great care not to trap or turn back the lip and then press the cup down the bore and onto the retainer. Replace dished piston washer 12 with its concave face towards the main cup.
5 Insert the piston, taking care not to damage or turn back the lip on the secondary cup. Push the piston down the bore, replace the pushrod and retaining circlip and fit the rubber boot.

FIG 9:9 Components of pressure regulating valve

Refitting the master cylinder:

Secure the master cylinder flange to the bulkhead with the two fixing bolts. Refit the pressure pipe. Connect the pushrod yoke to the pedal lever with the clevis pin and circlip.

Check the brake shoe adjustment, refill and bleed the system, apply the brakes hard and at the same time check the system for leaks.

9:7 Removing a flexible hose

Never try to release a flexible hose by turning the ends with a spanner. The correct procedure is as follows:

Unscrew the metal pipeline union nut from its connection with the hose. Hold the adjacent hexagon on the hose with a spanner and remove the locknut which secures the hose to the bracket. The hose can now be turned without twisting the flexible part, by using a spanner on the hexagon at the other end.

9:8 Pressure regulating valve

This is fitted in the brake fluid line and is illustrated in **FIG 9:9**. When pressure in the line reaches a certain figure the valve closes and prevents further pressure from being applied to the rear brakes to obviate wheel locking. Any further rise in fluid pressure is transferred to the front brakes only. The valve closes at 450 lb/sq in. with fixed caliper front brakes.

Removing:

Disconnect the three pressure lines from their connections on the valve body. Remove the nut and washer to release the valve from the rear subframe front cross-member.

Dismantling:

Clean the outside then unscrew the end plug. Extract the valve assembly and return spring. Examine the rubber seals. Fit a new piston and seal assembly if there is wear or damage to either.

Reassembling:

Clean all parts in brake fluid and assemble the parts wet with the fluid. Fit a new taper seal and piston seal, making certain that the taper seal is fitted with the small diameter entering the bore first. Refit the return spring and valve assembly, securing in place with the end plug and sealing washer.

Note that if the sealing washer is an aluminium one it must be replaced by one made of copper. At the same time fit a new end plug and a new short pipe from the valve to the chassis.

Refitting:

After the assembly has been secured to the cross-member and the three pipelines reconnected, bleed the system as described in **Section 9:5**.

9:9 The handbrake

Normally, adjustment of the rear brakes will automatically take up excessive handbrake travel. If there is still too much travel after adjustment, suspect worn brake shoe linings or stretched handbrake cables. Examine the linings and fit replacement shoes if they are worn. Check the action of the handbrake again and if there is still too much travel before the brakes are applied it is permissible to take it up as follows:

It is essential to make sure that the rear shoes are correctly adjusted as instructed in Section 9:2 and to follow these further instructions carefully.

Apply the handbrake until the pawl engages with the ratchet at the third notch. Locate the nuts on the handbrake lever trunnion and adjust them until it is just possible to turn the road wheels by heavy hand pressure. **It is important that both rear road wheels offer the same resistance to turning.**

Return the lever to fully 'OFF' and check that both wheels are quite free. If a brake tends to bind, remove the brake drum and hub unit and check that the brake shoe pull-off springs are correctly fitted. Also check for suspected seizure of the wheel cylinder. When all is well, refit the hub and drum, readjust and recheck.

Removing the handbrake cables:

Chock the front wheels and release the handbrake. Remove the cable adjusting nuts from the handbrake lever trunnion. Remove the cable fair-lead located in the centre of the floor between the front seats. From under the car, draw the cable through the floor and release it from the guide channel on the rear subframe front crossmember.

Jack-up the car under the rear subframe and remove the road wheel. Remove the nut securing the cable swivel sector to the radius arm and remove the sector and cable. Draw the cable through the frame and release it from the actuating lever on the brake backplate.

When fitting a new cable make sure that the corners of the sector are 'nipped'. Refitting is a reversal of the removing instructions but make sure that the guide channel is well lubricated. Readjust the handbrake as just detailed.

9:10 Fault diagnosis

(a) 'Spongy' pedal

1 Leak in the system
2 Worn master cylinder
3 Leaking wheel cylinders
4 Air in the fluid system
5 Gaps between rear shoes and underside of linings

(b) Excessive pedal movement

1 Check 1 and 4 in (a)
2 Excessive lining wear
3 Very low fluid level in supply tank
4 Too much free movement of pedal

(c) Brakes grab or pull to one side

1 Distorted discs or drums
2 Wet or oily pads or linings
3 Rear brake backplate loose
4 Disc loose on hub
5 Worn suspension or steering connections
6 Mixed linings of different grades
7 Uneven tyre pressures
8 Broken shoe return springs
9 Seized handbrake cable
10 Seized piston in wheel cylinder
11 Loose caliper fixings

CHAPTER 10

THE ELECTRICAL SYSTEM

10 : 1 Description

All models covered by this manual have 12 volt electrical systems in which the positive battery terminal is earthed. There are three units in the regulator box to control the charging circuit; a cut-out, a current regulator and a voltage regulator. These are fitted with adjusting devices, but it must be stressed that accurate meters are required when checking or altering the settings. Cheap and unreliable instruments will make accurate adjustment impossible.

There are wiring diagrams in Technical Data at the end of this manual to enable those with electrical experience to trace and correct wiring faults.

For the UK market the headlamps are of the double-filament dipping, sealed beam type with adjustments for beam setting. The fuel and temperature gauges are voltage-controlled by a bi-metal resistance unit which supplies a stabilized and predetermined voltage to the instruments and equipment.

The battery and the fuses are mounted on the righthand side of the engine compartment.

Detailed instructions for servicing the electrical equipment will be found in this chapter, but it must be pointed out that it is not sensible to try to repair that which is seriously defective, electrically or mechanically. Such equipment should be replaced by new units which can be obtained on an Exchange basis.

10 : 2 The battery

This is of the 12 volt lead/acid type and has to meet heavy demands for current particularly in the winter. To maintain the performance of the battery at its maximum it is essential to carry out the following operations.

Keep the top of the battery and surrounding parts dry and clean, as dampness can cause leakage between the securing strap and the negative terminal. Clean off corrosion from the metal parts of the battery mounting with diluted ammonia and paint them with anti-sulphuric paint. If the terminal posts are corroded, remove the cables and clean with diluted ammonia. Smear the posts with petroleum jelly before remaking the connections and fit the terminal screws securely. High electrical resistance due to corrosion at the terminal posts is often responsible for lack of sufficient current to operate the starter motor.

Remove the manifold and check that it is not cracked. A defective manifold might cause leakage of electrolyte and consequent corrosion. Test the condition of the cells after topping up the electrolyte level with distilled water to just above the tops of the separators. **Never add neat acid. If it is necessary to make new electrolyte due to loss by spillage, add sulphuric acid to distilled water. It is highly dangerous to add water to acid.**

To test the condition of the cells use an hydrometer to check the specific gravity of the electrolyte. The method is shown in **FIG 10 : 1** and the indications from the readings are as follows:

For climates below 27°C or 80°F
Cell fully charged — Specific gravity 1.270 to 1.290
Cell half-discharged — Specific gravity 1.190 to 1.210
Cell discharged — Specific gravity 1.110 to 1.130

For climates above 27°C or 80°F
Cell fully charged — Specific gravity 1.210 to 1.230
Cell half-discharged — Specific gravity 1.130 to 1.150
Cell discharged — Specific gravity 1.050 to 1.070

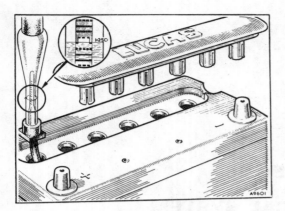

FIG 10 : 1 Checking specific gravity of battery electrolyte with hydrometer

These figures are given assuming an electrolyte temperature of 16°C or 60°F. If the temperature of the electrolyte exceeds this, add .002 to the readings for each 3°C or 5°F rise. Subtract .002 if it drops below 16°C or 60°F.

All six cells should read approximately the same. If one differs radically from the rest it may be due to an internal fault or to spilling or leakage of the electrolyte.

If the battery is in a low state of charge take the car for a long daylight run or put it on a charger at 4 amps until it gasses freely. When putting a battery on a charger, take out the vent plugs and refrain from using a naked light when it is gassing. If the battery is to stand unused for long periods, give a freshening-up charge every month. It will be ruined if it is left discharged.

10 : 3 The generator

An exploded view of the generator is given in **FIG 10 : 2**. Note that bearings 4 and 21 are pressed into their respective end covers.

Testing when generator is not charging:

1 Check that belt slip is not the cause of the trouble. Tension should be such that the belt can be deflected about ½ inch with moderate hand pressure at the centre of the longest run between two pulleys. To tighten a slack belt loosen the two top mounting bolts on the generator brackets and the bolt of the slotted adjustment link lower down. Lift the generator with a gentle hand pull and tighten the three bolts. Do not over-tighten the belt or excessive loading will be placed on the generator bearings.

2 Check the connections. Generator terminal **D** must be connected to control box terminal **D** and generator terminal **F** to control box terminal **F**. Switch off all lights and accessories and disconnect the cables from the generator terminals **D** and **F**. Connect the two terminals with a short length of wire. Run the engine at normal idling speed and clip the negative lead of a 0-20 volt moving coil meter to one generator terminal and the other lead to a good earth on the generator body. Gradually increase engine speed up to about 1000 rev/min. The voltmeter reading should rise

steadily and without fluctuation, but do not let it reach 20 volts and do not race the engine in an attempt to increase the reading.

3 If there is no reading check the brushgear. If the reading is about ½ to 1 volt the field winding may be faulty. If approximately 4 to 5 volts the armature may be faulty.

4 If the generator is in good order, leave the temporary link in position between the terminals and restore the original connections correctly. Remove the **D** lead from the control box and connect the voltmeter between this lead and a good earth on the car. Run the engine as before. The reading should be the same as that measured directly on the generator. No reading indicates a break in the cable from generator to control box. Repeat the test on the **F** cable. Finally, remove the temporary link from the generator. If the readings are correct, test the control box as in **Section 10 : 5**.

Removing generator:

Disconnect the leads from the generator. Slacken all attachment bolts, press the generator towards the cylinder block and remove the belt. Remove the attachment bolts and lift away the generator.

Dismantling generator:

Remove nut 12 in **FIG 10 : 2** and pull off the driving pulley. Remove key 11 from the shaft. Unscrew and remove through-bolts 17 and lift off commutator end bracket 1. Tap off driving end bracket 23 which will bring with it armature 19. Unless the bearing 21 is faulty it need not be removed. To remove the armature from the end bracket use a suitable hand press.

Servicing brushes:

Lift the brushes up in the boxes and hold them in that position by letting each brush spring bear on the side of its brush. Fit the commutator end bracket over the commutator end of the armature shaft and release the brushes by hooking up the springs with a thin screwdriver. Hold back each spring in turn and move the brush by pulling gently on its flexible connector. If the brush moves sluggishly, remove it and polish the sides on a smooth file. Mark it before removal so that it will be replaced in its original working position.

The minimum permissible length of a brush is $\frac{9}{32}$ inch, so renew any which are less than that. Test the brush springs with a spring tension scale. New springs should have a tension of 18 to 24 oz. In service this value may fall to 15 oz before performance is affected. Bed-in new brushes by wrapping fine sandpaper round the commutator, pressing down on the brush and rotating the commutator under it, or draw the paper to and fro.

Servicing the commutator:

One in good condition will be smooth and free from pitting or burned segments. Clean with a rag moistened in petrol. If necessary, polish with fine glasspaper while rotating the armature. **Do not use emery cloth.**

If the commutator is badly worn it may be skimmed in a lathe. Use a high speed, take a light cut and see that the tool is sharp. Remove only enough metal to clean up and then polish with fine glasspaper. To undercut the insulation between the segments, grind a hacksaw blade

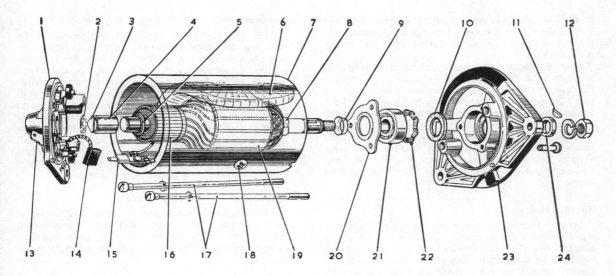

FIG 10:2   Components of the generator

Key to Fig 10:2   1 Commutator end bracket   2 Felt ring   3 Felt ring retainer   4 Bronze bush
5 Thrust washer   6 Field coils   7 Yoke   8 Shaft collar   9 Shaft collar retaining cup   10 Felt ring
11 Shaft key   12 Shaft nut   13 Output terminal D   14 Brushes   15 Field terminal F   16 Commutator
17 Through bolts   18 Pole shoe securing screws   19 Armature   20 Bearing retaining plate   21 Ballbearing
22 Corrugated washer   23 Driving end bracket   24 Pulley spacer

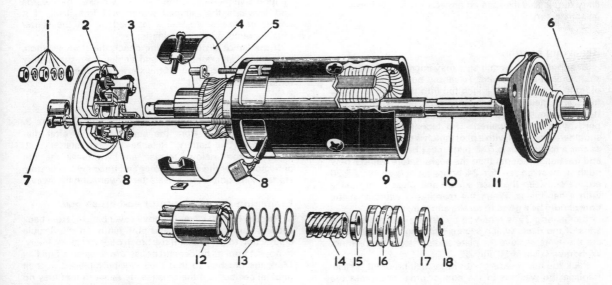

FIG 10:3   Components of the starter motor

Key to Fig 10:3   1 Terminal nuts and washers   2 Brush spring   3 Through-bolt   4 Band cover
5 Terminal post   6 Bearing bush   7 Bearing   8 Brushes   9 Yoke   10 Armature shaft
11 Driving end bracket   12 Pinion assembly   13 Restraining spring   14 Sleeve   15 Impact washer
16 Main spring   17 Locating washer   18 Circlip

on the sides until it is the thickness of the insulation and very carefully work between each pair of segments until the insulation has been cut to a depth of $\frac{1}{32}$ inch below the surface.

Some commutators are moulded instead of being built up with mica. These may be skimmed to a minimum diameter of 1.45 inch and then undercut .040 inch wide and .020 inch deep. It is important that the sides of the undercut clear the moulding material by a minimum of .015 inch.

Visual inspection may determine the cause of armature failure. Breaks in armature windings cause burnt commutator segments. Short-circuited windings are discoloured by overheating, with badly burnt commutator segments.

Testing field coils:

When tested with an ohmmeter the reading should be 6.0 to 6.3 ohms. Failing an ohmmeter, use a 12 volt supply and connect it in series with an ammeter across the field terminal 15 and the yoke or body 7. The meter should read about 2 amps. If there is no reading the field coil winding has a break in it. If the reading is much more than 2 amps or the ohmmeter records much less than 6 ohms it shows that field coil insulation has broken down. Renewal of the field coils is an operation best left to a Service Station.

The armature:

Apart from reconditioning the commutator, there is little which can be done to the armature itself. **Never try to straighten a bent shaft and do not machine the armature core.** Armature windings are tested with equipment normally not available to the car owner. The only check for a suspected faulty armature which he can carry out, is to substitute an armature which is known to be satisfactory.

Renewing bearings:

Bearings which permit side movement of the armature shaft should be renewed. To renew bush 4, remove the old one by screwing a $\frac{5}{8}$ inch tap into the bush for a few turns and then pull the bush out by means of the tap. It is not permissible to ream a bush after it is fitted or the porosity will be impaired. The technique is to use a shouldered mandrel with a pilot which is the same diameter as the armature shaft. The pilot must be highly polished and fractionally longer than the bush. Before fitting a new bush it must be left for 24 hours immersed in SAE.20 engine oil. Keep the bush square and press it into place with a handpress. When the mandrel is withdrawn the bore should be a good fit for the armature shaft.

Ballbearing 21 is renewed by drilling out the splayed ends of the rivets which secure retaining plate 20. Drive out the rivets, remove the plate and press out the bearing. Withdraw washers 10 and 22.

Pack the new bearing with high-melting point grease. Replace the washers in the correct order and press the bearing into the housing in the end bracket. Secure the retaining plate with new rivets.

When refitting the drive-end bracket to the armature shaft, do not press on the bracket itself. Use a length of tubing which will press on the inner race of the ballbearing.

Reassembling and refitting the generator:

This is a reversal of the dismantling procedure. To assemble the commutator end bracket to the yoke, partially withdraw the brushes and trap them in this position by letting the springs bear on the sides of the brushes. Fit the bracket to the armature shaft and when it is about $\frac{1}{2}$ inch from the yoke face, lift the springs with a thin screwdriver and this will let the brushes drop onto the commutator. Check that the springs now bear correctly on the tops of the brushes and push the bracket fully home. After completing the assembly add a few drops of 20W oil into the centre hole in the end boss. Note when refitting the generator that later models have plain washers under the heads of the upper mounting bolts.

Lubrication of the generator:

Every 6000 miles add two or three drops of 20W engine oil to the bearing at the commutator end by introducing them into the central hole in the boss on the end bracket. Over-oiling will lead to trouble with the commutator and brushes.

10:4 The starter

Tests for a starter which does not operate:

Check the condition of the battery and particularly the connections to the terminals and to earth. If the battery is charged, switch on the lights and operate the starter control. If the lights go dim but the starter does not turn it shows that current is reaching the starter. The probability is that the pinion on the starter shaft is jammed in mesh. It can often be released by using a spanner on the squared end of the starter shaft at the end farthest from the flywheel. Another method is to engage a gear with the ignition switched off. If the car is now rocked backwards and forwards the jammed pinion will free itself. If it proves impossible to free a jammed pinion the starter must be removed for examination.

If the lamps do not go dim, check the starter switch. Also check all connections and cables from the battery to the switch and starter. If the starter still does not work, remove it.

Removing the starter:

Remove the distributor as described in **Chapter 3**. Release the cable from the starter terminal after disconnecting the battery. Release the top starter bolt. Working from below, release and withdraw the dirt deflector under the starter motor and unscrew the bottom starter fixing bolt. Work the starter forward and lift away.

Examining the commutator and brush gear:

Refer to **FIG 10 : 3** and remove cover band 4. Hold back each of springs 2 in turn and pull gently on the flexible connection to the brush. If the brush does not move freely, remove it from its holder and polish the sides on a fine file. Mark the brushes so that they will be replaced in their original positions. If the brushes are so worn that they no longer bear on the commutator, or the brush connector has become exposed on the running face, the brushes must be renewed.

If the commutator is blackened clean it by turning it inside a petrol-moistened cloth. With the brushes and commutator overhauled, hold the body of the starter in a vice and connect it with thick cables to a 12 volt battery. One cable should go to the starter terminal and the other to the body of the starter. The starter should run at high speed. If it does not, it must be dismantled for further examination and testing.

Dismantling the starter:

Hold back the brush springs and take out the brushes. Remove terminal nuts and washers 1. Unscrew and withdraw through-bolts 3 and lift off the commutator end bracket, which is the one carrying the brushes. When end bracket 11 is removed it will take with it the armature and the pinion drive, which is shown below as items 12 to 18.

Servicing the brushes:

Test the brush springs with a balance, the parts being clearly shown in **FIG 10 : 4**. The correct tension is 25 to 15 oz according to the wear on the brushes. Fit a new spring if the tension is low.

The examination of the brushes was covered in a preceding paragraph. Note, however, that two of the brushes are connected to terminal sockets on the brush holders attached to the end bracket as shown in **FIG 10 : 4**. The other two brushes are connected to tappings on the field coils as shown in **FIG 10 : 5**. To renew brushes unsolder them one at a time. Secure each new brush in place, taking care not to let the solder run along the flexible leads. The brushes are preformed so that they do not need bedding-in to the curvature of the commutator.

Servicing the commutator:

Clean it with a cloth moistened in petrol. If still not clean, polish with fine glasspaper while rotating the commutator. **Do not use emery paper.** If it is pitted or burnt the commutator may be skimmed in a lathe using high speed and taking a light cut with a keen tool. Remove just enough metal to clean up and finally polish with fine glasspaper. **The mica insulation between the copper segments must not be undercut.**

Testing the field coils:

Use a 12 volt bulb in one lead of a 12 volt battery. Connect one lead to the tapping point **B** in **FIG 10 : 5** and the other to terminal post 5 in **FIG 10 : 3**. If the bulb does not light there is a break in the field coil windings. This is not a complete test as it is still possible for a coil to be earthed. Check this by removing the lead from the tapping **B** and holding it on a clean metal surface of the yoke or body. If the bulb lights it shows that the field coils are earthed.

The only cure for faulty field coils is to consult a Service Station.

Examining the armature:

The armature shaft may be bent due to the starter being operated while the engine is running. **Do not try to straighten a bent shaft or machine the armature core to obtain clearance.**

The starter may run at very high speeds if it is engaged while the engine is running and this may cause the copper wires to lift from the commutator. This could be a reason for failure.

Starter bearings:

Bearing bushes 7 are of porous bronze and must not be reamed after fitting. Withdraw worn bushes by screwing a tap into them and pulling on the tap. New bushes must be immersed in 20W engine oil for 24 hours before fitting. Press them into place using a shouldered mandrel which has a polished spigot the length of the bearing and the diameter of the starter shaft. When this is withdrawn after fitting, the bore of the bush should be correct in size.

The pinion drive:

Refer to parts 12 to 18 in **FIG 10 : 3**. The chief sources of trouble are likely to be dirt, broken springs or a worn sleeve.

To dismantle the drive compress spring 16 and remove circlip 18. Pull off the parts and unscrew sleeve 14 from assembly 12. Check for worn, cracked or broken springs. If the screwed sleeve is worn or damaged it is necessary to renew both the sleeve and the pinion assembly.

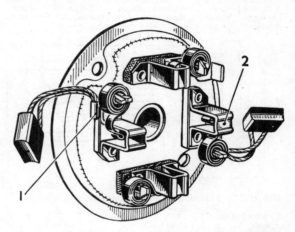

FIG 10 : 4   Commutator end bracket of starter motor showing terminal socket 1 and brush holder 2

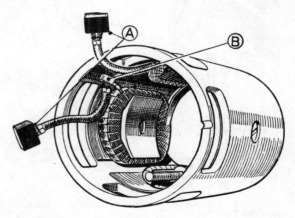

FIG 10 : 5   Brushes A and connection to field coils B on starter motor yoke

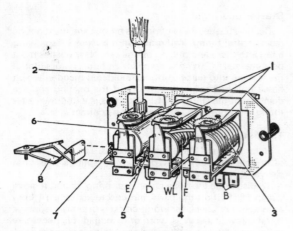

FIG 10:6 The control box RB.340

Key to Fig 10:6   1 Adjustment cams   2 Setting tool
3 Cut-out relay   4 Current regulator   5 Current regulator
contacts   6 Voltage regulator   7 Voltage regulator contacts
8 Clip

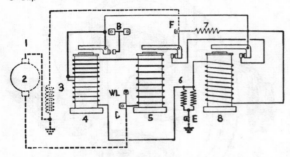

FIG 10:7 Control box charging circuit

Key to Fig 10:7   1 Generator   2 Armature
3 Field   4 Cut-out relay   5 Current regulator
6 Swamp resistor   7 Field resistor   8 Voltage regulator

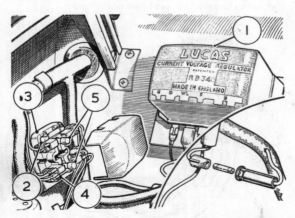

**FIG 10:8 Control box and fuses. Inset shows the pilot
and tail light fuse**

Key to Fig 10:8   1 Cover   2 AUX fuse (35 amp)
3 Fuse block   4 AUX.IGN fuse (35 amp)   5 Spare fuses

After cleaning, reassemble the drive. Do not use lubricant on the screwed sleeve or the pinion assembly, as this causes dirt to adhere to the running surfaces and this is often the cause of a sticking drive.

Reassembling and refitting the starter:

In both cases this is a simple reversal of the dismantling procedure.

10:5 The control box

Description:

This is the Lucas RB.340 box which has three units, a cut-out 3 in **FIG 10:6,** a current regulator 4 and a voltage regulator 6. Vibrating armatures and contacts are the control mechanisms. Adjustment is effected through cams 1, using a Special Tool. Normally the works settings will be perfectly satisfactory and the cover should not be removed unnecessarily.

Checking charging circuit:

If there is trouble with the charging circuit do not disturb the control box until the following simple tests have been made:
1 Check that the driving belt is not slipping.
2 Check the battery by substitution, or use an hydrometer. A heavy-discharge tester can be used to see how the battery stands up to demand.
3 Check the generator by substitution or by testing with a voltmeter. Disconnect the cables from the generator and join terminals **D** and **F** together with wire. Connect the voltmeter between this link and earth. Run the generator up to about 1000 rev/min when a steadily rising voltage should be indicated.
4 Check all wiring between the generator, the control box and the ammeter for continuity and all connections for security.
5 Check all earth connections particularly that of the control box and the battery.
6 Make certain that the low state of a battery is not just due to under-charging from running the car for low mileages only.

If the tests indicate that the control box may be at fault, the following tests and adjustments may be tried:

Adjusting voltage regulator:

All adjustments must be completed as rapidly as possible to avoid errors due to heating up of the operating coil.
1 Refer to the wiring diagram in **FIG 10:7** for connections and **FIG 10:6** for a view of the control box. Withdraw the cables from terminal blades **B.** So that the engine can be started, join together the ignition and battery feeds with a suitable lead.
2 Connect a first-grade 0-20 moving coil voltmeter between control box terminal **D** and a good earth. A good way to do this is to withdraw the ignition warning light feed from control box terminal **WL** and to clip the voltmeter lead of correct polarity to the small blade thus exposed, as this is electrically common with terminal **D.**
3 Start up and run the generator at 3000 rev/min, at which speed the meter needle should be steady at the following readings, according to the temperature:

Ambient temperature			Voltage reading
10°C or 50°F	..	..	14.9 to 15.5
20°C or 68°F	..	..	14.7 to 15.3
30°C or 86°F	..	..	14.5 to 15.1

An unsteady reading may be due to dirty contacts. Clean them as instructed later. If the reading is steady but outside the limits just given, adjust the regulator as follows:

4 Stop the engine and remove the control box cover. Restart the engine and run the generator up to 3000 rev/min. Using the tool 2 indicated in **FIG 10 : 6** turn the cam until the correct reading is obtained. Turning the tool clockwise will raise the setting and anticlockwise will lower it. Always check by stopping the engine and then restarting and running the generator up to the required speed. When adjustment is completed refit the cover and restore the connections.

Adjusting current regulator:

1 The generator must be made to deliver its maximum output of 22 amps whatever the state of charge of the battery at the time. This is done by making the voltage regulator inoperative by using clip 8 to hold contacts 7 together.

2 Withdraw the cables from terminal blades **B** and connect a high-grade 0-40 moving coil ammeter between these cables and one of the blades **B**. It is important that blade **B** carries only this one connection. All other load connections, including the ignition coil feed must be made to the battery side of the ammeter.

3 Switch on all lights and accessories, start the engine and run the generator up to 4500 rev/min. The meter needle should be steady at a reading of 21 to 23 amps. An unsteady reading may be due to dirty contacts which may be cleaned by following the instructions given later. If the reading is too high or too low, adjust as follows:

4 Using the Special Tool, turn the adjustment cam until the reading is correct. Turn the tool clockwise to raise the setting and anticlockwise to lower it. Stop the engine, restore the connections and fit the cover.

Adjusting the cut-out:

1 First check the cutting-in, making all adjustments as rapidly as possible to avoid errors due to overheating of the coil winding.

2 Connect a high-grade 0-20 moving coil voltmeter between control box terminal **D** and a good earth. A convenient way to do this is to withdraw the ignition warning light feed from control box terminal **WL** and to clip the voltmeter lead of the correct polarity to the small terminal blade thus exposed, as the terminal is electrically common with terminal **D**. Switch on the headlamps to provide a load, start the engine and gradually increase its speed. Voltage should rise steadily and then drop slightly at the moment of contact closure. The cut-in voltage is that which is indicated just before the needle drops back and should lie between 12.7 and 13.3 volts. If the cut-in occurs outside these limits an adjustment must be made as follows:

3 Remove the control box cover. Use the Special Tool and turn the cam until the correct reading is obtained. Turn the tool clockwise to raise the setting or anti-clockwise to lower it. Stop the engine, restore the connections and fit the cover.

4 Check the drop-off adjustment. Withdraw the control box cables from blade **B**. To start the engine it will be necessary to join the ignition and battery feeds together with a suitable lead. Connect a first-grade 0-20 moving coil voltmeter between control box terminal **B** and a good earth. Start the engine and run up to approximately 3000 rev/min.

5 Slowly decelerate and watch the meter needle. When it drops to zero it indicates that the contacts have opened. This should occur between 9.5 and 11 volts. If the drop-off takes place outside these limits, adjust as follows:

6 Stop the engine and remove the control box cover. Adjust by bending the bracket for the fixed contact. A reduction in contact gap will raise the drop-off voltage and increasing the gap will lower it. Check again and readjust if necessary until satisfied. When the contacts 'make' there should be a 'follow through' or blade deflection of .010 to .020 inch. Restore the connections and refit the cover.

Adjustment of air gap settings:

These are accurately set during manufacture and should not need attention. If the original settings have been disturbed, readjust as follows:

Armature-to-bobbin core gap of voltage and current regulators:

1 Disconnect the battery. Using the Special Tool turn the adjustment cam of the regulator which requires adjustment to the point which gives minimum lift to the armature tensioning spring. This is done by turning the tool anticlockwise to the fullest extent.

2 Slacken the contact locknut and unscrew the contact. Insert a .056 inch feeler gauge between the armature and the regulator head as far back as the two rivet heads on the underside of the armature. Keep the gauge in this position and press down squarely on the armature. Screw in the contact until it just touches the armature contact. Tighten the locknut and withdraw the feeler. Repeat the operation on the other regulator.

Note that early regulators having copper shims on the regulator heads need a different setting. Use a .045 inch feeler and take care when inserting it that the copper shim is not damaged.

When all mechanical adjustments are completed, check the electrical settings as described earlier.

Contact 'follow-through' and armature-to-bobbin core gap of cut-out:

1 Press the armature squarely down against the copper separation on the core face. Bend the fixed contact bracket until the 'follow-through' or blade deflection of the moving contact is between .010 and .020 inch.

2 Adjust the armature back stop to give a core gap of .035 to .045 inch.

3 Check the cut-in and drop-off voltage settings as previously described.

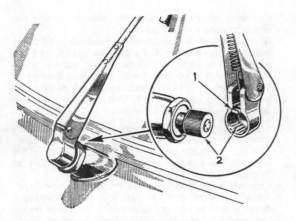

FIG 10:9 Fitting the wiper arm. Inset shows the retaining clip 1 and splined drive 2

Cleaning contact points, current or voltage regulators:

Use a fine carborundum stone or silicon carbide paper and clean off all dust with methylated spirits.

Cleaning contact points, cut-out:

These points are soft and must not be cleaned with carborundum stone or emery paper. Use a strip of fine glasspaper and clean off all dust with methylated spirits.

10:6 Fuses

The location of the fuse unit is shown in **FIG 10:8** where it is seen to be on the righthand wing inside the engine compartment. The moulding carries two 35 amp fuses in spring clips and two spares. The fuse across terminals 1 and 2 protects the circuits such as the horn which operate independently of the ignition switch. The fuse across terminals 3 and 4 protects the circuits such as the fuel gauge, wiper motor and flashers which operate only when the ignition is switched on. The inset to the illustration shows the separate fuse for the pilot and tail lights. This is housed in a cylindrical tube which is part of the wiring loom beneath the battery or facia. To renew this fuse, hold one end of the tube then twist and pull off the other end.

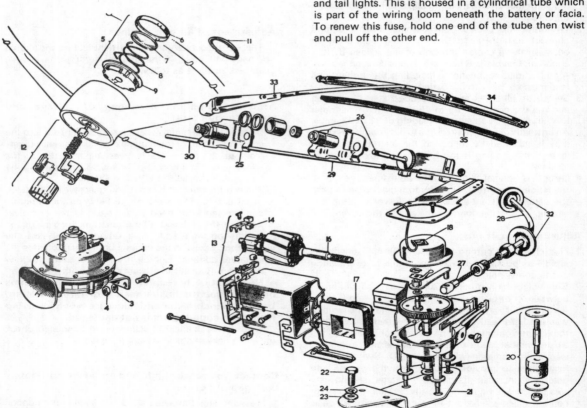

FIG 10:10 Components of the horn and the wiper mechanism

Key to Fig 10:10   1 Horn   2 Screw   3 Washer   4 Nut   5 Horn-push   6 Retaining ring
7 Contact (upper)   8 Motif spring   9 Cover and contact   11 Motif   12 Slip ring and rotor   13 Brush gear
14 Brush   15 Brush spring   16 Armature   17 Field coil   18 Switch   19 Shaft and gear   20 Stud
21 Mounting bracket   22 Bracket screw   23 Plain washer   24 Spring washer   25 Wheelbox
26 Spindle and gear   27 Crosshead and rack   28 Drive casing (motor to box)   29 Drive casing (wheelbox)
30 Drive casing (end)   31 Ferrule   32 Grommet   33 Wiper arm   34 Wiper blade   35 Rubber

10:7 Flasher unit

On Mk I models this is located on the righthand side of the engine compartment and is controlled by a switch on the steering column. Warning lights are provided on the instrument panel on early models, or on the end of the switch lever on later models. The function of the lamp or lamps is to indicate that the flasher is operating and also to show when a bulb has failed. The reduction in bulb current flowing through the coil in the unit reduces the magnetism acting on the secondary armature to prevent closure of the pilot light contacts.

Faulty operation of flashers:

In cases of trouble check the bulbs for broken filaments. Refer to the wiring diagrams in Technical Data and check all flasher circuit cables and connections. Check the appropriate fuse.

Switch on the ignition and check with a voltmeter between flasher unit terminal **B** (or +) and earth to see if battery voltage is present.

Connect together flasher unit terminals **B** (or +) and **L** and operate the direction indicator switch. If the flasher lamps now light, the flasher unit is defective and must be renewed. It is not possible to dismantle and repair faulty flasher units. Before removing, make a note of the connections so that they will be replaced correctly when the new unit is installed.

Before making the connections it is advisable to check the circuits to ensure that the new flasher unit is not damaged by wrong connections. Test by joining together the cables normally connected to the unit and operate the switch. If the connections are wrong the auxiliaries fuse will blow but no damage will be done to the flasher unit.

10:8 Windscreen wipers

General maintenance is confined to changing the blades when they have deteriorated and occasionally lubricating the rubber grommet round the spindle with a few drops of glycerine. The blade arm fixing is shown in **FIG 10:9**. The motor gearbox and the operating cable rack are packed with grease during manufacture and should need no further attention.

Setting the limit switch:

If the limit switch 18 in **FIG 10:10** is incorrectly set it might be possible for the wiper motor to overrun the open-circuit position and continue to draw current. To set the switch, slacken the four cover screws and turn the domed switch cover until the setting pip on top is in line with the central groove in the gearbox cover. To park the blades on the opposite side turn the switch through 180 deg. in one direction only.

Checking current consumption:

Insert a 0-15 amp moving coil meter in the wiper circuit and switch on. Normal running demand should be 2.7 to 3.4 amps.

Wiper motor takes no current:

Check the fuse. the wiring and all connections. If the fuse is intact, check the wiring for breaks and make sure that the wiper switch is operating correctly. If the car is fitted with a current-operated thermostat, check it by connecting an ohmmeter across its terminals in place of the two cables. If a closed circuit is indicated the thermostat is in order and the cables must be refitted. An open circuit shows that the thermostat has operated but has not reset, and the best check for this is by substitution. It is not possible to adjust a faulty thermostat. If the thermostat proves to be in order proceed on the lines suggested for a wiper taking abnormally high current.

Wiper motor takes abnormally low current:

Make sure that the battery is fully charged. Remove the cover at the commutator end and examine the brush gear 13. Clean the commutator with a petrol-moistened cloth. Check that the brushes bear firmly on the commutator. The brush levers should move freely on their pivots. Work them to and fro if they are tight. Also check the tension of the brush lever spring and renew it if faulty. The best check for a faulty armature is by substitution.

Wiper motor takes abnormally high current:

Excessive friction may account for this. When cold the motor will stall at 14 amps and at 8 amps when hot.

If no wiper blade is stuck, check the motor gearbox. Remove the cover and check the end float of the armature shaft 16. The adjusting screw should be set so that end float is between .008 and .012 inch.

Sluggish action with high current consumption may be due to excessive friction in the tubes carrying the inner rack 27. There is a Lucas Special Tool to check this, consisting of a cable which is .010 inch larger in diameter than the working rack. This will show whether the outer tube or casing is kinked or has curves which are too sharp.

Another cause of excessive friction might be the alignment of the wheelboxes 25. Removal of these is covered under a separate heading later.

Removing and refitting the motor:

Remove the wiper arms, and the electrical connections to the motor. Take off the gearbox cover and separate the outer casing 28 from the gearbox housing. Release the motor from the wing valance, drawing the rack 27 out of its casing. When refitting, it may be necessary to twist the rack to engage it with the worm wheels 26. If a replacement motor is being fitted, remove the gearbox cover and check that the final drive gear is stamped '150' which indicates the correct area of blade wipe.

Removing wheelboxes:

Remove the motor and gearbox, the facia panel as described in **Chapter 11**, and then the lefthand demister duct. Remove the nut, front bush and washer from the outside round the blade spindle, and lift the wheelboxes away from under the top panel as an assembly complete with rear bushes, spindle tubes and outer rack casings.

Refitting wheelboxes:

Reverse the removal sequence but take care that the wheelboxes are correctly aligned. Twist the cable rack

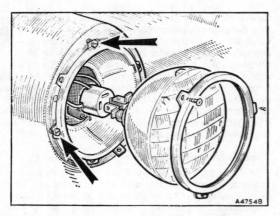

FIG 10:11   Sealed beam light unit showing adjustment screws

if necessary to ensure that it meshes correctly with the worm wheels 26.

Dismantling the wiper motor and gearbox:

Remove the gearbox cover and then the end cover by unscrewing the through-bolts. Lift off cover 13. The brush gear can be taken off as a unit but mark it to ensure that the brushes are correctly replaced. Check the condition of the commutator and make sure that no particles of carbon are short-circuiting the segments. Check the insulation and continuity of the internal wiring and look for the charring which shows overheating.

To dismantle the gearing remove the circlip and washer from the link pin and lift off the link and inner cable rack. From under the gearbox remove the circlip and washer from the final gear shaft. Remove burrs from the shaft and lift out the gear. The armature and worm drive 16 can now be withdrawn. Examine the gears for wear and renew if necessary.

Reassembling the wiper motor and gearbox:

Reverse the dismantling procedure. Lubricate the following points:

Armature bearings with SAE.20 engine oil, immersing the bearings for 24 hours before reassembly.
Armature shaft at the commutator end with a very little SAE.20 engine oil.
Felt lubricator in gearbox, apply SAE.20 engine oil.
Final gear bearings, crosshead and guide channel, connecting link, link pin and gears with grease.

Fitting a wiper arm:

Refer to **FIG 10:9** and set the spindles in the parked position by switching on the ignition and turning the wiper control on and then off. Press the heads onto the spindle splines at the correct parking angle until the retaining clip snaps over the end of the splines. Operate the wipers to check that they park correctly. Adjustment can be made by removing the heads and trying another position. Moving round one spline makes a difference in angle of 5 deg.

10:9 The headlamps

The sealed-beam headlamp is illustrated in **FIG 10:11**. The light unit is serviced only as an assembly.

To remove a unit remove the retaining screw at the bottom of the rim and lift the rim away. Take out the inner rim securing screws shown, pull the unit forward, disconnect the three-pin socket from the back and the unit will be free.

When refitting the unit ensure that the registers moulded on the rear edge of it engage in the slots in the back shell. Fit the rear edge of the rim first, pressing it over the two raised sections of the back shell. Press it downwards and inwards and replace the retaining screw.

Beam setting:

Accurate setting is best left to a Service Station equipped with the necessary devices. The main beams must be set parallel to the road surface or in accordance with local regulations. Adjustment is made by turning the top screw indicated in **FIG 10:11** for vertical setting. For horizontal setting, turn the lower screw.

10:10 Panel and warning lights

When removing the instrument panel disconnect the battery positive terminal. Gain access to the bulbs as follows:

On Morris cars, remove the instrument cowling (four Phillips screws). Release the combined instrument panel (three Phillips screws). Pull the panel forward to reach the bulb holders.

On Wolseley, Riley and MG cars, remove the access hole cover from inside the glovebox. From the rear of the ashtray remove the nut and bracket. Remove the ignition key escutcheon and disconnect the choke control. Remove the direction indicator switch and cowling and let the switch hang on its lead. Disconnect the steering column support bracket from the facia and pull the instrument panel forward to reach the bulb holders.

Austin and MG Sedan: From under the facia, withdraw the push-in bulb holders from the rear of the instrument panel.

On the 'Princess', remove the bezels and push out the ignition/starter and wiper/wash switches. Remove the wingnut just below the ball-mounted air duct on the driver's side. Remove the glovebox and lid. Remove the wingnut from the centre of the facia and the one just below and behind the ball-mounted air duct on the passenger's side.

Disconnect the steering column-to-body-crossmember steady bracket and lower the column. Pull the facia board forward at the bottom and lift it away from the facia surround. The bulb holders can then be pulled out from behind the instrument panel.

Refitting is a reversal of dismantling on all models.

10:11 The horn

Before removing an apparently faulty horn check the wiring and connections. Check that the mounting bolts are tight and that the horn does not foul any adjacent part.

The horn cannot normally be dismantled. **It is essential not to disturb the slotted centre core and locknut.**

There is a serrated adjustment screw provided. Turn

this anticlockwise until the horn just fails to sound when the horn-push is depressed. It is wise to remove fuse 1 to 2 and replace it with a link of wire to avoid constant blowing of the fuse. Do not keep the finger on the push too long. Now turn the adjustment screw back about a quarter of a turn.

When two horns are fitted, disconnect one while adjusting the other. Keep the disconnected leads from contacting any earthed metal parts.

The horn-push is readily levered out of the steering wheel with a screwdriver (see **FIG 10 : 10**).

10 : 12 Fuel and temperature gauges

The circuit of the bi-metal resistance instrumentation is given in **FIG 10 : 12**. The fuel and coolant transmitters are wired to indicating heads and to a common voltage stabilizer which ensures a steady supply of 10 volts to the equipment.

Faulty action:

When checking for continuity between terminals with the wiring disconnected, do not shortcircuit a gauge to earth.

Checking battery voltage:

Connect a voltmeter to control box terminal **B** and earth. Meter should read 12 volts with engine not running. With engine running at 1000 rev/min and the ignition warning light out the reading should be 12 to 13 volts approximately.

Checking wiring:

Check for continuity between each unit and check for a leak to earth. Check for shortcircuits in the wiring to each transmitter. Check that the voltage stabilizer and transmitters are earthed.

Voltage stabilizer:

Disconnect the lead from the stabilizer to the gauge, at the gauge, and connect it to the 'I' terminal of a Smiths Automotive Instrument Tester. The earth terminal of the Tester must be connected to the chassis. After two minutes with the ignition switched on, the reading should be 10 volts. If the voltage stabilizer is removed, replace it with terminals **B** and **E** uppermost and see that it is not more than 20 deg. from the vertical. Substitute a faulty stabilizer with a new one.

Transmitters:

Check for continuity between the terminal and the case with the lead disconnected. Substitute a faulty transmitter with a new one.

10 : 13 Impulse tachometer

This equipment consists of an indicator head and a pulse lead. The circuit is given in **FiG 10 : 13**. The pulse lead is connected in series between the ignition switch and the ignition coil, transmitting voltage impulses to the indicator head.

To check for faults, try the wiring for continuity and test the connections to the indicator head. The pulse lead should form a symmetrical loop as shown inset in

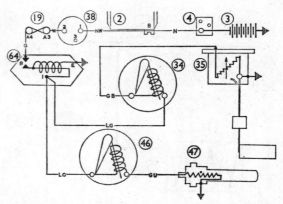

FIG 10 : 12 The bi-metal resistance instrumentation circuit

Key to Fig 10 : 12 2 Control box   3 Battery (12 volt)
4 Starter solenoid   19 Fuse (A3–A4)   34 Fuel gauge
35 Fuel tank unit   38 Ignition switch   46 Coolant
temperature gauge   47 Coolant temperature transmitter
64 Voltage stabilizer

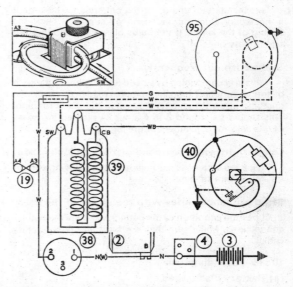

FIG 10 : 13 Circuit of impulse tachometer. Inset shows symmetrical appearance of pulse lead

Key to Fig 10 : 13   2 Control box   3 Battery (12 volt)
4 Starter solenoid   19 Fuse (A3–A4)   38 Ignition switch
39 Ignition coil   40 Distributor   95 Tachometer

FIG 10 : 13, and should not be tight against the plastic forms.

10 : 14 Electrically heated backlight

The circuit is shown in **FIG 10 : 14**. To remove the backlight refer to **Chapter 11**.

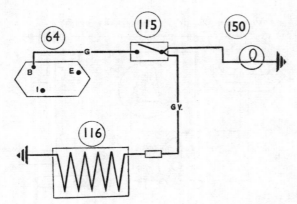

FIG 10:14   Circuit for heated backlight

Key to Fig 10:14   64 Instrument voltage stabilizer
115 Switch   116 Heated backlight   150 Warning light
(if fitted)

10:15 Lighting circuits

Lamps give insufficient light:

Test the state of charge of the battery and recharge it if necessary from an independent supply. Check the setting of the lamps. If the bulbs have darkened through age fit new ones.

Bulbs burn out frequently:

If this is accompanied by a need for frequent topping up of the battery and high hydrometer readings, check the charging rate with an ammeter when the car is running. This should be around 3 to 4 amps. A reading in excess of this calls for adjustment of the regulator.

Lamps light when switched on but gradually fade:

Check the battery as it is incapable of supplying current for any length of time.

Lamp brilliance varies with the speed of the car:

Check the condition of the battery. Examine the battery connections. Make sure they are tight and renew faulty cables.

10:16 Fault diagnosis

(a) Battery discharged

1 Terminal connections loose or dirty
2 Shorts in lighting circuit
3 Generator not charging
4 Regulator or cut-out units not working properly
5 Battery internally defective

(b) Insufficient charging current

1 Check 1 in (a)
2 Driving belt slipping

(c) Battery will not hold charge

1 Low electrolyte level
2 Battery plates sulphated
3 Electrolyte leakage from cracked case or top sealing compound
4 Plate separators defective

(d) Battery overcharged

1 Regulators need adjusting

(e) Generator output low or nil

1 Belt broken or slipping
2 Regulator unit out of adjustment
3 Worn bearings, loose pole pieces
4 Commutator worn, burned or shorted
5 Armature shaft bent or worn
6 Insulation proud between commutator segments
7 Brushes sticking, springs weak or broken
8 Field coil windings broken, shorted or burned

(f) Starter motor lacks power or will not operate

1 Battery discharged, loose cable connections
2 Starter pinion jammed in flywheel gear
3 Starter switch faulty
4 Brushes worn or sticking, leads detached or shorting
5 Commutator dirty or worn
6 Starter shaft bent
7 Engine abnormally stiff, perhaps due to rebore

(g) Starter motor runs but does not turn engine

1 Pinion sticking on screwed sleeve
2 Broken teeth on pinion or flywheel gears

(h) Noisy starter pinion when engine is running

1 Restraining spring weak or broken

(j) Starter motor inoperative

1 Check 1 and 4 in (f)
2 Armature or field coils faulty

(k) Starter motor rough or noisy

1 Mounting bolts loose
2 Damaged pinion or flywheel gear teeth
3 Main pinion spring broken

(l) Lamps inoperative or erratic

1 Battery low, bulbs burned out
2 Faulty earthing of lamps or battery
3 Lighting switch faulty, loose or broken connections

(m) Wiper motor sluggish, taking high current

1 Faulty armature
2 Bearings out of alignment
3 Commutator dirty or shortcircuited
4 Wheelbox spindle binding, cable rack tight in outer casing
5 Lack of lubrication
6 No end float to armature spindle

(n) Wiper motor runs but does not drive arms

1 Wheelbox gear and spindle worn
2 Cable rack faulty
3 Gearbox components worn

(o) Fuel or temperature gauges do not work

1 Check wiring for continuity

2 Voltage stabilizer faulty
3 **Check** instruments and transmitters for continuity

(p) Faulty impulse type tachometer

1 **Check** wiring and connections to indicator head
2 Pulse lead incorrectly fitted

CHAPTER 11

BODYWORK

11 : 1 Bodywork finish

Large-scale repairs to body panels are best left to expert panel beaters. Even small dents can be tricky, as too much hammering will stretch the metal and make things worse instead of better. Filling minor dents and scratches is probably the best method of restoring the surface. The touching-up of paintwork is well within the powers of most car owners, particularly as self-spraying cans of paint in the correct colours are now readily available. It must be remembered, however, that paint changes colour with age and it is better to spray a whole wing rather than try to touch-up a small area.

Before spraying it is essential to remove all traces of wax polish with white sprit. More drastic treatment is required if silicone polishes have been applied. Use a primer surfacer or paste stopper according to the amount of filling required, and when it is dry, rub it down with 400 grade 'Wet or Dry' paper until the surface is smooth and flush with the surrounding area. Spend time on getting the best finish as this will control the final effect. Apply the retouching paint, keeping it wet in the centre and light and dry round the edges.

After a few hours of drying, use a cutting compound to remove the dry spray and finish with liquid polish.

11 : 2 Fitting seat belts

It is dangerous to tackle this job in a slipshod way. If an owner feels that his skill and equipment may not enable him to make a safe installation of the belts, he is strongly advised to give the work to an Authorized Dealer.

Fitting to centre pillar:

Refer to **FIG 11 : 1** and locate the top fixing hole. It may be behind the trim or there may be a snap button concealing it. Cut a hole in the trim to coincide with the hole in the pillar. On Vanden Plas models make sure that the hole in the hardboard liner also coincides with the hole in the pillar.

Take one of the $\frac{7}{16}$ inch bolts and place on it the bracket, a waved washer and a shouldered distance piece the smaller diameter of which will slot into the bracket, see inset 1. Screw the assembly to the pillar, making sure that no fabric interferes with the metal-to-metal contact between the distance piece and the pillar.

Sill fixing for static belts:

Refer to inset 2. Locate the fixing hole and cut the carpet so that there will be metal-to-metal contact between the distance piece and the sill. Take a $\frac{7}{16}$ inch bolt and fit to it the bracket, a waved washer and the shouldered distance piece so that the small diameter will slot into the bracket. Screw the assembly to the hole in the sill.

Sill fixing for automatic belts:

Locate the fixing point and cut the covering immediately over the hole. Refer to inset 4 and fit over the $\frac{7}{16}$ inch bolt the belt bracket, a waved washer, the shouldered distance piece so that its smaller diameter will slot into the bracket, the reel fixing bracket and the distance piece. Screw the assembly into the hole in the sill. Drill holes in the sill through the $\frac{3}{16}$ inch holes in the bracket and screw in the self-tapping screws.

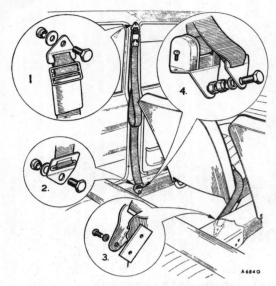

FIG 11 : 1   Seat belt attachments to pillar 1, to sill 2 (static belt), to tunnel 3 and to sill 4 (automatic belt)

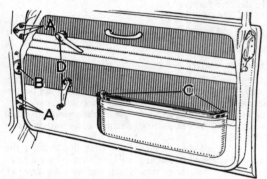

FIG 11 : 2   The door assembly

Key to Fig 11 : 2   **A** Hinge screws   **B** Check link
C Door map pocket screws   **D** Door handle and window regulator screws

Secure the reel to the bracket so that the belt will unwind on the pillar side. The base of the reel must be mounted in a horizontal position to ensure that it works properly.

Tunnel fixing:

Lift the carpet and remove the two plugs in the side of the tunnel nearest to the seat being fitted, inset 3. Position the tapping plate under the floor panel, making sure no pipelines are trapped by it. Under the carpet and felt, secure the bracket of the short belt to the plate with the screws and lockwashers provided. Cut a slit in the carpet and the felt to allow the belt to pass through, locating the slit by buckling the belt in the wearing position.

Testing automatic belts

The reel will only lock under conditions of sharp deceleration or when inclined at an angle of 45 deg. After installation, check that the reel will lock when the car is subjected to hard braking or sharp cornering.

To unlock the reel, apply slight forward body pressure against the belt and then release by a rearward movement of the body. **The reel end covers must not be removed at any time.**

11 : 3 Removing door trim pad

Austin, Morris, Wolseley, Riley and MG:

Refer to **FIG 11 : 2** and remove the window regulator handle, door pull (or armrest), and the inner door handle.
Remove the map pocket screws and lever the trim pad away with a screwdriver.

Princess:

Remove the door lock and window regulator handles and the drive screws securing the chrome door pull to the armrest. Remove the woodscrews securing the armrest to the map pocket and then remove the pocket. Remove the drive screws securing the trim panel and lever it away from the door. If required, remove the drive screws and lift off the wooden door finishers.
On all models, refitting is the reverse of removal.

11 : 4 Servicing door fittings

Hinges, except Traveller:

Mark the position of the hinges on the door pillar for easier refitting. Remove the splitpin, washer and clevis pin from the check link. Support the door and remove the setscrews securing the hinges to the door pillar.

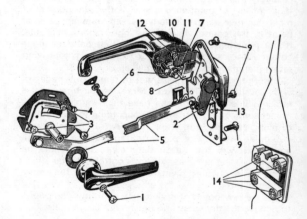

FIG 11 : 3   Door lock and striker mechanism

Key to Fig 11 : 3   1 Inner door handle retaining screw
2 Lock operating lever   3 Remote control to door retaining screws   4 Self-tapping screw   5 Connecting link
6 Outer door handle retaining screws   7 Key operating arm
8 Lock frame   9 Lock to door retaining screws
10 Push-button plunger bolt   11 Lock contactor   12 Locknut
13 Children's safety catch   14 Striker to door pillar retaining screws

Hinges, Traveller and Countryman rear doors:

Support the door and remove the locknut and bolt from each of the two door brackets. Remove the three captive screws from each of the two hinge plates in the drain channel and lift the door away.

Door locks, two-door and four-door models:

The mechanism is illustrated in **FIG 11 : 3. Before removing any part of the door lock mechanism because of faulty operation, make sure that the trouble is not caused by incorrect installation.**

To remove, take off the inner door handle, the door pull and the window regulator handle. Remove the door trim pad assembly as in **Section 11 : 3.** Remove the remote control link 5 from lever 2 by taking off the spring clip and wavy washer. Remove setscrews 9 and pull the lock away from the door panel. Refit in the reverse order.

If it is necessary to remove the striker, mark its position first and then remove screws 14.

To remove the outer door handle take out screws 6. The push button assembly is contained in the outer handle.

Rear door locks, Countryman and Traveller:

To remove the lock and remote control, remove the six metal thread screws with flat and spring washers from the lock, remote control and link bar. Lift the lock and remote control from the panel. Reverse the instructions when refitting.

To remove the outer door handle, remove the trim pad by levering the fixing clips away from the interior panel. Remove the two 2BA nuts with flat and spring washers from the outer handle studs and lift off the handle.

Window glass regulators; four-door models

To remove the regulator refer to **FIG 11 : 4.** Remove the interior handles, fittings and trim pad. Remove the seven screws **B.** Release the regulator arc **E** from the bottom of the glass, lift up the glass to clear the regulator and remove the regulator and bracket assembly. Refit in the reverse order.

Window glass and regulator; two-door models:

Remove the inner handles, the door pull or armrest, the trim pad and liner. Remove screws and withdraw the door glass stop, then lower the glass to the bottom of the door.

Lever off the outer weatherstrip and the inner door waist rail. Remove ventilator screw, the screw on the top edge of the door and lift out the fixed quarter-light assembly. Centre the bottom control channel, then twist the glass forwards and upwards to remove it.

Remove the ten screws which secure the window winder mechanism and withdraw it. Reverse the instructions when refitting.

11 : 5 Removing door glass
On four-door models:

Remove the interior handles, the door pull or armrest and the trim pad by following the instructions in

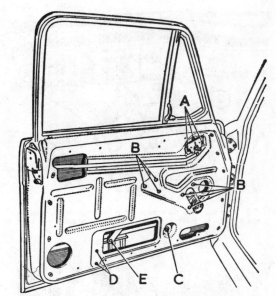

FIG 11 : 4   Door with trim pad removed

Key to Fig 11 : 4   **A** Door lock remote control
B Window regulator and bracket screws   **C** Ventilator screw
D Door stop screws   **E** Door glass regulator arc

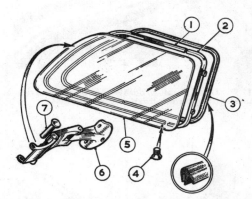

FIG 11 : 5   Rear quarter light components

Key to Fig 11 : 5   1 Frame assembly (rear righthand)
2 Frame assembly (front righthand)   3 Glazing rubber
4 Screw   5 Glass   6 Catch assembly   7 Rivet

Section 11 : 3. Lever off the waist finisher strips and release the glass channel attached to the regulator assembly (see **FIG 11 : 4**). Remove the glass stop (screws **D**) and lower the glass to the bottom of the door. Remove the regulator arc from the glass regulator channel at **E.** Remove the top and vertical felt channels. Release the ventilator securing screws and remove the assembly. Withdraw the door glass assembly up through the top of the door panel. Refit in the reverse order.

FIG 11 : 6 Luggage compartment lock showing notched locking ring 1, fixing screws 2 and connecting link 3

FIG 11 : 7 Using Service Tool 18G.468 to ease the rubber channel lip over a windscreen or backlight glass

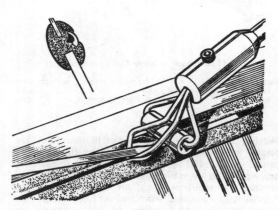

FIG 11 : 8 Threading the locking filler strip into the rubber channel with the glazing tool and eye. Inset section is through the channel and filler strip

On two-door models:

Refer to the instructions at the end of **Section 11 : 4**.

Removing ventilators:

Follow the preceding instructions to the point where the window assembly has been released. Do not remove the window, but lift out the ventilator assembly.

11 : 6 Removing rear side windows

On the Countryman and Traveller:

Unscrew and remove the two window catches. Remove the two closing clips and detach the inner and outer finishers. Remove the eight inner finisher retaining clips.

Drill out the five rivets holding the glass channel retainer to the body. Remove the assembly by levering the glass channel retainer up and out from the bottom.

To remove the glass from the assembly, carefully flex the spring steel channel retainer and lift it out. When replacing the windows use Glasticon Dum-Dum Putty, Part No. 97H.2727 as a sealer in the body aperture. When sealing between the glass channel retainer and the body, take care not to seal over the water outlets.

On the two-door saloon:

Refer to **FIG 11 : 5**. Remove the screws securing catch 6 to the body and swing the window open slightly. Grip the top and bottom firmly and pull the glass and frame out of the glazing rubber. Refit in the reverse manner.

11 : 7 Luggage compartment lock

Do not close the lid while the lock mechanism is being removed or refitted. Refer to **FIG 11 : 6**.

To remove the lock, remove the notched locking ring 1 and withdraw the push button assembly. Unhook connecting link 3, remove screws 2 and withdraw the catch assembly. Reverse the instructions when refitting.

11 : 8 Fitting windscreen glass

To remove the original glass, lift the wiper arms clear. The filler strip locks in a groove in the front face of the rubber surround and can be seen in the Section in **FIG 11 : 8**. Prise up the end of this strip and carefully pull it out of the channel in the rubber. Wearing gloves as protection, press the glass from inside the car, starting at a corner and easing the rubber surround from the metal flange of the body.

To fit a new glass when the original one has been broken, it is first essential to remove all particles of glass which remain in the rubber channel. It is also possible for tiny particles of glass to fall into the demister ducts and tubes and these will be discharged into the driver's or passenger's face when the blower motor is switched on. **It is most important to disconnect the demister ducts and tubing from the heater box and blow out all particles of glass before the new windscreen is fitted.**

The following instructions will apply to fitting either a new windscreen or a backlight glass. Note that the rubber on the backlight of a Countryman or Traveller is sealed and must always be renewed.

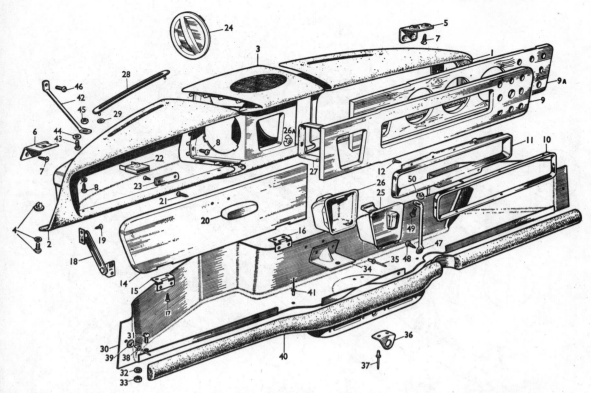

FIG 11:9   Facia panel components for MG, Riley and Wolseley models

Key to Fig 11:9   1 Facia panel assembly (righthand)   2 Facia panel assembly (lefthand)
3 Facia panel assembly (centre)   4 Screw, washer, nylon nut   5 Bracket   6 Bracket   7 Screw   8 Screw
9 Instrument panel assembly (Wolseley, MG)   9A Instrument panel assembly (Riley)   10 Instrument panel finisher (Wolseley, MG)
11 Instrument bezel (Wolseley, MG)   12 Screw (Wolseley, MG)   14 Glovebox lid assembly   15 Outer hinge
16 Inner hinge   17 Screw   18 Glovebox lid support   19 Screw   20 Handle   21 Screw
22 Magnetic lock   23 Magnetic lock keeper   24 Plug   25 Ashtray assembly   26 Ashtray case assembly
26A Wing nut   27 Ashtray retaining strap   28 Demister slot finisher   29 Push-on fix   30 Facia tray
31 Screw   32 Washer   33 Nut   34 Bracket   35 Rivet   36 Bracket   37 Rivet   38 Rivet
39 Washer   40 Support rail   41 Rivet   42 Stay   43 Screw   44 Plain washer   45 Nut
46 Screw   47 Stay   48 Screw   49 Screw   50 Nylon nut

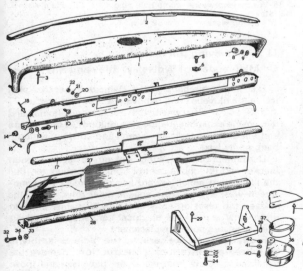

FIG 11:10   Facia panel components for Austin models

Key to Fig 11:10 1 Top facia panel 2 Panel retaining channel
3 Rivet   4 Lower facia panel   5 Screw   6 Nut
7 Nut   8 Spring washer   9 Plain washer   10 Screw
11 Screw   12 Plain washer   13 Spring washer   14 Nut
15 Finisher   16 Rivet   17 Crash rail (lower facia panel)
18 Rivet   19 Radio aperture mask   20 Plain washer
21 Spring washer   22 Nut   23 Steering column bracket
24 Screw   25 Plain washer   26 Spring washer
27 Parcel shelf   28 Crash pad (parcel shelf)   29 Rivet
30 Ashtray frame shield   31 Rivet   32 Screw
33 Plain washer   34 Spring washer   35 Screw
36 Ashtray   37 Ashtray case   38 Spring clip
39 Distance piece   40 Screw   41 Plain washer
42 Curved washer

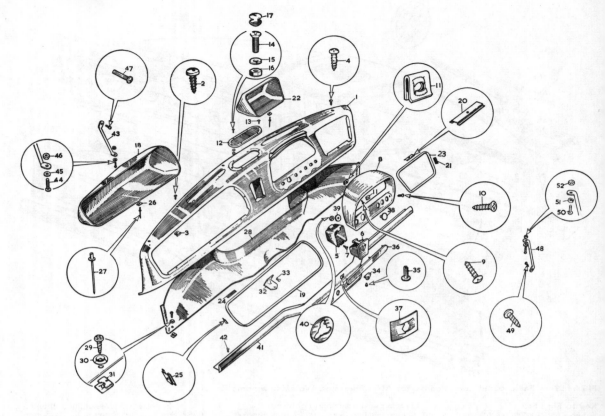

FIG 11 : 11   Facia panel components for Morris models

Key to Fig 11 : 11   1 Facia panel assembly   2 Screw   3 Nut   4 Screw   5 Ashtray case
6 Ashtray   7 Screw   8 Instrument cowl   9 Screw   10 Screw   11 Nut   12 Speaker fret
13 Screw   14 Screw   15 Spring washer   16 Nut   17 Cap (screw)   18 Facia pocket
19 Facia pocket finisher   20 Finisher strip (long)   21 Finisher strip (short)   22 Glovebox   23 Glovebox finisher
24 Finisher strip (long)   25 Finisher strip (short)   26 Clip   27 Rivet   28 Facia tray   29 Screw
30 Cup washer   31 Nut   32 Support bracket   33 Rivet   34 Bulb holder bracket   35 Rivet
36 Heater control blanking escutcheon   37 Push-on fix   38 Windscreen washer pump hole plug   39 Plain washer
40 Push-on fix   41 Facia support rail   42 Rivet   43 Stay   44 Screw   45 Plain washer   46 Nut
47 Screw   48 Stay   49 Screw   50 Screw   51 Spring washer   52 Nut

Fit the surround rubber to the body aperture flange
and lubricate the channel for the glass with a soap-and-
water solution. Fit the glass into the lower channel and
start at one corner to lift the lip of the rubber over the glass,
using the short peg on the handle of Service Tool
18G.468 for this purpose as shown in **FIG 11 : 7**.

Refer to **FIG 11 : 8** for the method of fitting the locking
filler strip. First apply a soap-and-water solution to the
channel. Use Service Tool 18G.468 with adaptor 468A
and thread the end of the filler strip through the eye of
the adaptor and under the roller. Lie the filler strip over the
groove in the rubber, insert the eye of the tool in the
groove, and holding the filler strip in place, push the tool
along the groove to roll the strip into position. Slight
side-to-side action will help when rounding corners.

When the circuit is completed, cut off any surplus strip
to make a neat butt joint on the centre line of the glass.
Make sure to fit the filler strip with its thicker section
facing the glass, see inset in the illustration.

11 : 9 Removing the facia

On Mk I models of Wolseley, Riley and MG :

Disconnect the battery lead. Remove the access plug
inside the glovebox and remove nut 26A, and bracket 27
in **FIG 11 : 9**. Disconnect the ashtray bulb holder and
remove the assembly. Remove the ignition key escutcheon
and the direction indicator switch and cowling, letting it
hang on its lead.

Disconnect the steering column-to-facia support
bracket and the choke control from the carburetter. Pull
the instrument panel forward and disconnect the windscreen washer pipes, the speedometer drive cable, the
mileage trip reset on early cars, the oil gauge pipe on
Rileys only and all the electrical connections, marking
them to ensure correct replacement.

**From now on take care, as the facia assembly is
of Fibreglass interlock construction.** Remove the
panel fixing screw from inside the glovebox and those

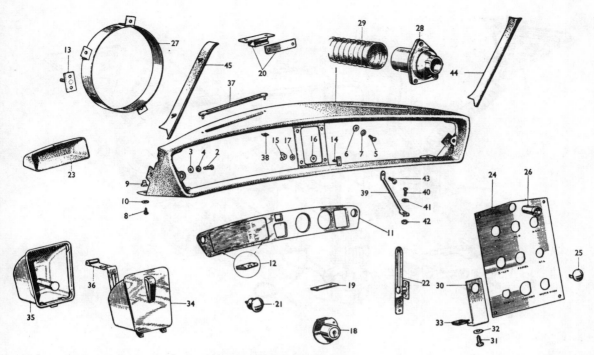

FIG 11:12   Facia panel components for Vanden Plas Princess models

Key to Fig 11:12   **1** Facia surround   **2** Screw   **3** Plain washer   **4** Shakeproof washer   **5** Screw
6 Plain washer   **7** Shakeproof washer   **8** Screw   **9** Nut   **10** Plain washer   **11** Facia board
12 Hinge   **13** Stud and plate   **14** Stud and plate   **15** Wingnut   **16** Plain washer   **17** Spring washer
18 Lock   **19** Lock striker plate   **20** Magnetic catch   **21** Knob   **22** Quadrant   **23** Box
24 Switch panel   **25** Blanking plug   **26** Panel illumination light casing   **27** Instrument surround
28 Fresh-air louvre   **29** Fresh-air hose   **30** Mixture control bracket   **31** Screw   **32** Plain washer
33 Nut   **34** Ashtray   **35** Ashtray case   **36** Ashtray clip and tray   **37** Demister finisher slot
38 Push-on fix   **39** Facia support stay   **40** Screw   **41** Plain washer   **42** Nut   **43** Screw
44 Finisher A post (righthand)   **45** Finisher A post (lefthand)

screws located beneath the box. Lift away the glove box. Remove the fixing screws from above and below the centre section and lift away the assembly.

On Austin and MG Sedan:

Refer to **FIG 11:10** which shows the top padded panel 1 and the lower panel 4 which carries the instruments and controls. These panels must be removed and refitted separately.

Disconnect the battery, and the choke control cable from the carburetter. On early models the panels are joined by nuts on studs at each end and by countersunk screws where the panels meet. On later models there are four drive screws with hinged metal caps on their heads. Remove the fixings and lift off the top panel.

Remove the locking rings from the ignition switch and the windscreen washer control. Undo the hexagon locknuts and release the light switches and wiper switch. Disconnect the speedometer cable and all electrical connections to the instruments after marking them for correct replacement. Pull out the warning and panel lamp bulb holders.

On early models remove the six lower screws and lift out the panel, manoeuvring it from the passenger's side.

Ensure that the back of the instrument casing clears the mounting bracket for the steering column.

On later models remove the two drive screws on the windscreen scuttle and four screws from beneath the facia. Release the steering column bracket and lift out the panel assembly.

On Morris cars:

Refer to **FIG 11:11**. Disconnect the battery. Remove the bolt from the clamp at the lower end of the steering column and the setscrews from the column bracket under the facia.

Disconnect the flashing indicator and horn connections under the parcel shelf and remove the column assembly. Remove instrument cowling 8 and disconnect the instrument panel. Remove the combined instrument panel assembly and the facia securing screws on the facia surround. Pull the facia forward, disconnect the demister ducts and remove the facia panel assembly.

On Princess cars:

Refer to **FIG 11:12**. Disconnect the battery, and the mixture control cable. Inside the car, remove the bezels

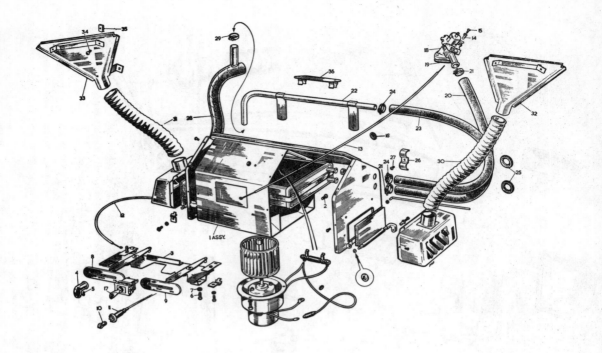

FIG 11:13   Layout of heater components

Key to Fig 11:13   1 Heater unit assembly   2 Screw   3 Heater and demister control   4 Control lever knob
5 Screw   6 Screw   7 Shakeproof washer   8 Air control escutcheon   9 Temperature control escutcheon
10 Bulb   11 Bulb holder   12 Air flap control cable   13 Water valve control cable   14 Cable trunnion
15 Screw   16 Grommet   17 Heater switch   18 Water valve   19 Joint washer   20 Hose
21 Hose clip   22 Pipe assembly   23 Hose   24 Hose clip   25 Grommet   26 Hose clip   27 Screw
28 Hose   29 Clip   30 Demister tube (righthand)   31 Demister tube (lefthand)   32 Duct assembly (righthand)
33 Duct assembly (lefthand)   34 Screw   35 Nut   36 Heater instruction plate

and push out the ignition/starter and wiper/wash switches.

Remove the wingnut directly below and behind the ball-mounted air duct on the driver's side. Remove the glovebox lid and the drive screws securing the glovebox to the facia. Remove two wingnuts, one from below and behind the ball-mounted air duct on the passenger's side and the other from the centre of the facia.

Disconnect the steering column-to-body crossmember bracket and lower the column. Pull the facia board 11 forward at the bottom and lift away.

Disconnect all instruments and switches, marking the electrical cables for correct replacement, and then remove the facia board complete with instruments and switches.

Remove the drive screws securing facia surround 1 to the body crossmember, to the 'A' posts and to the top crossmember. Remove the 'A' post finishers 44 and 45 and lift away the surround.

Refitting; all models:

This is a reversal of the removal instructions. On Princess cars the facia panel must be fitted with the board-securing clips located in the facia surround.

11:10 The heater

This is shown in component form in **FIG 11:13**. The controls and positions for various requirements are illustrated in **FIG 11:14**. For extreme conditions an electric blower can be used to increase the quantity of air fed into the heater. It may be used when the car is stationary or travelling slowly to compensate for the lack of intake air. The blower switch has two positions for running the fan at half and full boost.

The lefthand control regulates the quantity of air delivered to the car interior or to the windscreen for demisting or defrosting. The righthand control regulates the temperature of the air.

To prevent windscreen misting and provide maximum warm air to the car interior, set the air control between 'SCREEN' and 'CAR' positions and the temperature control at 'MAX'. When starting from cold leave the air control at 'OFF' until the engine has warmed up. Use the blower if the car is stationary or travelling slowly.

To remove ice from the screen set the air control to 'SCREEN' and the temperature control to 'MAX'. From cold, leave the air control at 'OFF' until the engine has warmed up. Switch on the blower if stationary or travelling slowly.

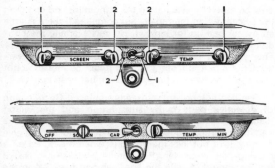

FIG 11:14 Heater controls 'OFF' in position 1, giving maximum interior heating 2 and for windscreen demisting in lower view

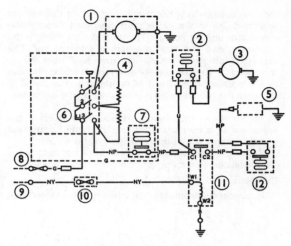

FIG 11:17 Wiring diagram of air conditioning electrical system

Key to Fig 11:17   1 Fan motor   2 High pressure cut-in
3 Fan motor   4 Resistor assembly   5 Clutch
6 Control switch   7 Temperature sensing switch
8 Fuse 3 (ignition controlled accessories)   9 Terminal D on
control box 10 Line fuse 11 Relay 12 High pressure cut-out

Cable colour code: **NY** Brown/Yellow **NP** Brown/Purple
G Green   **U** Blue   **B** Black
When a cable has two colour code letters, the first denotes the main colour, and the second denotes the tracer colour

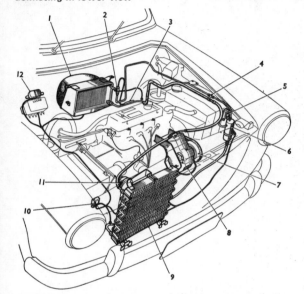

FIG 11:15 Layout of air conditioning components. Part numbers are used in the text

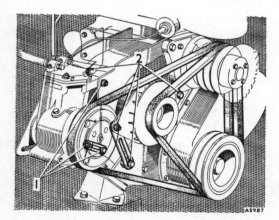

FIG 11:16 Use adjusting points 1 for compressor belt and points 2 for generator belt

For cooling purposes move the air control to 'CAR' and the temperature control to 'MIN'. Use the blower for extra air.

In hot weather, move the air control to 'SCREEN' to get cool air at head level with the temperature control at 'MIN'. Use the blower for extra air.

On Princess cars there are ball-mounted ducts on either side of the facia panel. Move these to direct air to any desired position except outwards. In this position the air flow is cut off.

11:11 Air conditioning

The layout of the system is shown in **FIG 11:15**. Note the compressor 8 which is driven by belt from the crankshaft. An electro-magnetic clutch 7 is incorporated in the drive. The liquid refrigerant is condensed in a heat exchanger 9, provided with an electric fan 11. 6 is a liquid receiver, and high-pressure switch 5 controls the compressor clutch. A second high-pressure switch 10 controls condenser pressure. Sight glass 4 permits inspection of the refrigerant charge. 2 and 3 are expansion valves. Relay 12 energizes the clutch solenoid. The evaporator unit 1 is the air condition component of the system and is mounted below the facia. The unit has four control switches 'OFF', 'LOW', 'MED' and 'HIGH', an electrically driven fan, a temperature phial and a temperature sensing switch.

When the engine is running at or above a fast idle and the system is switched on at one of the fan speeds, the relay energizes the clutch solenoid and the compressor is started. **Air in the car is then** circulated through the evaporator unit by the fan. The air is drawn through the cooling matrix and then discharged into the car. The vaporized refrigerant having absorbed heat from the air is drawn into the compressor and passed under pressure to the condenser where it is condensed. The liquid is stored in the receiver until it is required by the evaporator unit.

To decrease the interior temperature quickly the windows must be closed, the 'HIGH' button depressed and the engine run at approximately 1500 rev/min.

When the air conditioning system is not required it should be operated for about 15 minutes every week.

Servicing:

As almost every defect in the working of the system can only be cured by evacuating the refrigerant and charging the system when the repairs are completed, there is little an owner can do for himself. He can examine the condition of the drive belt which is shown in **FIG 11:16**. The adjusting points are clearly shown. Do not overtighten the belt, but set it so that it can be moved about $\frac{1}{2}$ to $\frac{3}{4}$ inch midway in the longest run between pulleys.

Electrical components are readily replaced. Rectification of defective parts is by substitution and the wiring diagram in **FIG 11:17** will be found helpful. With the engine running at 1500 rev/min the generator should give an output of not less than 9 volts when measured on a moving-coil voltmeter. Preliminary checks in case of trouble should include the line fuse and fuse 3-4 in the fusebox. Check all cables for continuity and connections for security.

APPENDIX

TECHNICAL DATA

WIRING DIAGRAMS

HINTS ON MAINTENANCE AND OVERHAUL

GLOSSARY OF TERMS

INDEX

Inches	Decimals	Milli-metres	Inches to Millimetres		Millimetres to Inches	
			Inches	mm	mm	Inches
1/64	.015625	.3969	.001	.0254	.01	.00039
1/32	.03125	.7937	.002	.0508	.02	.00079
3/64	.046875	1.1906	.003	.0762	.03	.00118
1/16	.0625	1.5875	.004	.1016	.04	.00157
5/64	.078125	1.9844	.005	.1270	.05	.00197
3/32	.09375	2.3812	.006	.1524	.06	.00236
7/64	.109375	2.7781	.007	.1778	.07	.00276
1/8	.125	3.1750	.008	.2032	.08	.00315
9/64	.140625	3.5719	.009	.2286	.09	.00354
5/32	.15625	3.9687	.01	.254	.1	.00394
11/64	.171875	4.3656	.02	.508	.2	.00787
3/16	.1875	4.7625	.03	.762	.3	.01181
13/64	.203125	5·1594	.04	1.016	.4	.01575
7/32	.21875	5.5562	.05	1.270	.5	.01969
15/64	.234375	5.9531	.06	1.524	.6	.02362
1/4	.25	6.3500	.07	1.778	.7	.02756
17/64	.265625	6.7469	.08	2.032	.8	.03150
9/32	.28125	7.1437	.09	2.286	.9	.03543
19/64	.296875	7.5406	.1	2.54	1	.03937
5/16	.3125	7.9375	.2	5.08	2	.07874
21/64	.328125	8.3344	.3	7.62	3	.11811
11/32	.34375	8.7312	.4	10.16	4	.15748
23/64	.359375	9.1281	.5	12.70	5	.19685
3/8	.375	9.5250	.6	15.24	6	.23622
25/64	.390625	9.9219	.7	17.78	7	.27559
13/32	.40625	10.3187	.8	20.32	8	.31496
27/64	.421875	10.7156	.9	22.86	9	.35433
7/16	.4375	11.1125	1	25.4	10	.39370
29/64	.453125	11.5094	2	50.8	11	.43307
15/32	.46875	11.9062	3	76.2	12	.47244
31/64	.484375	12.3031	4	101.6	13	.51181
1/2	.5	12.7000	5	127.0	14	.55118
33/64	.515625	13.0969	6	152.4	15	.59055
17/32	.53125	13.4937	7	177.8	16	.62992
35/64	.546875	13.8906	8	203.2	17	.66929
9/16	.5625	14.2875	9	228.6	18	.70866
37/64	.578125	14.6844	10	254.0	19	.74803
19/32	.59375	15.0812	11	279.4	20	.78740
39/64	.609375	15.4781	12	304.8	21	.82677
5/8	.625	15.8750	13	330.2	22	.86614
41/64	.640625	16.2719	14	355.6	23	.90551
21/32	.65625	16.6687	15	381.0	24	.94488
43/64	.671875	17.0656	16	406.4	25	.98425
11/16	.6875	17.4625	17	431.8	26	1.02362
45/64	.703125	17.8594	18	457.2	27	1.06299
23/32	.71875	18.2562	19	482.6	28	1.10236
47/64	.734375	18.6531	20	508.0	29	1.14173
3/4	.75	19.0500	21	533.4	30	1.18110
49/64	.765625	19.4469	22	558.8	31	1.22047
25/32	.78125	19.8437	23	584.2	32	1.25984
51/64	.796875	20.2406	24	609.6	33	1.29921
13/16	.8125	20.6375	25	635.0	34	1.33858
53/64	.828125	21.0344	26	660.4	35	1.37795
27/32	.84375	21.4312	27	685.8	36	1.41732
55/64	.859375	21.8281	28	711.2	37	1.4567
7/8	.875	22.2250	29	736.6	38	1.4961
57/64	.890625	22.6219	30	762.0	39	1.5354
29/32	.90625	23.0187	31	787.4	40	1.5748
59/64	.921875	23.4156	32	812.8	41	1.6142
15/16	.9375	23.8125	33	838.2	42	1.6535
61/64	.953125	24.2094	34	863.6	43	1.6929
31/32	.96875	24.6062	35	889.0	44	1.7323
63/64	.984375	25.0031	36	914.4	45	1.7717

UNITS	Pints to Litres	Gallons to Litres	Litres to Pints	Litres to Gallons	Miles to Kilometres	Kilometres to Miles	Lbs. per sq. In. to Kg. per sq. Cm.	Kg. per sq. Cm. to Lbs. per sq. In.
1	.57	4.55	1.76	.22	1.61	.62	.07	14.22
2	1.14	9.09	3.52	.44	3.22	1.24	.14	28.50
3	1.70	13.64	5.28	.66	4.83	1.86	.21	42.67
4	2.27	18.18	7.04	.88	6.44	2.49	.28	56.89
5	2.84	22.73	8.80	1.10	8.05	3.11	.35	71.12
6	3.41	27.28	10.56	1.32	9.66	3.73	.42	85.34
7	3.98	31.82	12.32	1.54	11.27	4.35	.49	99.56
8	4.55	36.37	14.08	1.76	12.88	4.97	.56	113.79
9		40.91	15.84	1.98	14.48	5.59	.63	128.00
10		45.46	17.60	2.20	16.09	6.21	.70	142.23
20				4.40	32.19	12.43	1.41	284.47
30				6.60	48.28	18.64	2.11	426.70
40				8.80	64.37	24.85		
50					80.47	31.07		
60					96.56	37.28		
70					112.65	43.50		
80					128.75	49.71		
90					144.84	55.92		
100					160.93	62.14		

UNITS	Lb ft to kgm	Kgm to lb ft	UNITS	Lb ft to kgm	Kgm to lb ft
1	.138	7.233	7	.967	50.631
2	.276	14.466	8	1.106	57.864
3	.414	21.699	9	1.244	65.097
4	.553	28.932	10	1.382	72.330
5	.691	36.165	20	2.765	144.660
6	.829	43.398	30	4.147	216.990

TECHNICAL DATA

Dimensions are in inches unless otherwise stated

ENGINE

Bore and stroke:
1098cc (types 10AMW, 10GR, 10V) ...	...	...	64.58 x 83.72 mm

Compression ratio (low):
Single carburetter	7.5:1
Twin carburetter	8.1:1

Compression ratio (high):
Single carburetter	8.5:1
Twin carburetter	8.9:1
Automatic transmission, type 10AG	8.9:1

Crankshaft:
Main journal diameter	1.7505 to 1.751
Main bearings	Three thinwall, steel-backed
Main bearing material	Lead/bronze, lead/indium plated
Diametrical clearance	.001 to .0027
Undersizes	—.010, —.020, —.030, —.040
End float	.002 to .003
Crankpin journal diameter	1.6254 to 1.6259
Crankpin minimum regrind diameter	1.5854

Connecting rods:
Length between centres	5.75
Big-end bearings	Thinwall, steel-backed
Big-end bearing material	Lead/bronze, lead/indium plated
Big-end bearing diametrical clearance...	.001 to .0025
Big-end float	.008 to .012

Pistons:
Type	Aluminium, solid skirt
Clearance, top of skirt	.0021 to .0037
Clearance, bottom of skirt	.0005 to .0011
Suitable bore size (standard)	64.576 to 64.635 mm
Oversizes available	+.010 and +.020
Piston rings	Three compression, one oil control
Top ring	Internally chamfered, chrome faced
Second and third rings	Tapered
Oil control ring:	
Early	Slotted scraper
Later	Duaflex 61
Width, top ring	.062 to .0625
Width, second and third rings	.0615 to .0625
Width, oil control ring:	
Slotted scraper	.124 to .125
Fitted gap, top, second and third	.007 to .012
Fitted gap, oil control:	
Slotted scraper	.007 to .012
Duaflex 61	Rails .012 to .028, side springs .100 to .150
Ring to groove clearance:	
Top, second and third	.002 to .004
Slotted scraper	.0015 to .0035
Gudgeon pin type	Fully floating
Gudgeon pin fit in piston	Hand-push

Camshaft:

Journal diameters:	
Front	1.6655 to 1.666
Centre	1.62275 to 1.62325
Rear...	1.3725 to 1.3735
End float	.003 to .007
Bearing type	Three steel-backed, whitemetal lined
Bearing diametrical clearance	.001 to .002
Drive	Chain, $\frac{3}{8}$ pitch x 52 pitches

Tappets:

Outside diameter	.81125 to .81175
Length...	1.495 to 1.505

Valves:

Seat angle, inlet and exhaust	45 deg.
Head diameter, inlet	1.151 to 1.156
Later models, twin carburetter applications	1.213 to 1.218
Head diameter, exhaust	1.00 to 1.005
Stem diameter, inlet	.2793 to .2798
Stem diameter, exhaust	.2788 to .2793
Valve lift	.312
Stem to guide clearance:	
Inlet	.0015 to .0025
Exhaust	.002 to .003

Valve guides:

Length, inlet and exhaust	1.531
Fitted height above spring seat	$\frac{19}{32}$

Valve springs:

Free length:	
Single carburetter	1.75
Twin carburetters	1.75 outer, 1.672 inner
Load at fitted length:	
Single carburetter	52.5 lb
Twin carburetters	52 lb outer, 18 lb inner

Valve timing and clearance:

Timing marks	Dimples on timing wheels, marks on flywheel
Rocker clearance, running	.012 cold
Rocker clearance **for timing only**	.029
Inlet valve opens	5 deg. BTDC
Inlet valve closes	45 deg. ABDC
Exhaust valve opens	51 deg. BBDC
Exhaust valve closes	21 deg. ATDC

Oil pump:

Type	Internal gear or vane
Pressure relief valve lifts	60 lb/sq in
Relief valve spring length	Free $2\frac{55}{64}$, fitted $2\frac{5}{32}$

Oil filter... ... ... Fullflow with renewable element

Capacity	One pint

Oil pressure ... ... Running 60 lb/sq in, idling (min.) 15 lb/sq in

COOLING SYSTEM

Thermostat settings:

Standard	82°C or 180°F
Cold climate	88°C or 190°F
Hot climate	74°C or 165°F

FUEL SYSTEM

Carburetter(s):

Type:
    Synchromesh ... ... SU, HS2 single or twin
    Automatic ... ... SU, HS4 single

Choke diameter:
    Synchromesh ... ... $1\frac{1}{4}$
    Automatic ... ... $1\frac{1}{2}$

Needle, standard:
    Synchromesh ... ... AN single, D3 twin
    Automatic ... ... DL

Needle, weak:
    Synchromesh ... ... EB single, GV twin
    Automatic ... ... ED

Needle, rich:
    Synchromesh ... ... H6 single, D6 weak
    Automatic ... ... BQ

Piston spring, single carburetters ... ... Red
Piston spring, twin carburetters ... ... Blue

Fuel pump:

Type ... ... SU electric, SP or AUF.200

IGNITION SYSTEM

Sparking plugs:

Type ... ... Champion N5
Gap ... ... .024 to .026

Coil ... ... Lucas LA.12

Distributor:

Type ... ... Lucas 25.D4
Contact points gap ... ... .014 to .016

Static timing:
    Synchromesh (single carburetter) ... ... 3 deg. BTDC
    Synchromesh (twin carburetters) ... ... 5 deg. BTDC
    Automatic (distributor number 41134A) ... ... 7 deg. BTDC
    Automatic (distributor number 41181A) ... ... 5 deg. BTDC

Stroboscopic timing:
    Automatic (distributor number 41134A) ... ... 10 deg. BTDC at 600 rev/min
    Automatic (distributor number 41181A) ... ... 8 deg. BTDC at 600 rev/min

CLUTCH

Clutch:

Type (early cars) ... ... Single dry plate with coil springs
Type (later cars) ... ... Single dry plate, diaphragm spring
Diameter of plate ... ... $7\frac{1}{8}$
Number of coil springs 6
Colour of coil springs ... ... Black with white spot
Colour of diaphragm spring ... ... Green
Fluid ... ... Lockheed Disc Brake Fluid,
                               Series II

TRANSMISSION

Gearbox:

Number of forward speeds ... ... Four
Synchromesh ... ... Second, third and top gears

Overall gearbox ratios:
Synchromesh:
Top ...	...	...	...	...	...	...	4.133:1
Third	...	...	...	...	...	...	5.83:1
Second	...	...	...	...	...	...	8.98:1
First...	...	...	...	...	...	...	14.99:1
Reverse	...	...	...	...	...	...	14.99:1

Automatic, (early):
Top ...	...	...	...	...	...	...	4:1
Third	...	...	...	...	...	...	5.84:1
Second	...	...	...	...	...	...	7.38:1
First...	...	...	...	...	...	...	10.76:1
Reverse	...	...	...	...	...	...	10.76:1

Automatic (later):
Top ...	...	...	...	...	...	...	3.76:1
Third	...	...	...	...	...	...	5.49:1
Second	...	...	...	...	...	...	6.94:1
First...	...	...	...	...	...	...	10.11:1
Reverse	...	...	...	...	...	...	10.11:1

Differential ratio:
Synchromesh ...	...	...	...	...	...	4.133:1
Automatic (early)	...	...	...	...	...	3.48:1
Automatic (later)	...	...	...	...	...	3.27:1

Torque converter:
Type ...	...	...	...	...	...	...	Three-element
Ratio ...	...	...	...	...	...	...	2:1 maximum
Converter output gear ratio	...	...	...	...			1.15:1
End float ...	...	...	...	...	...		.0035 to .0065

STEERING

Steering:
Type ...	...	...	...	...	...	...	Rack and pinion
Steering wheel turns, lock to lock	...	...	...				$3\frac{1}{8}$

Steering angles, static unladen condition:
Camber	...	...	...	...	...	...	$\frac{3}{4}$ deg. positive ± 1 deg.
Castor ...	...	...	...	...	...	...	$5\frac{1}{2}$ deg. positive $\pm\frac{1}{2}$ deg.
Swivel hub inclination...	...	...	...	...			10 deg.
Toe-out ...	...	...	...	...	...		$\frac{1}{16}$

SUSPENSION

Fluid pressure, front (unladen):
Austin, Morris, MG	...	...	...	...	...	205 ± 2 lb/sq in
MG (Normalair)	...	...	...	...	...	$220 + 10\text{-}0$ lb/sq in
Princess	...	...	...	...	...	$230 + 2$ lb/sq in

Rear suspension:
Toe-out	...	...	...	...	...	$\frac{1}{8}$
Camber	...	...	...	...	...	1 deg. positive

BRAKES

Brakes:
Type ...	...	...	...	...	...	...	Lockheed hydraulic, disc front and drum rear

Front disc brakes:
Diameter ...	...	...	...	...	...		8
Pad lining material ...	...	...	...	...			Ferodo M.78
Minimum pad thickness	...	...	...	...			$\frac{1}{16}$

Rear drum brakes:

Diameter	8
Lining material (early)	Ferodo AM.8
Lining material (later)	Ferodo AM.8.FF
Brake fluid	Lockheed Disc Brake Fluid, Series II

ELECTRICAL EQUIPMENT

Battery:

Type, early models	Lucas N9 or NZ9
Type, later models	Lucas D9 or DZ9
Capacity	12 volt, 40 amp/hr at 20 hr rate
Earthing system	Positive
Starter motor	Lucas M.35G
Generator	Lucas C.40
Generator maximum output	22 amp

Control box:

Type	RB.340
Units	Voltage regulator, current regulator and cut-out

Regulator open-circuit setting at 1500 rev/min of generator:

At 20°C or 68°F	14.2 to 14.8 volts

(For ambient temperatures every 10°C or 18°F **above** this temperature, subtract .2 volt. For the same **below** this temperature, add .2 volt)

Cut-out:

Cut-in voltage	12.6 to 13.4
Drop-off voltage	9.3 to 11.2

CAPACITIES

Transmission casing, including filter	8½ pints
Automatic transmission casing, including filter	13 pints (refill capacity 9 pints)
Cooling system without heater	5¾ pints
Heater	1 pint
Fuel tank	8 gallons
Hydrolastic suspension	5 pints

DIMENSIONS

Overall length	12 ft 2¾ inch
Track, static and unladen:	
Front	4 ft 3½ inch
Rear	4 ft 2⅞ inch
Turning circle	34 ft 9 inch

TORQUE WRENCH SETTINGS

Engine and transmission:

Cylinder head stud nuts	40 lb ft
Big-end bolts	35 lb ft
Main bearing bolts	60 lb ft
Flywheel centre bolt	110/115 lb ft
Rocker bracket nuts	25 lb ft
Transmission case to crankcase	6 lb ft
Cylinder side covers (early)	2 lb ft
Cylinder side covers (deep pressed type)	5 lb ft
Timing cover ¼ UNF bolts	6 lb ft
Timing cover $\frac{5}{16}$ UNF bolts	14 lb ft

Water pump	...	...	...	...	...	17 lb ft
Water outlet elbow	...	...	...	...	...	8 lb ft
Oil filter	...	...	...	...	...	10 to 15 lb ft
Oil pump	...	...	...	...	...	9 lb ft
Manifold to cylinder head	...	...	...	...	15 lb ft
Rocker cover	...	...	...	...	...	4 lb ft
Crankshaft pulley nut	...	...	...	...	70 lb ft
Transmission case studs, $\frac{3}{8}$ UNC	...	...	...	8 lb ft
Transmission case studs, $\frac{5}{16}$ UNC	...	...	...	6 lb ft
Transmission case stud nuts, $\frac{3}{8}$ UNF	...	...	...	25 lb ft
Transmission case stud nuts, $\frac{5}{16}$ UNF	...	...	...	18 lb ft
Bottom cover setscrews, changespeed tower, $\frac{1}{4}$ UNC	...	6 lb ft
First motion shaft nut	...	...	...	...	15 lb ft
Third motion shaft nut	...	...	...	...	150 lb ft
Flywheel housing bolts and stud nuts	...	...	...	18 lb ft
Distributor clamp bolt, fixed nut	...	...	...	50 lb in
Distributor clamp bolt, fixed bolt	...	...	...	30 lb in
Driven gear to differential cage	...	...	...	55 to 60 lb ft
Drive shaft flange nuts	...	...	...	...	70 lb ft and align to next splitpin hole
End cover bolts, differential housing	...	...	...	18 lb ft
Drive shaft U-bolt nuts	...	...	...	...	10 to 12.5 lb ft
Drain plug	...	...	...	...	...	40 to 50 lb ft

Suspension and steering:

Steering lever to hub bolts	...	...	...	...	30 to 35 lb ft
Steering lever ball joint nut	...	...	...	...	25 lb ft
Steering knuckle ball pin, bottom nut	...	...	...	35 to 40 lb ft
Steering knuckle ball pin, top nut	...	...	...	35 to 40 lb ft
Steering knuckle ball pin retainer	...	...	...	70 lb ft
Front hub nut (drive shaft)	...	...	...	...	150 lb ft and align to next splitpin hole
Rear suspension anti-roll bar fixing bolts	...	...	70 lb ft
Rear suspension stub axle nut	...	...	...	...	60 lb ft and align to next splitpin hole
Front suspension upper arm pivot pin nut	...	...	35 to 40 lb ft
Front suspension lower arm pivot pin nut	...	...	35 to 40 lb ft
Steering-wheel nut	...	...	...	...	...	50 lb ft
Road wheel nuts	...	...	...	...	...	42 lb ft
Disc to hub	...	...	...	...	...	40 to 45 lb ft
Front swivel hub to caliper	...	...	...	...	45 to 50 lb ft
Steering column clamp bolt	...	...	...	...	8 to 9 lb ft

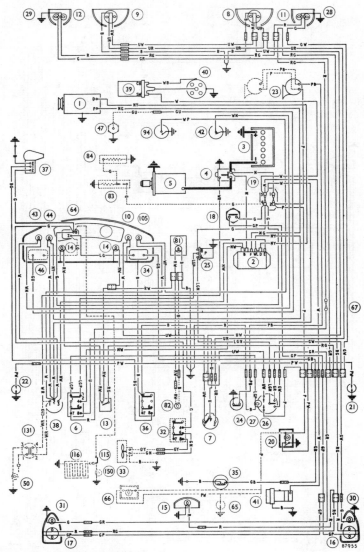

FIG 12:1   Wiring diagram for Morris Saloon and Traveller

Key to Fig 12:1   1 Generator   2 Control box   3 Battery (12 volt)   4 Starter solenoid   5 Starter motor
6 Lighting switch   7 Headlight dip switch   8 Righthand headlamp   9 Lefthand headlamp   10 Main beam warning light
11 Righthand sidelamp   12 Lefthand sidelamp   13 Panel light switch   14 Panel lights   15 Number plate lamp
16 Righthand stop and tail lamp   17 Lefthand stop and tail lamp   18 Stop lamp switch   19 Fuse unit (35 amp)
20 Interior lamp   21 Righthand door switch   22 Lefthand door switch   23 Horn (twin horns when fitted)
24 Horn-push   25 Flasher unit   26 Direction indicator switch   27 Direction indicator/headlight flasher warning light
28 Righthand front flasher lamp   29 Lefthand front flasher lamp   30 Righthand rear flasher lamp   31 Lefthand rear flasher lamp
32 Heater or fresh-air motor switch (when fitted)   33 Heater or fresh-air motor (when fitted)   34 Fuel gauge
35 Fuel gauge tank unit   36 Windscreen wiper switch   37 Windscreen wiper   38 Ignition/starter switch
39 Ignition coil   40 Distributor   41 Fuel pump   42 Oil pressure switch   43 Oil pressure warning light
44 Ignition warning light   45 Speedometer   46 Water temperature gauge (when fitted)   47 Water temperature
transmitter (when fitted)   50 Reverse lamp (when fitted)   64 Bi-metal instrument voltage stabilizer
65 Rear compartment light switch (Traveller)   66 Rear compartment light (Traveller)   67 Line fuse (35 amp)
81 Ashtray light   82 Heater switch or fresh-air switch light   83 Induction heater and thermostat   84 Suction chamber heater
94 Oil filter switch   105 Lubrication warning light   115 Rear window demister switch (when fitted)
116 Rear window demister unit (when fitted)   131 Combined reverse switch/automatic gearbox safety switch (when fitted)
150 Rear window demister warning light (when fitted)

Cable colour code: **N** Brown   **P** Purple   **W** White   **U** Blue   **G** Green   **Y** Yellow
R Red   **LG** Light Green   **B** Black
When a cable has two colour code letters, the first denotes the main colour, and the second denotes the tracer colour

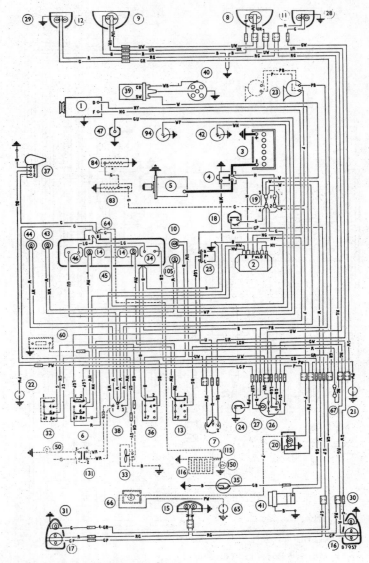

FIG 12:2   Wiring diagram for Austin Saloon and Countryman

Key to Fig 12:2   1 Generator   2 Control box   3 Battery (12 volt)   4 Starter solenoid   5 Starter motor
6 Lighting switch   7 Headlight dip switch   8 Righthand headlamp   9 Lefthand headlamp   10 Main beam warning light
11 Righthand sidelamp   12 Lefthand sidelamp   13 Panel light switch   14 Panel lights   15 Number plate lamp
16 Righthand stop and tail lamp   17 Lefthand stop and tail lamp   18 Stop lamp switch   19 Fuse unit (35 amp)
20 Interior lamp   21 Righthand door switch   22 Lefthand door switch   23 Horn (twin horns when fitted)
24 Horn-push   25 Flasher unit   26 Direction indicator switch   27 Direction indicator warning light
28 Righthand front flasher lamp   29 Lefthand front flasher lamp   30 Righthand rear flasher lamp
31 Lefthand rear flasher lamp   32 Heater or fresh-air motor switch (when fitted)   33 Heater or fresh-air motor (when fitted)
34 Fuel gauge   35 Fuel gauge tank unit   36 Windshield wiper switch   37 Windshield wiper
38 Ignition/starter switch   39 Ignition coil   40 Distributor   41 Fuel pump   42 Oil pressure switch
43 Oil pressure warning light   44 Ignition warning light   45 Speedometer   46 Water temperature gauge (when fitted)
47 Water temperature transmitter (when fitted)   50 Reverse lamp (when fitted)   60 Radio (if fitted)
64 Bi-metal instrument voltage stabilizer   65 Rear compartment light switch (Traveller)   66 Rear compartment light (Traveller)
67 Line fuse (35 amp)   83 Induction heater and thermostat   84 Suction chamber heater   94 Oil filter switch
105 Lubrication warning light   115 Rear window demister switch (when fitted)   116 Rear window demister unit (when fitted)
131 Combined reverse switch/automatic gearbox switch (when fitted)   150 Rear window demister warning light (when fitted)

Cable colour code: **N** Brown   **P** Purple   **W** White   **U** Blue   **G** Green   **Y** Yellow
R Red   **LG** Light Green   **B** Black
When a cable has two colour code letters, the first denotes the main colour, and the second denotes the tracer colour

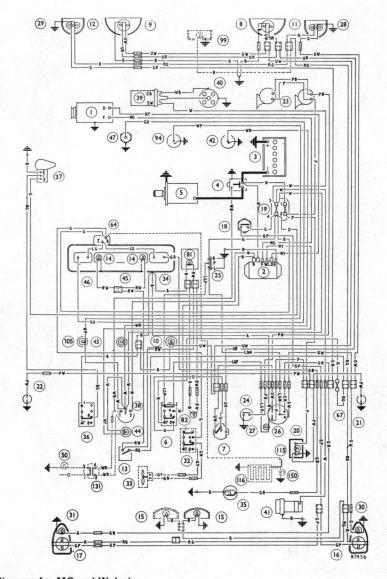

FIG 12:3 Wiring diagram for MG and Wolseley

Key to Fig 12:3 1 Generator 2 Control box 3 Battery (12 volt) 4 Starter solenoid 5 Starter motor
6 Lighting switch 7 Headlight dip switch 8 Righthand headlamp 9 Lefthand headlamp 10 Main-beam warning light
11 Righthand sidelamp 12 Lefthand sidelamp 13 Panel light switch 14 Panel lights 15 Number-plate lamp
16 Righthand stop and tail lamp 17 Lefthand stop and tail lamp 18 Stop lamp switch 19 Fuse unit (35 amp)
20 Interior lamp 21 Righthand door switch 22 Lefthand door switch 23 Horn 24 Horn-push
25 Flasher unit 26 Direction indicator switch 27 Direction indicator warning lights 28 Righthand front flasher lamp
29 Lefthand front flasher lamp 30 Righthand rear flasher lamp 31 Lefthand rear flasher lamp
32 Heater or fresh-air motor switch (when fitted) 33 Heater or fresh-air motor (when fitted)
35 Fuel gauge tank unit 36 Windscreen wiper switch 37 Windscreen wiper 38 Ignition/starter switch
39 Ignition coil 40 Distributor 41 Fuel pump 42 Oil pressure switch 43 Lubrication warning light
44 Ignition warning light 45. Speedometer 46 Water temperature gauge 47 Water temperature transmitter
50 Reverse lamp (when fitted) 64 Bi-metal instrument voltage stabilizer 67 Line fuse (35 amp) 81 Ashtray illumination
82 Heater or fresh-air switch light (when fitted) 94 Oil filter switch 99 Radiator badge illumination lamp (Wolseley)
105 Lubrication warning light 115 Rear window demister switch (when fitted) 116 Rear window demister unit (when fitted)
131 Combined reverse switch/automatic gearbox safety switch (when fitted) 150 Rear window demister warning light (when fitted)

Cable colour code: **N** Brown **P** Purple **W** White **U** Blue **G** Green **Y** Yellow
R Red **LG** Light Green **B** Black
When a cable has two colour code letters, the first denotes the main colour, and the second denotes the tracer colour

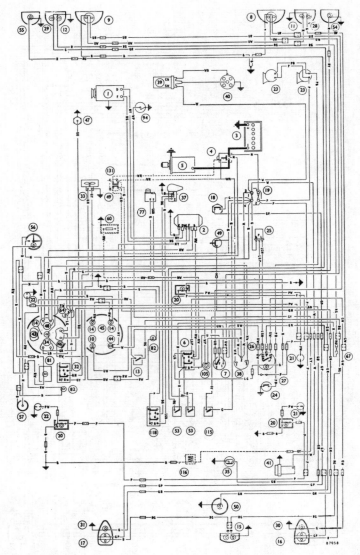

FIG 12:4 Wiring diagram for Princess cars

Key to Fig 12:4   1 Generator   2 Control box   3 Battery (12 volt)   4 Starter solenoid   5 Starter motor
6 Lighting switch   7 Headlamp dip switch   8 Righthand headlamp   9 Lefthand headlamp   10 Main-beam warning lamp
11 Righthand sidelamp   12 Lefthand sidelamp   13 Panel lamps switch   14 Panel lamps
15 Number plate illumination lamp   16 Righthand stop and tail lamp   17 Lefthand stop and tail lamp   18 Stop lamp switch
19 Fuse unit (35 amp 1-2, 35 amp 3-4)   20 Interior lights   21 Righthand door switch   22 Lefthand door switch
23 Horn   24 Horn-push   25 Flasher unit   26 Direction indicator and headlamp flasher switch
27 Direction indicator warning lamp   28 Righthand front flasher lamp   29 Lefthand front flasher lamp
30 Righthand rear flasher lamp   31 Lefthand rear flasher lamp   32 Heater or fresh-air motor switch
33 Heater or fresh-air motor   34 Fuel gauge   35 Fuel gauge tank unit   37 Windscreen wiper motor
38 Ignition/starter switch   39 Ignition coil   40 Distributor   41 Fuel pump   43 Oil pressure gauge
44 Ignition warning lamp   45 Speedometer   46 Water temperature gauge   47 Water temperature transmitter
48 Ammeter   49 Reverse lamp switch   50 Reverse lamp   53 Foglamps switch   54 Righthand foglamp
55 Lefthand foglamp   56 Clock   57 Cigar lighter   60 Radio (when fitted)   64 Bi-metal instrument voltage stabilizer
67 Line fuse (35 amp)   77 Electric windscreen washer   81 Ashtray illumination lamp   82 Illumination lamps switch
94 Oil filter switch   105 Lubrication warning lamp   115 Rear window demist switch   116 Rear window demist unit
118 Combined windscreen washer and wiper switch   131 Combined reverse switch/automatic gearbox safety switch (when fitted)

Cable colour code: **N** Brown   **P** Purple   **W** White   **U** Blue   **G** Green   **Y** Yellow
R Red   **LG** Light Green   **B** Black
When a cable has two colour code letters, the first denotes the main colour, and the second denotes the tracer colour

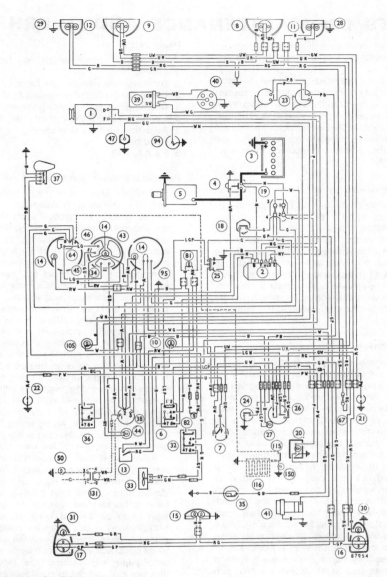

FIG 12:5   Wiring diagram for Riley cars

Key to Fig 12:5
1 Generator   2 Control box   3 Battery (12 volt)   4 Starter solenoid   5 Starter motor
6 Lighting switch   7 Headlight dip switch   8 Righthand headlamp   9 Lefthand headlamp
10 Main-beam warning light   11 Righthand sidelamp   12 Lefthand sidelamp   13 Panel lights switch
14 Panel lights   15 Number-plate lamp   16 Righthand stop and tail lamp   17 Lefthand stop and tail lamp
18 Stop lamp switch   19 Fuse unit (35 amp)   20 Interior lamp   21 Righthand door switch   22 Lefthand door switch
23 Horns   24 Horn-push   25 Flasher unit   26 Direction indicator and headlight flasher switch
27 Direction indicator warning light   28 Righthand front flasher   29 Lefthand front flasher   30 Righthand rear flasher
31 Lefthand rear flasher   32 Heater or fresh-air motor switch (when fitted)   33 Heater or fresh-air motor (when fitted)
34 Fuel gauge   35 Fuel gauge tank unit   36 Windscreen wiper switch   37 Windscreen wiper
38 Starter and ignition switch   39 Ignition coil   40 Distributor   41 Fuel pump   43 Oil pressure gauge
44 Ignition warning light   45 Speedometer   46 Water temperature gauge   47 Water temperature transmitter
50 Reverse lamp (when fitted)   64 Bi-metal instrument voltage stabilizer   67 Line fuse (35 amp)
81 Ashtray light   82 Heater switch or fresh-air switch light   94 Oil filter switch   95 Tachometer
105 Lubrication warning light   115 Rear window demister switch (when fitted)   116 Rear window demister unit (when fitted)
131 Combined reverse switch/automatic gearbox safety switch (when fitted)   150 Rear window demister warning light (when fitted)

Cable colour code: **N** Brown   **P** Purple   **W** White   **U** Blue   **G** Green   **Y** Yellow
R Red   **LG** Light Green   **B** Black
When a cable has two colour code letters, the first denotes the main colour, and the second denotes the tracer colour

HINTS ON MAINTENANCE AND OVERHAUL

There are few things more rewarding than the restoration of a vehicle's original peak of efficiency and smooth performance.

The following notes are intended to help the owner to reach that state of perfection. Providing that he possesses the basic manual skills he should have no difficulty in performing most of the operations detailed in this manual. It must be stressed, however, that where recommended in the manual, highly-skilled operations ought to be entrusted to experts, who have the necessary equipment, to carry out the work satisfactorily.

Quality of workmanship:

The hazardous driving conditions on the roads to-day demand that vehicles should be as nearly perfect, mechanically, as possible. It is therefore most important that amateur work be carried out with care, bearing in mind the often inadequate working conditions, and also the inferior tools which may have to be used. It is easy to counsel perfection in all things, and we recognize that it may be setting an impossibly high standard. We do, however, suggest that every care should be taken to ensure that a vehicle is as safe to take on the road as it is humanly possible to make it.

Safe working conditions:

Even though a vehicle may be stationary, it is still potentially dangerous if certain sensible precautions are not taken when working on it while it is supported on jacks or blocks. It is indeed preferable not to use jacks alone, but to supplement them with carefully placed blocks, so that there will be plenty of support if the car rolls off the jacks during a strenuous manoeuvre. Axle stands are an excellent way of providing a rigid base which is not readily disturbed. Piles of bricks are a dangerous substitute. Be careful not to get under heavy loads on lifting tackle, the load could fall. It is preferable not to work alone when lifting an engine, or when working underneath a vehicle which is supported well off the ground. To be trapped, particularly under the vehicle, may have unpleasant results if help is not quickly forthcoming. Make some provision, however humble, to deal with fires. Always disconnect a battery if there is a likelihood of electrical shorts. These may start a fire if there is leaking fuel about. This applies particularly to leads which can carry a heavy current, like those in the starter circuit. While on the subject of electricity, we must also stress the danger of using equipment which is run off the mains and which has no earth or has faulty wiring or connections. So many workshops have damp floors, and electrical shocks are of such a nature that it is sometimes impossible to let go of a live lead or piece of equipment due to the muscular spasms which take place.

Work demanding special care:

This involves the servicing of braking, steering and suspension systems. On the road, failure of the braking system may be disastrous. Make quite sure that there can be no possibility of failure through the bursting of rusty brake pipes or rotten hoses, nor to a sudden loss of pressure due to defective seals or valves.

Problems:

The chief problems which may face an operator are:
1. External dirt.
2. Difficulty in undoing tight fixings.
3. Dismantling unfamiliar mechanisms.
4. Deciding in what respect parts are defective.
5. Confusion about the correct order for reassembly.
6. Adjusting running clearances.
7. Road testing.
8. Final tuning.

Practical suggestion to solve the problems:

1. Preliminary cleaning of large parts—engines, transmissions, steering, suspensions, etc.,—should be carried out before removal from the car. Where road dirt and mud alone are present, wash clean with a high-pressure water jet, brushing to remove stubborn adhesions, and allow to drain and dry. Where oil or grease is also present, wash down with a proprietary compound (Gunk, Teepol etc.,) applying with a stiff brush—an old paint brush is suitable—into all crevices. Cover the distributor and ignition coils with a polythene bag and then apply a strong water jet to clear the loosened deposits. Allow to drain and dry. The assemblies will then be sufficiently clean to remove and transfer to the bench for the next stage.

    On the bench, further cleaning can be carried out, first wiping the parts as free as possible from grease with old newspaper. Avoid using rag or cotton waste which can leave clogging fibres behind. Any remaining grease can be removed with a brush dipped in paraffin. If necessary, traces of paraffin can be removed by carbon tetrachloride. Avoid using paraffin or petrol in large quantities for cleaning in enclosed areas, such as garages, on account of the high fire risk.

    When all exteriors have been cleaned, and not before, dismantling can be commenced. This ensures that dirt will not enter into interiors and orifices revealed by dismantling. In the next phases, where components have to be cleaned, use carbon tetrachloride in preference to petrol and keep the containers covered except when in use. After the components have been cleaned, plug small holes with tapered hard wood plugs cut to size and blank off larger orifices with grease-proof paper and masking tape. Do not use soft wood plugs or matchsticks as they may break.

2. It is not advisable to hammer on the end of a screw thread, but if it must be done, first screw on a nut to protect the thread, and use a lead hammer. This applies particularly to the removal of tapered cotters. Nuts and bolts seem to 'grow' together, especially in exhaust systems. If penetrating oil does not work, try the judicious application of heat, but be careful of starting a fire. Asbestos sheet or cloth is useful to isolate heat.

    Tight bushes or pieces of tail-pipe rusted into a silencer can be removed by splitting them with an open-ended hacksaw. Tight screws can sometimes be started by a tap from a hammer on the end of a suitable screwdriver. Many tight fittings will yield to the judicious use of a hammer, but it must be a soft-faced hammer if damage is to be avoided, use a heavy block on the opposite side to absorb shock. Any parts of the steering system which have been damaged should be renewed, as attempts to repair them may lead to cracking and subsequent failure, and steering ball joints should be disconnected using a recommended tool to prevent damage.

3 If often happens that an owner is baffled when trying to dismantle an unfamiliar piece of equipment. So many modern devices are pressed together or assembled by spinning-over flanges, that they must be sawn apart. The intention is that the whole assembly must be renewed. However, parts which appear to be in one piece to the naked eye, may reveal close-fitting joint lines when inspected with a magnifying glass, and, this may provide the necessary clue to dismantling. Left-handed screw threads are used where rotational forces would tend to unscrew a right-handed screw thread.

Be very careful when dismantling mechanisms which may come apart suddenly. Work in an enclosed space where the parts will be contained, and drape a piece of cloth over the device if springs are likely to fly in all directions. Mark everything which might be reassembled in the wrong position, scratched symbols may be used on unstressed parts, or a sequence of tiny dots from a centre punch can be useful. Stressed parts should never be scratched or centre-popped as this may lead to cracking under working conditions. Store parts which look alike in the correct order for reassembly. Never rely upon memory to assist in the assembly of complicated mechanisms, especially when they will be dismantled for a long time, but make notes, and drawings to supplement the diagrams in the manual, and put labels on detached wires. Rust stains may indicate unlubricated wear. This can sometimes be seen round the outside edge of a bearing cup in a universal joint. Look for bright rubbing marks on parts which normally should not make heavy contact. These might prove that something is bent or running out of true. For example, there might be bright marks on one side of a piston, at the top near the ring grooves, and others at the bottom of the skirt on the other side. This could well be the clue to a bent connecting rod. Suspected cracks can be proved by heating the component in a light oil to approximately 100°C, removing, drying off, and dusting with french chalk, if a crack is present the oil retained in the crack will stain the french chalk.

4 In determining wear, and the degree, against the permissible limits set in the manual, accurate measurement can only be achieved by the use of a micrometer. In many cases, the wear is given to the fourth place of decimals; that is in ten-thousandths of an inch. This can be read by the vernier scale on the barrel of a good micrometer. Bore diameters are more difficult to determine. If, however, the matching shaft is accurately measured, the degree of play in the bore can be felt as a guide to its suitability. In other cases, the shank of a twist drill of known diameter is a handy check.

Many methods have been devised for determining the clearance between bearing surfaces. To-day the best and simplest is by the use of Plastigage, obtainable from most garages. A thin plastic thread is laid between the two surfaces and the bearing is tightened, flattening the thread. On removal, the width of the thread is compared with a scale supplied with the thread and the clearance is read off directly. Sometimes joint faces leak persistently, even after gasket renewal. The fault will then be traceable to distortion, dirt or burrs. Studs which are screwed into soft metal frequently raise burrs at the point of entry. A quick cure for this is to chamfer the edge of the hole in the part which fits over the stud.

5 **Always check a replacement part with the original one before it is fitted.**

If parts are not marked, and the order for reassembly is not known, a little detective work will help. Look for marks which are due to wear to see if they can be mated. Joint faces may not be identical due to manufacturing errors, and parts which overlap may be stained, giving a clue to the correct position. Most fixings leave identifying marks especially if they were painted over on assembly. It is then easier to decide whether a nut, for instance, has a plain, a spring, or a shakeproof washer under it. All running surfaces become 'bedded' together after long spells of work and tiny imperfections on one part will be found to have left corresponding marks on the other. This is particularly true of shafts and bearings and even a score on a cylinder wall will show on the piston.

6 Checking end float or rocker clearances by feeler gauge may not always give accurate results because of wear. For instance, the rocker tip which bears on a valve stem may be deeply pitted, in which case the feeler will simply be bridging a depression. Thrust washers may also wear depressions in opposing faces to make accurate measurement difficult. End float is then easier to check by using a dial gauge. It is common practice to adjust end play in bearing assemblies, like front hubs with taper rollers, by doing up the axle nut until the hub becomes stiff to turn and then backing it off a little. Do not use this method with ballbearing hubs as the assembly is often preloaded by tightening the axle nut to its fullest extent. If the splitpin hole will not line up, file the base of the nut a little.

Steering assemblies often wear in the straight-ahead position. If any part is adjusted, make sure that it remains free when moved from lock to lock. Do not be surprised if an assembly like a steering gearbox, which is known to be carefully adjusted outside the car, becomes stiff when it is bolted in place. This will be due to distortion of the case by the pull of the mounting bolts, particularly if the mounting points are not all touching together. This problem may be met in other equipment and is cured by careful attention to the alignment of mounting points.

When a spanner is stamped with a size and A/F it means that the dimension is the width between the jaws and has no connection with ANF, which is the designation for the American National Fine thread. Coarse threads like Whitworth are rarely used on cars to-day except for studs which screw into soft aluminium or cast iron. For this reason it might be found that the top end of a cylinder head stud has a fine thread and the lower end a coarse thread to screw into the cylinder block. If the car has mainly UNF threads then it is likely that any coarse threads will be UNC, which are not the same as Whitworth. Small sizes have the same number of threads in Whitworth and UNC, but in the $\frac{1}{2}$ inch size for example, there are twelve threads to the inch in the former and thirteen in the latter.

7 After a major overhaul, particularly if a great deal of work has been done on the braking, steering and suspension systems, it is advisable to approach the problem of testing with care. If the braking system has been overhauled, apply heavy pressure to the brake pedal and get a second operator to check every possible source of leakage. The brakes may work extremely well, but a leak could cause complete failure after a few miles.

Do not fit the hub caps until every wheel nut has been checked for tightness, and make sure the tyre pressures are correct. Check the levels of coolant, lubricants and hydraulic fluids. Being satisfied that all is well, take the car on the road and test the brakes at once. Check the steering and the action of the handbrake. Do all this at moderate speeds on quiet roads, and make sure there is no other vehicle behind you when you try a rapid stop.

Finally, remember that many parts settle down after a time, so check for tightness of all fixings after the car has been on the road for a hundred miles or so.

8 It is useless to tune an engine which has not reached its normal running temperature. In the same way, the tune of an engine which is stiff after a rebore will be different when the engine is again running free. Remember too, that rocker clearances on pushrod operated valve gear will change when the cylinder head nuts are tightened after an initial period of running with a new head gasket.

Trouble may not always be due to what seems the obvious cause. Ignition, carburation and mechanical condition are interdependent and spitting back through the carburetter, which might be attributed to a weak mixture, can be caused by a sticking inlet valve.

For one final hint on tuning, never adjust more than one thing at a time or it will be impossible to tell which adjustment produced the desired result.

GLOSSARY OF TERMS

Allen key   Cranked wrench of hexagonal section for use with socket head screws.

Alternator   Electrical generator producing alternating current. Rectified to direct current for battery charging.

Ambient temperature   Surrounding atmospheric temperature.

Annulus   Used in engineering to indicate the outer ring gear of an epicyclic gear train.

Armature   The shaft carrying the windings, which rotates in the magnetic field of a generator or starter motor. That part of a solenoid or relay which is activated by the magnetic field.

Axial   In line with, or pertaining to, an axis.

Backlash   Play in meshing gears.

Balance lever   A bar where force applied at the centre is equally divided between connections at the ends.

Banjo axle   Axle casing with large diameter housing for the crownwheel and differential.

Bendix pinion   A self-engaging and self-disengaging drive on a starter motor shaft.

Bevel pinion   A conical shaped gearwheel, designed to mesh with a similar gear with an axis usually at 90 deg. to its own.

bhp   Brake horse power, measured on a dynamometer.

bmep   Brake mean effective pressure. Average pressure on a piston during the working stroke.

Brake cylinder   Cylinder with hydraulically operated piston(s) acting on brake shoes or pad(s).

Brake regulator   Control valve fitted in hydraulic braking system which limits brake pressure to rear brakes during heavy braking to prevent rear wheel locking.

Camber   Angle at which a wheel is tilted from the vertical.

Capacitor   Modern term for an electrical condenser. Part of distributor assembly, connected across contact breaker points, acts as an interference suppressor.

Castellated   Top face of a nut, slotted across the flats, to take a locking splitpin.

Castor   Angle at which the kingpin or swivel pin is tilted when viewed from the side.

cc   Cubic centimetres. Engine capacity is arrived at by multiplying the area of the bore in sq cm by the stroke in cm by the number of cylinders.

Clevis   U-shaped forked connector used with a clevis pin, usually at handbrake connections.

Collet   A type of collar, usually split and located in a groove in a shaft, and held in place by a retainer. The arrangement used to retain the spring(s) on a valve stem in most cases.

Commutator   Rotating segmented current distributor between armature windings and brushes in generator or motor.

Compression   The ratio, or quantitative relation, of the total volume (piston at bottom of stroke) to the unswept volume (piston at top of stroke) in an engine cylinder.

Condenser   See capacitor.

Core plug   Plug for blanking off a manufacturing hole in a casting.

Crownwheel   Large bevel gear in rear axle, driven by a bevel pinion attached to the propeller shaft. Sometimes called a 'ring wheel'.

'C'-spanner   Like a 'C' with a handle. For use on screwed collars without flats, but with slots or holes.

Damper   Modern term for shock-absorber, used in vehicle suspension systems to damp out spring oscillations.

Depression   The lowering of atmospheric pressure as in the inlet manifold and carburetter.

Dowel   Close tolerance pin, peg, tube, or bolt, which accurately locates mating parts.

Drag link   Rod connecting steering box drop arm (pitman arm) to nearest front wheel steering arm in certain types of steering systems.

Dry liner   Thinwall tube pressed into cylinder bore

Dry sump   Lubrication system where all oil is scavenged from the sump, and returned to a separate tank.

Dynamo   See Generator.

Electrode   Terminal, part of an electrical component, such as the points or 'Electrodes' of a sparking plug.

Electrolyte   In lead-acid car batteries a solution of sulphuric acid and distilled water.

End float   The axial movement between associated parts, end play.

EP   Extreme pressure. In lubricants, special grades for heavily loaded bearing surfaces, such as gear teeth in a gearbox, or crownwheel and pinion in a rear axle.

Fade	Of brakes. Reduced efficiency due to overheating.
Field coils	Windings on the polepieces of motors and generators.
Fillets	Narrow finishing strips usually applied to interior bodywork.
First motion shaft	Input shaft from clutch to gearbox.
Fullflow filter	Filters in which all the oil is pumped to the engine. If the element becomes clogged, a bypass valve operates to pass unfiltered oil to the engine.
FWD	Front wheel drive.
Gear pump	Two meshing gears in a close fitting casing. Oil is carried from the inlet round the outside of both gears in the spaces between the gear teeth and casing to the outlet, the meshing gear teeth prevent oil passing back to the inlet, and the oil is forced through the outlet port.
Generator	Modern term for 'Dynamo'. When rotated produces electrical current.
Grommet	A ring of protective or sealing material. Can be used to protect pipes or leads passing through bulkheads.
Grubscrew	Fully threaded headless screw with screwdriver slot. Used for locking, or alignment purposes.
Gudgeon pin	Shaft which connects a piston to its connecting rod. Sometimes called 'wrist pin', or 'piston pin'.
Halfshaft	One of a pair transmitting drive from the differential.
Helical	In spiral form. The teeth of helical gears are cut at a spiral angle to the side faces of the gearwheel.
Hot spot	Hot area that assists vapourisation of fuel on its way to cylinders. Often provided by close contact between inlet and exhaust manifolds.
HT	High Tension. Applied to electrical current produced by the ignition coil for the sparking plugs.
Hydrometer	A device for checking specific gravity of liquids. Used to check specific gravity of electrolyte.
Hypoid bevel gears	A form of bevel gear used in the rear axle drive gears. The bevel pinion meshes below the centre line of the crownwheel, giving a lower propeller shaft line.
Idler	A device for passing on movement. A free running gear between driving and driven gears. A lever transmitting track rod movement to a side rod in steering gear.
Impeller	A centrifugal pumping element. Used in water pumps to stimulate flow.
Journals	Those parts of a shaft that are in contact with the bearings.
Kingpin	The main vertical pin which carries the front wheel spindle, and permits steering movement. May be called 'steering pin' or 'swivel pin'.
Layshaft	The shaft which carries the laygear in the gearbox. The laygear is driven by the first motion shaft and drives the third motion shaft according to the gear selected. Sometimes called the 'countershaft' or 'second motion shaft.'
lb ft	A measure of twist or torque. A pull of 10 lb at a radius of 1 ft is a torque of 10 lb ft.
lb/sq in	Pounds per square inch.
Little-end	The small, or piston end of a connecting rod. Sometimes called the 'small-end'.
LT	Low Tension. The current output from the battery.
Mandrel	Accurately manufactured bar or rod used for test or centring purposes.
Manifold	A pipe, duct, or chamber, with several branches.
Needle rollers	Bearing rollers with a length many times their diameter.
Oil bath	Reservoir which lubricates parts by immersion. In air filters, a separate oil supply for wetting a wire mesh element to hold the dust.
Oil wetted	In air filters, a wire mesh element lightly oiled to trap and hold airborne dust.
Overlap	Period during which inlet and exhaust valves are open together.
Panhard rod	Bar connected between fixed point on chassis and another on axle to control sideways movement.
Pawl	Pivoted catch which engages in the teeth of a ratchet to permit movement in one direction only.
Peg spanner	Tool with pegs, or pins, to engage in holes or slots in the part to be turned.
Pendant pedals	Pedals with levers that are pivoted at the top end.
Phillips screwdriver	A cross-point screwdriver for use with the cross-slotted heads of Phillips screws.
Pinion	A small gear, usually in relation to another gear.
Piston-type damper	Shock absorber in which damping is controlled by a piston working in a closed oil-filled cylinder.
Preloading	Preset static pressure on ball or roller bearings not due to working loads.
Radial	Radiating from a centre, like the spokes of a wheel.

Radius rod	Pivoted arm confining movement of a part to an arc of fixed radius.
Ratchet	Toothed wheel or rack which can move in one direction only, movement in the other being prevented by a pawl.
Ring gear	A gear tooth ring attached to outer periphery of flywheel. Starter pinion engages with it during starting.
Runout	Amount by which rotating part is out of true.
Semi-floating axle	Outer end of rear axle halfshaft is carried on bearing inside axle casing. Wheel hub is secured to end of shaft.
Servo	A hydraulic or pneumatic system for assisting, or, augmenting a physical effort. See 'Vacuum Servo'.
Setscrew	One which is threaded for the full length of the shank.
Shackle	A coupling link, used in the form of two parallel pins connected by side plates to secure the end of the master suspension spring and absorb the effects of deflection.
Shell bearing	Thinwalled steel shell lined with anti-friction metal. Usually semi-circular and used in pairs for main and big-end bearings.
Shock absorber	See 'Damper'.
Silentbloc	Rubber bush bonded to inner and outer metal sleeves.
Socket-head screw	Screw with hexagonal socket for an Allen key.
Solenoid	A coil of wire creating a magnetic field when electric current passes through it. Used with a soft iron core to operate contacts or a mechanical device.
Spur gear	A gear with teeth cut axially across the periphery.
Stub axle	Short axle fixed at one end only.
Tachometer	An instrument for accurate measurement of rotating speed. Usually indicates in revolutions per minute.
TDC	Top Dead Centre. The highest point reached by a piston in a cylinder, with the crank and connecting rod in line.
Thermostat	Automatic device for regulating temperature. Used in vehicle coolant systems to open a valve which restricts circulation at low temperature.
Third motion shaft	Output shaft of gearbox.
Threequarter floating axle	Outer end of rear axle halfshaft flanged and bolted to wheel hub, which runs on bearing mounted on outside of axle casing. Vehicle weight is not carried by the axle shaft.
Thrust bearing or washer	Used to reduce friction in rotating parts subject to axial loads.
Torque	Turning or twisting effort. See 'lb ft'.
Track rod	The bar(s) across the vehicle which connect the steering arms and maintain the front wheels in their correct alignment.
UJ	Universal joint. A coupling between shafts which permits angular movement.
UNF	Unified National Fine screw thread.
Vacuum servo	Device used in brake system, using difference between atmospheric pressure and inlet manifold depression to operate a piston which acts to augment brake pressure as required. See 'Servo'.
Venturi	A restriction or 'choke' in a tube, as in a carburetter, used to increase velocity to obtain a reduction in pressure.
Vernier	A sliding scale for obtaining fractional readings of the graduations of an adjacent scale.
Welch plug	A domed thin metal disc which is partially flattened to lock in a recess. Used to plug core holes in castings.
Wet liner	Removable cylinder barrel, sealed against coolant leakage, where the coolant is in direct contact with the outer surface.
Wet sump	A reservoir attached to the crankcase to hold the lubricating oil.

INDEX

THE AUTOBOOK SERIES OF WORKSHOP MANUALS

Make				Author	Title

ALFA ROMEO

Make				Author	Title
1600 Giulia TI 1961–67	..	..	..	Ball	Alfa Romeo Giulia 1962–71 Autobook
1600 Giulia Sprint 1962–68	..	..	..	Ball	Alfa Romeo Giulia 1962–71 Autobook
1600 Giulia Spider 1962–68	..	..	..	Ball	Alfa Romeo Giulia 1962–71 Autobook
1600 Giulia Super 1965–70	..	..	..	Ball	Alfa Romeo Giulia 1962–71 Autobook
1750 Giulia Saloon 1968–71	..	..	..	Ball	Alfa Romeo Giulia 1962–71 Autobook
1750 Giulia Spider 1968–71	..	..	..	Ball	Alfa Romeo Giulia 1962–71 Autobook
1750 Giulia Coupé 1968–71	..	..	..	Ball	Alfa Romeo Giulia 1962–71 Autobook

ASTON MARTIN

All models 1921–58	..	..	..	Coram	Aston Martin 1921–58 Autobook

AUDI

Auto Union Audi 100	..	..	..	Ball	Audi 100 1969–71 Autobook
Audi 100 1969–71	..	..	..	Ball	Audi 100 1969–71 Autobook
Audi 100 S 1969–71	..	..	..	Ball	Audi 100 1969–71 Autobook
Audi 100 LS 1969–71	..	..	..	Ball	Audi 100 1969–71 Autobook

AUSTIN

A30 1951–56	..	..	..	Ball	Austin A30, A35, A40 Autobook
A35 1956–62	..	..	..	Ball	Austin A30, A35, A40 Autobook
A40 Farina 1957–67	..	..	..	Ball	Austin A30, A35, A40 Autobook
A40 Cambridge 1954–57	..	..	..	Ball	BMC Autobook Three
A50 Cambridge 1954–57	..	..	..	Ball	BMC Autobook Three
A55 Cambridge Mk 1 1957–58	..	..	..	Ball	BMC Autobook Three
A55 Cambridge Mk 2 1958–61	..	..	..	Ball	Austin A55 Mk 2, A60 1958–69 Autobook
A60 Cambridge 1961–69	..	..	..	Ball	Austin A55 Mk 2, A60 1958–69 Autobook
A99 1959–61	..	..	..	Ball	Austin A99, A110 1959–68 Autobook
A110 1961–68	..	..	..	Ball	Austin A99, A110 1959–68 Autobook
Mini 1959–71	..	..	..	Ball	Mini 1959–71 Autobook
Mini Clubman 1969–71	..	..	..	Ball	Mini 1959–71 Autobook
Mini Cooper 1961–70	..	..	..	Ball	Mini Cooper 1961–70 Autobook
Mini Cooper S 1963–70	..	..	..	Ball	Mini Cooper 1961–70 Autobook
1100 Mk 1 1963–67	..	..	..	Ball	1100 Mk 1 1962–67 Autobook
1100 Mk 2 1968–70	..	..	..	Ball	1100 Mk 2, 1300 Mk 1, 2, America 1968–71 Autobook
1300 Mk 1, 2 1968–71	..	..	..	Ball	1100 Mk 2, 1300 Mk 1, 2, America 1968–71 Autobook
America 1968–71	..	..	..	Ball	1100 Mk 2, 1300 Mk 1, 2, America 1968–71 Autobook
1800 Mk 1, 2 1964–71	..	..	..	Ball	1800 1964–71 Autobook
1800 S 1969–71	..	..	..	Ball	1800 1964–71 Autobook
Maxi 1500 1969–71	..	..	..	Ball	Austin Maxi 1969–71 Autobook
Maxi 1750 1970–71	..	..	..	Ball	Austin Maxi 1969–71 Autobook

AUSTIN HEALEY

100/6 1955–59	..	..	..	Ball	Austin Healey 100/6, 3000 1956–68 Autobook
Sprite 1958–71	..	..	..	Ball	Sprite, Midget 1958–71 Autobook
3000 Mk 1, 2, 3 1959–68	..	..	..	Ball	Austin Healey 100/6, 3000 1956–68 Autobook

BEDFORD

CA Mk 1 and 2 1957–64	..	..	..	Ball	Vauxhall Victor 1, 2 FB 1957–64 Autobook
Beagle HA 1964–66	..	..	..	Ball	Vauxhall Viva HA 1964–66 Autobook

BMW

1600 1966–70	..	..	..	Ball	BMW 1600 1966–70 Autobook
1600–2 1966–70	..	..	..	Ball	BMW 1600 1966–70 Autobook
1600TI 1966–70	..	..	..	Ball	BMW 1600 1966–70 Autobook
1800 1964–70	..	..	..	Ball	BMW 1800 1964–70 Autobook
1800TI 1964–67	..	..	..	Ball	BMW 1800 1964–70 Autobook
2000 1966–70	..	..	..	Ball	BMW 2000, 2002 1966–70 Autobook

Make					Author	Title
2000A 1966–70	..	..	..	..	Ball	BMW 2000, 2002 1966–70 Autobook
2000TI 1966–70	..	..	..	..	Ball	BMW 2000, 2002 1966–70 Autobook
2000CS 1967–70	..	..	..	..	Ball	BMW 2000, 2002 1966–70 Autobook
2000CA 1967–70	..	..	..	..	Ball	BMW 2000, 2002 1966–70 Autobook
2002 1968–70	..	..	..	..	Ball	BMW 2000, 2002 1966–70 Autobook

CITROEN

| DS19 1955–65 | .. | .. | .. | .. | Ball | Citroen DS19, ID19 1955–66 Autobook |
| ID19 1956–66 .. | .. | .. | .. | .. | Ball | Citroen DS19, ID19 1955–66 Autobook |

COMMER

Cob Series 1, 2, 3 1956–65	..	..	..	Ball	Hillman Minx 1 to 5 1956–65 Autobook
Imp Vans 1963–68	..	..	..	..	Smith	Hillman Imp 1963–68 Autobook
Imp Vans 1969–71	..	..	..	..	Ball	Hillman Imp 1969–71 Autobook

DAIMLER

| Daimler Sovereign 2.8, 4.2 litre 1970–72 | .. | Ball | Jaguar XJ6 1968–72 Autobook |

DE DION BOUTON

One-cylinder 1899–1907	..	..	..	Mercredy	De Dion Bouton Autobook One
Two-cylinder 1903–1907	..	..	..	Mercredy	De Dion Bouton Autobook One
Four-cylinder 1905–1907	..	..	..	Mercredy	De Dion Bouton Autobook One

DATSUN

1200 B 110 1970–72 ..	..	..	..	Ball	Datsun 1200 1970–72 Autobook
1200 KB 110 1970–72	..	..	..	Ball	Datsun 1200 1970–72 Autobook
1300 1968–70	..	..	..	..	Ball	Datsun 1300, 1600 1968–70 Autobook
1600 1968–70	..	..	..	..	Ball	Datsun 1300, 1600 1968–70 Autobook
240Z HLS 1970–71	..	..	..	Ball	Datsun 240Z Sport 1970–71 Autobook
240Z HS 1970–71	..	..	..	Ball	Datsun 240Z Sport 1970–71 Autobook

FIAT

500 1957–61 ..	..	..	..	..	Ball	Fiat 500 1957–69 Autobook
500D 1960–65	..	..	..	..	Ball	Fiat 500 1957–69 Autobook
500F 1965–69	..	..	..	..	Ball	Fiat 500 1957–69 Autobook
500L 1968–69	..	..	..	..	Ball	Fiat 500 1957–69 Autobook
600 633 cc 1955–61	..	..	..	Ball	Fiat 600, 600D 1955–69 Autobook
600D 767 cc 1960–69 ..	..	..	..	Ball	Fiat 600, 600D 1955–69 Autobook
850 1964–71 ..	..	..	..	..	Ball	Fiat 850 1964–71 Autobook
850S 1964–71	..	..	..	..	Ball	Fiat 850 1964–71 Autobook
850S Coupé 1965–68	..	..	..	Ball	Fiat 850 1964–71 Autobook
850S Special 1968–71	..	..	..	Ball	Fiat 850 1964–71 Autobook
850S Spyder 1965–68	..	..	..	Ball	Fiat 850 1964–71 Autobook
850 Sport 903 cc 1968–71	..	..	..	Ball	Fiat 850 1964–71 Autobook
1300 1961–66	..	..	..	..	Ball	Fiat 1300, 1500 1961–67 Autobook
1500 1961–67	..	..	..	..	Ball	Fiat 1300, 1500 1961–67 Autobook
124A 1966–71	..	..	..	..	Ball	Fiat 124 1966–71 Autobook
124AF 1967–71	..	..	..	..	Ball	Fiat 124 1966–71 Autobook
124 Special 1969–71 ..	..	..	..	Ball	Fiat 124 1966–71 Autobook
124 Spyder 1966–70	..	..	..	Ball	Fiat 124 Sport 1966–70 Autobook
124 Coupé 1967–69 ..	..	..	..	Ball	Fiat 124 Sport 1966–70 Autobook

FORD

Anglia 100E 1953–59 ..	..	..	..	Ball	Ford Anglia Prefect 100E Autobook
Anglia 105E 1959–67 ..	..	..	..	Smith	Ford Anglia 105E, Prefect 107E 1959–67 Autobook
Anglia Super 123E 1962–67	..	..	..	Smith	Ford Anglia 105E, Prefect 107E 1959–67 Autobook
Capri 109E 1962	..	..	..	..	Smith	Ford Classic, Capri 1961–64 Autobook
Capri 116E 1962–64 ..	..	..	..	Smith	Ford Classic, Capri 1961–64 Autobook
Capri 1300, 1300GT 1968–71	..	..	..	Ball	Ford Capri 1300, 1600 1968–71 Autobook
Capri 1600, 1600GT 1968–71	..	..	..	Ball	Ford Capri 1300, 1600 1968–71 Autobook
Capri 2000 GT 1969–71	..	..	..	Ball	Ford Capri 2000 GT, 3000 GT 1969–71 Autobook

Make				Author	Title
Capri 3000 GT 1969–71	..	..	..	Ball	Ford Capri 2000 GT, 3000 GT 1969–71 Autobook
Capri 3000 E 1969–71	..	..	..	Ball	Ford Capri 2000 GT, 3000 GT 1969–71 Autobook
Classic 109E 1961–62	..	..	..	Smith	Ford Classic, Capri 1961–64 Autobook
Classic 116E 1962–63	..	..	..	Smith	Ford Classic, Capri 1961–64 Autobook
Consul Mk 1 1950–56	..	..	..	Ball	Ford Consul, Zephyr, Zodiac 1, 2 1950–62 Autobook
Consul Mk 2 1956–62	..	..	..	Ball	Ford Consul, Zephyr, Zodiac 1, 2 1950–62 Autobook
Corsair Straight Four 1963–65	..	..	..	Ball	Ford Corsair Straight Four 1963–65 Autobook
Corsair Straight Four GT 1963–65	..	..	..	Ball	Ford Corsair Straight Four 1963–65 Autobook
Corsair V4 3004E 1965–68	..	..	..	Smith	Ford Corsair V4 1965–68 Autobook
Corsair V4 GT 1965–66	..	..	..	Smith	Ford Corsair V4 1965–68 Autobook
Corsair V4 1663 cc 1969–70	..	..	..	Ball	Ford Corsair V4 1969–70 Autobook
Corsair 2000, 2000E 1966–68	..	..	..	Smith	Ford Corsair V4 1965–68 Autobook
Corsair 2000, 2000E 1969–70	..	..	..	Ball	Ford Corsair V4 1969–70 Autobook
Cortina 113E 1962–66	..	..	..	Smith	Ford Cortina 1962–66 Autobook
Cortina Super 118E 1963–66	..	..	..	Smith	Ford Cortina 1962–66 Autobook
Cortina Lotus 125E 1963–66	..	..	..	Smith	Ford Cortina 1962–66 Autobook
Cortina GT 118E 1963–66	..	..	..	Smith	Ford Cortina 1962–66 Autobook
Cortina 1300 1967–68	..	..	..	Smith	Ford Cortina 1967–68 Autobook
Cortina 1300 1969–70	..	..	..	Ball	Ford Cortina 1969–70 Autobook
Cortina 1500 1967–68	..	..	..	Smith	Ford Cortina 1967–68 Autobook
Cortina 1600 (including Lotus) 1967–68	..	..	..	Smith	Ford Cortina 1967–68 Autobook
Cortina 1600 1969–70	..	..	..	Ball	Ford Cortina 1969–70 Autobook
Cortina 1600 OHC Mk 3, GT 1971–72			..	Ball	Ford Cortina 1600 GT, 2000, OHC, Mk 3 1971–72 Autobook.
Cortina 2000 OHC HC Mk 3 1971–72		..		Ball	Ford Cortina 1600 GT, 2000, OHC, Mk 3 1971–72 Autobook
Escort 100E 1955–59 ..	..	..	..	Ball	Ford Anglia Prefect 100E Autobook
Escort 1100 1967–71 ..	..	..	..	Ball	Ford Escort 1967–71 Autobook
Escort 1300 1967–71	..	..	..	Ball	Ford Escort 1967–71 Autobook
Executive 1966–71	..	..	..	Ball	Ford Zephyr V4, V6, Zodiac 1966–71 Autobook
Prefect 100E 1954–59	..	..	..	Ball	Ford Anglia Prefect 100E Autobook
Prefect 107E 1959–61	..	..	..	Smith	Ford Anglia 105E, Prefect 107E 1959–67 Autobook
Popular 100E 1959–62	..	..	..	Ball	Ford Anglia Prefect 100E Autobook
Squire 100E 1955–59	..	..	..	Ball	Ford Anglia Prefect 100E Autobook
Taunus 1300 OHC LC and HC 1971–72		..		Ball	Ford Cortina 1600 GT, 2000, OHC, Mk 3, 1971–72 Autobook
Taunus 1600 OHC GT 1971–72	..		..	Ball	Ford Cortina 1600 GT, 2000, OHC, Mk 3 1971–72 Autobook
Zephyr Mk 1 1950–56	..	..	..	Ball	Ford Consul, Zephyr, Zodiac 1, 2 1950–62 Autobook
Zephyr Mk 2 1956–62	..	..	..	Ball	Ford Consul, Zephyr, Zodiac 1, 2 1950–62 Autobook
Zephyr 4 Mk 3 1962–66	..	..	..	Ball	Ford Zephyr, Zodiac Mk 3 1962–66 Autobook
Zephyr 6 Mk 3 1962–66	..	..	..	Ball	Ford Zephyr, Zodiac Mk 3 1962–66 Autobook
Zodiac Mk 3 1962–66 ..	..	..	..	Ball	Ford Zephyr, Zodiac Mk 3 1962–66 Autobook
Zodiac Mk 1 1953–56 ..	..	..	..	Ball	Ford Consul, Zephyr, Zodiac 1, 2 1950–62 Autobook
Zodiac Mk 2 1956–62 ..	..	..	..	Ball	Ford Consul, Zephyr, Zodiac 1, 2 1950–62 Autobook
Zephyr V4 2 litre 1966–71	..	..	..	Ball	Ford Zephyr V4, V6, Zodiac 1966–71 Autobook
Zephyr V6 2.5 litre 1966–71	..	..	..	Ball	Ford Zephyr V4, V6, Zodiac 1966–71 Autobook
Zodiac V6 3 litre 1966–71	..	..	..	Ball	Ford Zephyr V4, V6, Zodiac 1966–71 Autobook

HILLMAN

Make				Author	Title
Avenger, 1970–71	..	..	..	Ball	Hillman Avenger 1970–71 Autobook
Avenger, GT 1970–71 ..	..	..	..	Ball	Hillman Avenger 1970–71 Autobook
Hunter, GT 1966–71	..	..	..	Ball	Hillman Hunter 1966–71 Autobook
Minx series 1, 2, 3 1956–59	..	..	..	Ball	Hillman Minx 1 to 5 1956–65 Autobook
Minx series 3A, 3B, 3C 1959–63	..	..	..	Ball	Hillman Minx 1 to 5 1956–65 Autobook
Minx series 5 1963–65	..	..	..	Ball	Hillman Minx 1 to 5 1956–65 Autobook
Minx series 6 1965–67	..	..	..	Ball	Hillman Minx 1965–67 Autobook
New Minx 1500, 1725 1966–70	..	..	..	Ball	Hillman Minx 1966–70 Autobook
Imp 1963–68 ..	..	..	..	Smith	Hillman Imp 1963–68 Autobook
Imp 1969–71 ..	..	..	..	Ball	Hillman Imp 1969–71 Autobook

Make					Author	Title
Husky series 1, 2, 3 1958–65	..	..		..	Ball	Hillman Minx 1 to 5 1956–65 Autobook
Husky Estate 1969–71		..	..	..	Ball	Hillman Imp 1969–71 Autobook
Super Minx Mk 1, 2, 3 1961–65		..		..	Ball	Hillman Super Minx 1961–65 Autobook
Super Minx Mk 4 1965–67	..		..	..	Ball	Hillman Minx 1965–67 Autobook

HUMBER

Sceptre Mk 1 1963–65		..	..	..	Ball	Hillman Super Minx 1961–65 Autobook
Sceptre Mk 2 1965–67		..	..	..	Ball	Hillman Minx 1965–67 Autobook
Sceptre 1967–71	..	..	..	..	Ball	Hillman Hunter 1966–71 Autobook

JAGUAR

XK 120 1948–54	..	..	..	..	Ball	Jaguar XK 120, 140, 150 Mk 7, 8, 9 1948–61 Autobook
XK 140 1954–57	..	..	..	..	Ball	Jaguar XK 120, 140, 150 Mk 7, 8, 9 1948–61 Autobook
XK 150 1957–61	..	..	..	..	Ball	Jaguar XK 120, 140, 150 Mk 7, 8, 9 1948–61 Autobook
XK 150S 1959–61	..		..	..	Ball	Jaguar XK 120, 140, 150 Mk 7, 8, 9 1948–61 Autobook
Mk 7, 7M, 8, 9 1950–61		..		..	Ball	Jaguar XK 120, 140, 150 Mk 7, 8, 9 1948–61 Autobook
2.4 Mk 1, 2 1955–67	..	..		..	Ball	Jaguar 2.4, 3.4, 3.8 Mk 1, 2 1955–69 Autobook
3.4 Mk 1, 2 1957–67	..	..		..	Ball	Jaguar 2.4, 3.4, 3.8 Mk 1, 2 1955–69 Autobook
3.8 Mk 2 1959–67		..	..	..	Ball	Jaguar 2.4, 3.4, 3.8 Mk 1, 2 1955–69 Autobook
240 1967–69	..	..		..	Ball	Jaguar 2.4, 3.4, 3.8 Mk 1, 2 1955–69 Autobook
340 1967–69	..	..		..	Ball	Jaguar 2.4, 3.4, 3.8 Mk 1, 2 1955–69 Autobook
E Type 3.8 1961–65	..	..		..	Ball	Jaguar E Type 1961–70 Autobook
E Type 4.2 1964–69	..		..	..	Ball	Jaguar E Type 1961–70 Autobook
E Type 4.2 2+2 1966–70		..		..	Ball	Jaguar E Type 1961–70 Autobook
E Type 4.2 Series 2 1969–70		..		..	Ball	Jaguar E Type 1961–70 Autobook
S Type 3.4 1963–68	..	..		..	Ball	Jaguar S Type and 420 1963–68 Autobook
S Type 3.8 1963–68	..	..		..	Ball	Jaguar S Type and 420 1963–68 Autobook
420 1963–68	..	..	..	..	Ball	Jaguar S Type and 420 1963–68 Autobook
XJ6 2.8 litre 1968–72	..		..	..	Ball	Jaguar XJ6 1968–72 Autobook
XJ6 4.2 litre 1968–72	..	..		..	Ball	Jaguar XJ6 1968–72 Autobook

JOWETT

Javelin PA 1947–49	..	..		..	Mitchell	Jowett Javelin Jupiter 1947–53 Autobook
Javelin PB 1949–50	..	..		..	Mitchell	Jowett Javelin Jupiter 1947–53 Autobook
Javelin PC 1950–51	..	..		..	Mitchell	Jowett Javelin Jupiter 1947–53 Autobook
Javelin PD 1951–52	..	..		..	Mitchell	Jowett Javelin Jupiter 1947–53 Autobook
Javelin PE 1952–53	..		..	..	Mitchell	Jowett Javelin Jupiter 1947–53 Autobook
Jupiter Mk 1 SA 1949–52		..		..	Mitchell	Jowett Javelin Jupiter 1947–53 Autobook
Jupiter Mk 1A SC 1952–53	..		..	..	Mitchell	Jowett Javelin Jupiter 1947–53 Autobook

LANDROVER

Series 1 1948–58	..	..		..	Ball	Landrover 1, 2 1948–61 Autobook
Series 2 1997 cc 1959–61		..	..	..	Ball	Landrover 1, 2 1948–61 Autobook
Series 2 2052 cc 1959–61		..	..	..	Ball	Landrover 1, 2 1948–61 Autobook
Series 2 2286 cc 1959–61		..	..	..	Ball	Landrover 2, 2A 1959–71 Autobook
Series 2A 2286 cc 1961–71		..	..	..	Ball	Landrover 2, 2A 1959–71 Autobook
Series 2A 2625 cc 1967–71		..	..	..	Ball	Landrover 2, 2A 1959–71 Autobook

MG

TA 1936–39	..	..	..	..	Ball	MG TA to TF 1936–55 Autobook
TB 1939	..	..	..	..	Ball	MG TA to TF 1936–55 Autobook
TC 1945–49	..	..	..	..	Ball	MG TA to TF 1936–55 Autobook
TD 1950–53	..	..	..	..	Ball	MG TA to TF 1936–55 Autobook
TF 1953–54	..	..	..	..	Ball	MG TA to TF 1936–55 Autobook
TF 1500 1954–55	..	..	..	..	Ball	MG TA to TF 1936–55 Autobook
Midget 1961–71	..	..	..	..	Ball	Sprite, Midget 1958–71 Autobook
Magnette ZA, ZB 1955–59	..	..		..	Ball	BMC Autobook Three
MGA 1500, 1600 1955–62	..	..		..	Ball	MGA, MGB 1955–68 Autobook
MGA Twin Cam 1958–60	..	..		..	Ball	MGA, MGB 1955–68 Autobook

Make				Author	Title
MGB 1962–68	..	..	..	Ball	MGA, MGB 1955–68 Autobook
MGB 1969–71			..	Ball	MG MGB 1969–71 Autobook
1100 Mk 1 1962–67	..	..	..	Ball	1100 Mk 1 1962–67 Autobook
1100 Mk 2 1968	..		..	Ball	1100 Mk 2, 1300 Mk 1, 2, America 1968–71 Autobook
1300 Mk 1, 2 1968–71	..	..	..	Ball	1100 Mk 2, 1300 Mk 1, 2, America 1968–71 Autobook

MERCEDES-BENZ

190B 1959–61	..	..	..	Ball	Mercedes-Benz 190 B, C, 200 1959–68 Autobook
190C 1961–65	..	..	..	Ball	Mercedes-Benz 190 B, C, 200 1959–68 Autobook
200 1965–68	..	..	..	Ball	Mercedes-Benz 190 B, C, 200 1959–68 Autobook
220B 1959–65	..	..	..	Ball	Mercedes-Benz 220 1959–65 Autobook
220SB 1959–65	..	..	..	Ball	Mercedes-Benz 220 1959–65 Autobook
220SEB 1959–65	..	..	..	Ball	Mercedes-Benz 220 1959–65 Autobook
220SEBC 1961–65	..	..	..	Ball	Mercedes-Benz 220 1959–65 Autobook
230 1965–67	..	..	..	Ball	Mercedes-Benz 230 1963–68 Autobook
230 S 1965–68	..	..	..	Ball	Mercedes-Benz 230 1963–68 Autobook
230 SL 1963–67	..	..	..	Ball	Mercedes-Benz 230 1963–68 Autobook
250 S 1965–68	..	..	..	Ball	Mercedes-Benz 250 1965–67 Autobook
250 SE 1965–67	..	..	..	Ball	Mercedes-Benz 250 1965–67 Autobook
250 SE BC 1965–67	..	..	..	Ball	Mercedes-Benz 250 1965–67 Autobook
250 SL 1967	..	..	..	Ball	Mercedes-Benz 250 1965–67 Autobook

MORGAN

Four wheelers 1936–69	..	..	..	Clarke	Morgan 1936–69 Autobook

MORRIS

Oxford 2. 3 1954–59	..	..	..	Ball	BMC Autobook Three
Oxford 5, 6 1959–70	..	..	..	Ball	Morris Oxford 5, 6 1959–70 Autobook
Marina 1.3, 1.3 TC 1971–72	..	..	..	Ball	Morris Marina 1971–72 Autobook
Marina 1.8, 1.8 TC 1971–72	..	..	..	Ball	Morris Marina 1971–72 Autobook
Minor series 2 1952–56	..	..	..	Ball	Morris Minor 1952–71 Autobook
Minor 1000 1957–71	..	..	..	Ball	Morris Minor 1952–71 Autobook
Mini 1959–71	..	..		Ball	Mini 1959–71 Autobook
Mini Clubman 1969–71	..	..	..	Ball	Mini 1959–71 Autobook
Minor series 2 1952–56	..	..	..	Ball	Morris Minor 1952–71 Autobook
Minor 1000 1957–71	..	..	..	Ball	Morris Minor 1952–71 Autobook
Mini Cooper 1961–70	..	..	..	Ball	Mini Cooper 1961–70 Autobook
Mini Cooper S 1963–70	..	..	..	Ball	Mini Cooper 1961–70 Autobook
1100 Mk 1 1962–67	..	..	..	Ball	1100 Mk 1 1962–67 Autobook
1100 Mk 2 1968–70	..	..	..	Ball	1100 Mk 2, 1300 Mk 1, 2, America 1968–71 Autobook
1300 Mk 1, 2 1968–71	..	..	..	Ball	1100 Mk 2, 1300 Mk 1, 2, America 1968–71 Autobook
1800 Mk 1, 2 1966–71	..	..	..	Ball	1800 1964–71 Autobook
1800 S 1968–71	..	..	..	Ball	1800 1964–71 Autobook

NSU

Prinz 1000 L, LS 1963–67	..	..	..	Ball	NSU 1000 1963–70 Autobook
Prinz TT, TTS 1965–70	..	..	..	Ball	NSU 1000 1963–70 Autobook
1000 C 1967–70	..	..	..	Ball	NSU 1000 1963–70 Autobook
TYP 110 1966–67	..	..	..	Ball	NSU 1000 1963–70 Autobook
110 SC 1967	..	..	..	Ball	NSU 1000 1963–70 Autobook
1200, C, TT 1967–70	..	..	..	Ball	NSU 1000 1963–70 Autobook

OPEL

Kadett 993cc 1962–65	..	..	..	Ball	Opel Kadett, Olympia 993cc and 1078cc 1962–71 Autobook
Kadett 1078cc 1965–71	..	..	..	Ball	Opel Kadett, Olympia 993cc and 1078cc 1962–71 Autobook
Kadett 1492cc 1967–71	..	..	..	Ball	Opel Kadett, Olympia 1492cc, 1698cc and 1897cc 1967–71 Autobook
Kadett 1698cc 1967–70	..	..	..	Ball	Opel Kadett, Olympia 1492cc, 1698cc and 1897cc 1967–71 Autobook

Make				Author	Title
Kadett 1897cc 1967–71	..	..	..	Ball	Opel Kadett, Olympia 1492cc, 1698cc and 1897cc 1967–71 Autobook
Olympia 1078cc 1967–70	..	..	..	Ball	Opel Kadett, Olympia 993cc and 1078cc 1962–71 Autobook
Olympia 1492cc 1967–70	..	..	..	Ball	Opel Kadett, Olympia 1492cc, 1698cc and 1897cc 1967–71 Autobook
Olympia 1698cc 1967–70	..	..	..	Ball	Opel Kadett, Olympia 1492cc, 1698cc and 1897cc 1967–71 Autobook
Olympia 1897cc 1967–70	..	..	..	Ball	Opel Kadett, Olympia 1492cc, 1698cc and 1897cc 1967–71 Autobook
Rekord C 1.5, 1.7, 1.9 1966–70	..	..	..	Ball	Opel Rekord C 1966–70 Autobook

PEUGEOT

Make				Author	Title
404 1960–69	..	..	..	Ball	Peugeot 404 1960–69 Autobook
504 1968–70 (incl. fuel injection)		..	..	Ball	Peugeot 504 1968–70 Autobook

PLYMOUTH

Make				Author	Title
Cricket 1971	..	..	..	..	Ball	Hillman Avenger 1970–71 Autobook

PORSCHE

Make				Author	Title
356A 1957–59	..	..	..	..	Ball	Porsche 356A, 356B, 356C 1957–65 Autobook
356B 1959–63	..	..	..	..	Ball	Porsche 356A, 356B, 356C 1957–65 Autobook
356C 1963–65	..	..	..	..	Ball	Porsche 356A, 356B, 356C 1957–65 Autobook
911 1964–67	..	..	..	..	Ball	Porsche 911 1964–69 Autobook
911L 1967–68	..	..	..	..	Ball	Porsche 911 1964–69 Autobook
911S 1966–69	..	..	..	..	Ball	Porsche 911 1964–69 Autobook
911T 1967–69	..	..	..	..	Ball	Porsche 911 1964–69 Autobook
911E 1968–69	..	..	..	..	Ball	Porsche 911 1964–69 Autobook
912 1582cc 1965–69	..	..	..	..	Ball	Porsche 912 1965–69 Autobook

RELIANT

Make				Author	Title
Regal Coupé 1952–56	..	..	..	Ball	Reliant Regal 1952–70 Autobook
Regal Mk 3, 4, 5, 6 1957–62	..	..	..	Ball	Reliant Regal 1952–70 Autobook
Regal 3/25 1962–68	..	..	..	Ball	Reliant Regal 1952–70 Autobook
Regal 3/30 1968–70	..	..	..	Ball	Reliant Regal 1952–70 Autobook
5 cwt, Super, Supervan 1956–70	..	..	Ball	Reliant Regal 1952–70 Autobook

RENAULT

Make				Author	Title
R4L 748cc, 845cc 1961–65	..	..	..	Ball	Renault R4, R4L, 4 1961–70 Autobook
R4 845cc 1962–66	..	..	..	Ball	Renault R4, R4L, 4 1961–70 Autobook
4 845cc 1966–70	..	..	..	Ball	Renault R4, R4L, 4 1961–70 Autobook
6 1968–70	..	..	..	Ball	Renault 6 1968–70 Autobook
R8 956cc 1962–65	..	..	..	Ball	Renault 8, 10, 1100 1962–70 Autobook
8 956cc, 1108cc 1965–70	..	..	..	Ball	Renault 8, 10, 1100 1962–70 Autobook
8S 1108cc, 1968–70	..	..	..	Ball	Renault 8, 10, 1100 1962–70 Autobook
1100 1108cc 1964–69	..	..	..	Ball	Renault 8, 10, 1100 1962–70 Autobook
R10 1108cc 1967–69	..	..	..	Ball	Renault 8, 10, 1100 1962–70 Autobook
10 1289cc 1969–70	..	..	..	Ball	Renault 8, 10, 1100 1962–70 Autobook
Dauphine (R1090) 1957–64	..	..	Ball	Renault Dauphine Floride 1957–67 Autobook
Gordini Models (R1091 and R1095) 1959–67		Ball	Renault Dauphine Floride 1957–67 Autobook
Floride (R1092) 1959–63	..	..	..	Ball	Renault Dauphine Floride 1957–67 Autobook
16 1470cc 1965–71	..	..	..	Ball	Renault R16 1965–71 Autobook
16TS 1968–71	..	..	..	..	Ball	Renault R16 1965–71 Autobook
16TL 1970–71	..	..	..	..	Ball	Renault R16 1965–71 Autobook
12L 1969–71	..	..	..	..	Ball	Renault 12 1969–71 Autobook
12TL 1969–71	..	..	..	..	Ball	Renault 12 1969–71 Autobook

1100 Mk I

Make						Author	Title

RILEY

Make						Author	Title
1.5 1957–65	..	..	..	..	..	Ball	BMC Autobook Three
Elf Mk 1, 2, 3 1961–69		..	..	..		Ball	Mini 1959–71 Autobook
1100 Mk 1 1965–67	..	..	..	..		Ball	1100 Mk 1 1962–67 Autobook
1100 Mk 2 1968	..	..	..	..		Ball	1100 Mk 2, 1300 Mk 1, 2 America 1968–71 Autobook
1300 Mk 1, 2 1968–69		..	..	..		Ball	1100 Mk 2, 1300 Mk 1, 2 America 1968–71 Autobook

ROVER

60 1953–59	..	..	..	..	..	Ball	Rover 60–110 1953–64 Autobook
75 1954–59	..	..	..	..		Ball	Rover 60–110 1953–64 Autobook
80 1959–62	..	..	..	..		Ball	Rover 60–110 1953–64 Autobook
90 1954–59	..	..	..	..		Ball	Rover 60–110 1953–64 Autobook
95 1962–64	..	..	..	..		Ball	Rover 60–110 1953–64 Autobook
100 1959–62	..	..	..	..		Ball	Rover 60–110 1953–64 Autobook
105R 1957–58	..	..	..	..		Ball	Rover 60–110 1953–64 Autobook
105S 1957–59	..	..	..	..		Ball	Rover 60–110 1953–64 Autobook
110 1962–64	..	..	..	..		Ball	Rover 60–110 1953–64 Autobook
2000 SC 1963–71	..	..	..	..		Ball	Rover 2000 1963–71 Autobook
2000 TC 1963–71	..	..	..	..		Ball	Rover 2000 1963–71 Autobook
3 litre Saloon Mk 1, 1A 1958–62		..	..		Ball		Rover 3 litre 1958–67 Autobook
3 litre Saloon Mk 2, 3 1962–67		..	..		Ball		Rover 3 litre 1958–67 Autobook
3 litre Coupé 1965–67		..	..	..		Ball	Rover 3 litre 1958–67 Autobook
3500, 3500S 1968–70		..	..	..		Ball	Rover 3500, 3500S 1968–70 Autobook

SAAB

95, 96 1960–64		..	..	..		Ball	Saab 95, 96 Sport 1960–68 Autobook
95(5), 96(5) 1964–68		..	..	..		Ball	Saab 95, 96 Sport 1960–68 Autobook
Sport 1962–66	..	..	..	..		Ball	Saab 95, 96 Sport 1960–68 Autobook
Monte Carlo 1965–66	..	..	..			Ball	Saab 95, 96 Sport 1960–68 Autobook
99 1969–70	..	..	..	..		Ball	Saab 99 1969–70 Autobook

SIMCA

1000 1961–65	..	..	..	..		Ball	Simca 1000 1961–71 Autobook
1000 Special 1962–63		..	..	..		Ball	Simca 1000 1961–71 Autobook
1000 GL 1964–71	..	..	..	..		Ball	Simca 1000 1961–71 Autobook
1000 GLS 1964–69	..	..	..	..		Ball	Simca 1000 1961–71 Autobook
1000 GLA 1965–69	..	..	..	..		Ball	Simca 1000 1961–71 Autobook
1000 LS 1965–71	..	..	..	..		Ball	Simca 1000 1961–71 Autobook
1000 L 1966–68	..	..	..	..		Ball	Simca 1000 1961–71 Autobook
1000 Special 1968–71		..	..	..		Ball	Simca 1000 1961–71 Autobook
1100 LS 1967–70	..	..	..	..		Ball	Simca 1100 1967–70 Autobook
1100 GL, GLS 1967–70		..	..	..		Ball	Simca 1100 1967–70 Autobook
1204 1970	..	..	..	..		Ball	Simca 1100 1967–70 Autobook
1300 GL 1963–65	..	..	..	..		Ball	Simca 1300, 1301, 1500, 1501 1963–71 Autobook
1300 LS 1965–66	..	..	..	..		Ball	Simca 1300, 1301, 1500, 1501 1963–71 Autobook
1301 GL 1966–71	..	..	..	..		Ball	Simca 1300, 1301, 1500, 1501 1963–71 Autobook
1301 LS 1966–68	..	..	..	..		Ball	Simca 1300, 1301, 1500, 1501 1963–71 Autobook
1500 L 1963–65	..	..	..	..		Ball	Simca 1300, 1301, 1500, 1501 1963–71 Autobook
1500 GL 1965–66	..	..	..	..		Ball	Simca 1300, 1301, 1500, 1501 1963–71 Autobook
1500 GLS 1965–66	..	..	..	..		Ball	Simca 1300, 1301, 1500, 1501 1963–71 Autobook
1501 GL 1966–70	..	..	..	..		Ball	Simca 1300, 1301, 1500, 1501 1963–71 Autobook
1501 GLS 1966–68	..	..	..	..		Ball	Simca 1300, 1301, 1500, 1501 1963–71 Autobook
1501 GLS 1970–71	..	..	..	..		Ball	Simca 1300, 1301, 1500, 1501 1963–71 Autobook
1501 Special 1968–71		..	..	..		Ball	Simca 1300, 1301, 1500, 1501 1963–71 Autobook

SINGER

Chamois 1964–68	..	..	..	..		Smith	Hillman Imp 1963–68 Autobook
Chamois 1969–70	..	..	..	..		Ball	Hillman Imp 1969–71 Autobook
Chamois Sport 1964–68		..	..	..		Smith	Hillman Imp 1963–68 Autobook
Chamois Sport 1969–70		..	..	..		Ball	Hillman Imp 1969–71 Autobook
Gazelle series 2A 1958		..	..	..		Ball	Hillman Minx 1 to 5 1956–65 Autobook
Gazelle 3, 3A, 3B, 3C 1958–63		..	..		Ball		Hillman Minx 1 to 5 1956–65 Autobook

Make				Author	Title
Gazelle series 5 1963–65	..	..	..	Ball	Hillman Minx 1 to 5 1956–65 Autobook
Gazelle series 6 1965–67	..	..	..	Ball	Hillman Minx 1965–67 Autobook
New Gazelle 1500, 1725 1966–70	..	..		Ball	Hillman Minx 1966–70 Autobook
Vogue Mk 1 to 3 1961–65	..	..	..	Ball	Hillman Super Minx 1961–65 Autobook
Vogue series 4 1965–67	..	..	..	Ball	Hillman Minx 1965–67 Autobook
New Vogue 1966–70	..	..	..	Ball	Hillman Hunter 1966–71 Autobook

SKODA

440, 445, 450 1957–69	..	..	..	Skoda	Skoda Autobook One

SUNBEAM

Alpine series 1, 2, 3, 4 1959–65	..	..	Ball	Sunbeam Rapie Alpine 1955–65 Autobook
Alpine series 5 1965–67	..	..	Ball	Hillman Minx 1965–67 Autobook
Alpine 1969–71	..	..	Ball	Hillman Hunter 1966–71 Autobook
Arrow 1969–71	..	..	Ball	Hillman Hunter 1966–71 Autobook
Rapier series 1, 2, 3, 3A, 4 1955–65	..		Ball	Sunbeam Rapier Alpine 1955–65 Autobook
Rapier series 5 1965–67	..	..	Ball	Hillman Minx 1965–67 Autobook
Rapier H.120 1967–71	..	..	Ball	Hillman Hunter 1966–71 Autobook
Imp Sport 1963–68	..	..	Smith	Hillman Imp 1963–68 Autobook
Imp Sport 1969–71	..	..	Ball	Hillman Imp 1969–71 Autobook
Stilletto 1967–68	..	..	Smith	Hillman Imp 1963–68 Autobook
Stilletto 1969–71	..	..	Ball	Hillman Imp 1969–71 Autobook
1250 1970–71	..	..	Ball	Hillman Avenger 1970–71 Autobook
1500 1970–71	..	..	Ball	Hillman Avenger 1970–71 Autobook

TOYOTA

Corolla 1100 1967–70	..	..	Ball	Toyota Corolla 1100 1967–70 Autobook
Corolla 1100 De luxe 1967–70	..	..	Ball	Toyota Corolla 1100 1967–70 Autobook
Corolla 1100 Automatic 1968–69	..	..	Ball	Toyota Corolla 1100 1967–70 Autobook
Corona 1500 Mk 1 1965–70	..	..	Ball	Toyota Corolla 1500 Mk 1 1965–70 Autobook
Corona 1900 Mk 2 1969–71	..	..	Ball	Toyota Corona 1900 Mk 2 1969–71 Autobook

TRIUMPH

TR2 1952–55	..	..	..	..	Ball	Triumph TR2, TR3, TR3A 1952–62 Autobook
TR3, TR3A 1955–62	..	..			Ball	Triumph TR2, TR3, TR3A 1952–62 Autobook
TR4, TR4A 1961–67	..	..			Ball	Triumph TR4, TR4A 1961–67 Autobook
TR5 1967–69	..	..			Ball	Triumph TR5, TR250, TR6 1967–70 Autobook
TR6 1969–70	..	..			Ball	Triumph TR5, TR250, TR6 1967–70 Autobook
TR250 1967–69	..	..			Ball	Triumph TR5, TR250, TR6 1967–70 Autobook
1300 1965–71	..	..			Ball	Triumph 1300, 1500 1965–71 Autobook
1300TC 1967–71	..	..			Ball	Triumph 1300, 1500 1965–71 Autobook
1500 1970–71	..	..			Ball	Triumph 1300, 1500 1965–71 Autobook
2000 Mk 1 1963–69	..	..			Ball	Triumph 2000 Mk 1, 2.5 PI Mk 1 1963–69 Autobook
2000 Mk 2 1969–71	..	..			Ball	Triumph 2000 Mk 2, 2.5 PI Mk 2 1969–71 Autobook
2.5 PI Mk 1 1963–69	..	..			Ball	Triumph 2000 Mk 1, 2.5 PI Mk 1 1963–69 Autobook
2.5 PI Mk 2 1969–71	..	..			Ball	Triumph 2000 Mk 2, 2.5 PI Mk 2 1969–71 Autobook
Herald 948 1959–64	..	..			Smith	Triumph Herald 1959–68 Autobook
Herald 1200 1961–68	..	..			Smith	Triumph Herald 1959–68 Autobook
Herald 1200 1969–70	..	..			Ball	Triumph Herald 1969–71 Autobook
Herald 12/50 1963–67	..	..			Smith	Triumph Herald 1959–68 Autobook
Herald 13/60 1967–68	..	..			Smith	Triumph Herald 1959–68 Autobook
Herald 13/60 1969–71	..	..			Ball	Triumph Herald 1969–71 Autobook
Spitfire 1962–68	..	..			Smith	Triumph Spitfire Vitesse 1962–68 Autobook
Spitfire Mk 3 1969–70	..	..			Ball	Triumph Spitfire Mk 3 1969–70 Autobook
Vitesse 1600 and 2 litre 1962–68	..	..		Smith	Triumph Spitfire Vitesse 1962–68 Autobook
Vitesse 2 litre 1969–70	..	..			Ball	Triumph GT6, Vitesse 2 litre 1969–70 Autobook
GT Six 2 litre 1966–68	..	..			Smith	Triumph Spitfire Vitesse 1962–68 Autobook
GT Six 1969–70	..	..			Ball	Triumph GT6, Vitesse 2 litre 1969–70 Autobook

1100 Mk l

Make				Author	Title

VANDEN PLAS

Make				Author	Title
3 litre 1959–64	..	..	..	Ball	Austin A99, A110 1959–68 Autobook
1100 Mk 1 1963–67	..	..	..	Ball	1100 Mk 1 1962–67 Autobook
1100 Mk 2 1968	..	..	..	Ball	1100 Mk 2, 1300 Mk 1, 2 America 1968–71 Autobook
1300 Mk 1, 2 1968–71	..	..	..	Ball	1100 Mk 2, 1300 Mk 1, 2 America 1968–71 Autobook

VAUXHALL

Make				Author	Title
Victor 1 1957–59	..	..	..	Ball	Vauxhall Victor 1, 2 FB 1957–64 Autobook
Victor 2 1959–61	..	..	..	Ball	Vauxhall Victor 1, 2 FB 1957–64 Autobook
Victor FB 1961–64	..	..	..	Ball	Vauxhall Victor 1, 2 FB 1957–64 Autobook
VX4/90 FBH 1961–64	..	..	..	Ball	Vauxhall Victor 1, 2 FB 1957–64 Autobook
Victor FC 101 1964–67	..	..	..	Ball	Vauxhall Victor 101 1964–67 Autobook
VX 4/90 FCH 1964–67	..	..	..	Ball	Vauxhall Victor 101 1964–67 Autobook
Victor FD 1599cc 1967–71	..	..	..	Ball	Vauxhall Victor FD 1600, 2000 1967–71 Autobook
Victor FD 1975cc 1967–71	..	..	..	Ball	Vauxhall Victor FD 1600, 2000 1967–71 Autobook
VX 4/90 1969–71	..	..	..	Ball	Vauxhall Victor FD 1600, 2000 1967–71 Autobook
Velox, Cresta PA 1957–62	..	..	..	Ball	Vauxhall Velox Cresta 1957–70 Autobook
Velox, Cresta PB 1962–65	..	..	..	Ball	Vauxhall Velox Cresta 1957–70 Autobook
Cresta PC 1965–70	..	..	..	Ball	Vauxhall Velox Cresta 1957–70 Autobook
Viscount 1966–70	..	..	..	Ball	Vauxhall Velox Cresta 1957–70 Autobook
Viva HA (including 90) 1964–66	..	..	..	Ball	Vauxhall Viva HA 1964–66 Autobook
Viva HB (including 90 and SL90) 1966–70	..	..	Ball	Vauxhall Viva HB 1966–70 Autobook
Viva HC 1159cc 1971	..	..	..	Ball	Vauxhall Viva HC, Firenza 1971 Autobook
Viva HC SL 1159cc 1971	..	..	..	Ball	Vauxhall Viva HC, Firenza 1971 Autobook
Firenza 1159cc 1971	..	..	..	Ball	Vauxhall Viva HC, Firenza 1971 Autobook
Firenza SL 1159cc 1971	..	..	..	Ball	Vauxhall Viva HC, Firenza 1971 Autobook

VOLKSWAGEN

Make				Author	Title
1200 Beetle 1954–67	..	..	..	Ball	Volkswagen Beetle 1954–67 Autobook
1200 Beetle 1968–71	..	..	..	Ball	Volkswagen Beetle 1968–71 Autobook
1200 Karmann Ghia 1955–65	..	..	..	Ball	Volkswagen Beetle 1954–67 Autobook
1200 Transporter 1954–64	..	..	..	Ball	Volkswagen Transporter 1954–67 Autobook
1300 Beetle 1965–67	..	..	..	Ball	Volkswagen Beetle 1954–67 Autobook
1300 Beetle 1968–71	..	..	..	Ball	Volkswagen Beetle 1968–71 Autobook
1300 Karmann Ghia 1965–66	..	..	..	Ball	Volkswagen Beetle 1954–67 Autobook
1500 Beetle 1966–67	..	..	..	Ball	Volkswagen Beetle 1954–67 Autobook
1500 Beetle 1968–70	..	..	..	Ball	Volkswagen Beetle 1968–71 Autobook
1500 1961–65	..	..	..	Ball	Volkswagen 1500 1961–66 Autobook
1500N 1963–65	..	..	..	Ball	Volkswagen 1500 1961–66 Autobook
1500S 1963–65	..	..	..	Ball	Volkswagen 1500 1961–66 Autobook
1500A 1965–66	..	..	..	Ball	Volkswagen 1500 1961–66 Autobook
1500 Karmann Ghia 1966–67	..	..	..	Ball	Volkswagen Beetle 1954–67 Autobook
1500 Transporter 1963–67	..	..	..	Ball	Volkswagen Transporter 1954–67 Autobook
1500 Karmann Ghia 1968–70	..	..	..	Ball	Volkswagen Beetle 1968–71 Autobook
1600 TL 1965–70	..	..	..	Ball	Volkswagen 1600 Fastback 1965–70 Autobook
1600 Variant 1965–66	..	..	..	Ball	Volkswagen 1600 Fastback 1965–70 Autobook
1600 L 1966–67	..	..	..	Ball	Volkswagen 1600 Fastback 1966–70 Autobook
1600 Variant L 1966–70	..	..	..	Ball	Volkswagen 1600 Fastback 1965–70 Autobook
1600 T 1968–70	..	..	..	Ball	Volkswagen 1600 Fastback 1965–70 Autobook
1600 TA 1969–70	..	..	..	Ball	Volkswagen 1600 Fastback 1965–70 Autobook
1600 Variant A, M	..	..	..	Ball	Volkswagen 1600 Fastback 1965–70 Autobook
1600 Karmann Ghia	..	..	..	Ball	Volkswagen 1600 Fastback 1965–70 Autobook
Delivery Van 1600 1968–71	..	..	..	Ball	Volkswagen Transporter 1968–71 Autobook
Pick-up 1600 1968–71	..	..	..	Ball	Volkswagen Transporter 1968–71 Autobook
Kombi 1600 1968–71	..	..	..	Ball	Volkswagen Transporter 1968–71 Autobook
Micro-Bus 1600 1968–71	..	..	..	Ball	Volkswagen Transporter 1968–71 Autobook

Make				Author	Title

VOLVO

Make				Author	Title
121, 131, 221 1962–68	..	..	..	Ball	Volvo P120 1961–68 Autobook
122, 132, 222 1961–68	..	..	..	Ball	Volvo P120 1961–68 Autobook
123 GT 1967–68	..	..	..	..	Ball	Volvo P120 1961–68 Autobook
142, 142S 1967–69	..	..	..	..	Ball	Volvo 140 1966–70 Autobook
144, 144S 1966–70	..	..	..	..	Ball	Volvo 140 1966–70 Autobook
145, 145S 1968–70	..	..	..	..	Ball	Volvo 140 1966–70 Autobook
P 1800 1961–63	..	..	..	..	Ball	Volvo 1800 1961–71 Autobook
1800S 1963–69	..	..	..	..	Ball	Volvo 1800 1961–71 Autobook
1800E 1969–71	..	..	..	..	Ball	Volvo 1800 1961–71 Autobook

WOLSELEY

1500 1959–65	..	..	..	..	Ball	BMC Autobook Three
15/50 1956–58	..	..	..	..	Ball	BMC Autobook Three
6/99 1959–61 ..	..	..	..	..	Ball	Austin A99, A110 1959–68 Autobook
6/110 1961–68	..	..	..	..	Ball	Austin A99, A110 1959–68 Autobook
Hornet Mk 1, 2, 3 1961–71	..	..	..	Ball	Mini 1959–71 Autobook
1100 Mk 1 1965–67 ..	..	..	..	Ball	1100 Mk 1 1962–67 Autobook
1100 Mk 2 1968	..	..	..	..	Ball	1100 Mk 2, 1300 Mk 1, 2 America 1968–71 Autobook
1300 Mk 1, 2 1968–71	..	..	..	Ball	1100 Mk 2, 1300 Mk 1, 2 America 1968–71 Autobook
18/85 Mk 1, 2 1967–71	..	..	..	Ball	1800 1964–71 Autobook
18/85 S 1969–71	..	..	..	..	Ball	1800 1964–71 Autobook

NOTES

NOTES

NOTES

NOTES